MURDER, INC., AND THE MORAL LIFE

MURDER, INC.,
AND THE MORAL LIFE

GANGSTERS AND GANGBUSTERS
IN LA GUARDIA'S NEW YORK

ROBERT WELDON WHALEN

 Empire State Editions
An imprint of Fordham University Press
New York 2016

Visit us online at:
www.fordhampress.com
www.empirestateeditions.com

Library of Congress Cataloging-in-Publication Data

Names: Whalen, Robert Weldon, 1950– author.
Title: Murder, Inc., and the moral life : gangsters and gangbusters in La Guar-
    dia's New York / Robert Weldon Whalen.
Description: New York : Empire State Editions, Fordham University Press,
    [2016] | Includes bibliographical references and index.
Identifiers: LCCN 2016014319 | ISBN 9780823271559 (hardback)
Subjects: LCSH: Organized crime—New York (State)—New York—History—
    20th century. | Gangsters—New York (State)—New York—History—20th
    century. | Crime—New York (State)—New York—History—20th century.
    | New York (N.Y.)—History—1898–1951. | BISAC: HISTORY / United
    States / 20th Century. | TRUE CRIME / Organized Crime. | SOCIAL
    SCIENCE / Regional Studies.
Classification: LCC HV6452.N7 W43 2016 | DDC
    364.106/6097472309043—dc23
LC record available at https://lccn.loc.gov/2016014319

Printed in the United States of America

18 17 16   5 4 3 2 1

First edition

Contents

Abbreviations

BE	*Brooklyn Eagle*
BPL	Brooklyn Public Library
FBI files	FBI files, available through BACM Research/ Paperless Archives
JJC	John Jay College of Criminal Law, City University of New, Lloyd Sealy Library, Special Collections
NYCMA	New York City Municipal Archives
NYDN	*New York Daily News*
NYHT	*New York Herald-Tribune*
NYJA	*New York Journal-American*
NYDM	*New York Daily Mirror*
NYS	*New York Sun*
NYSA	New York State Archives
NYT Archives	*New York Times* online archive
NYWT	*New York World-Telegram*
TNR	*The New Republic*
TDP	Thomas E. Dewey Papers, River Campus Libraries, Department of Rare Books, Special Collections, and Preservation, University of Rochester
TNY	*The New Yorker*

Illustrations

Characters

Gangsters

The Brownsville Gang

Frank "the Dasher" Abbandando: active in both East New York and Brownsville, an associate of Harry Maione; according to one story, he earned his nickname, "the Dasher" because of his speed as a prison baseball team infielder.

Martin "Buggsy" Goldstein: close to Abe Reles and Harry Strauss, Goldstein was known for his goofy jokes and bad aim.

Harry "Happy" Maione: his perpetual frown earned him his ironic nickname; he ran his own gang, with Frank Abbandando and others, in East New York before joining forces with Abe Reles.

Abe "Kid Twist" Reles: the leading hoodlum in Brooklyn's Brownsville neighborhood in the 1930s and 1940s; the nominal chief of "Murder, Inc."

Harry "Pittsburgh Phil" Strauss: Reles's chief ally; famous for his dapper good looks and his murderous temper.

Anthony "Dukey" Maffetore, Angelo "Julie" Catalano, Seymour "Blue Jaw" Magoon, Abraham "Pretty" Levine: neighborhood "kids" who ran errands and did things for the major figures in Murder, Inc.

Brooklyn

Albert Anastasia: he and his brothers dominated the Brooklyn docks; his power extended east into Brownsville and beyond. Reles and the Brownsville gang always "checked with Albert" before they did anything big.

Manhattan

Louis "Lepke" Buchalter: dominated both the needle trades and New York's trucking industry; in the mid-1930s, he and Albert Anastasia would use Abe Reles and the Brownsville gang to eliminate witnesses

Frank Costello: the "Prime Minister" of gangland, Costello was primarily a bootlegger and a gambler, not a killer.

Meyer Lansky: the mathematical wizard of the New York gangs; during Prohibition, he and Bugsy Siegel formed the "Bugs & Meyer Gang."

Charlie "Lucky" Luciano: became leader of several Italian gangs but worked closely with criminals of all ethnic backgrounds.

Benjamin "Bugsy" Siegel: handsome as a movie star; Meyer Lansky's key ally; Siegel would extend New York gangsterism to the West Coast.

Emmanuel "Mendy" Weiss: Lepke Buchalter's chief lieutenant; he worked closely with Albert Anastasia and Abe Reles.

The Bronx

Dutch Schulz: the "Beer Baron of the Bronx," Schulz was involved in a host of other activities. His violent and impulsive temper would be a problem Luciano and others would have to solve.

Other Gangsters

Vincent "Mad Dog" Coll: the son of Irish immigrants, Coll worked for a variety of gang leaders. He allegedly killed a child in a gangland shootout, earning the name "Mad Dog."

Jack "Legs" Diamond: a thief, Diamond was a successful bootlegger. Chronically entangled in feuds with other gangsters, most notably with Dutch Schulz, Diamond was regularly shot at by someone or other.

Gangbusters

Tom Dewey: first as a federal attorney, later as the Manhattan District Attorney, Dewey would become famous as the "gangbuster."

Fiorello La Guardia: elected mayor of New York in 1933 on a Progressive-Republican ticket, La Guardia vowed to run the gangsters out of New York. La Guardia was reelected in 1937 and for a third time in 1941.

Lewis Valentine: New York police commissioner under Mayor La Guardia, Valentine waged an often-ferocious war against the gangs.

Bill O'Dwyer: an Irish immigrant, O'Dwyer went from day laborer to police officer to lawyer to politician. Brooklyn's district attorney during the Murder, Inc., trials, O'Dwyer, like Dewey, parlayed his gangbusting career into higher political office. He never could shake accusations that he had, in fact, ongoing links with organized crime.

Burton Turkus: Brooklyn's assistant district attorney for homicide, he prosecuted most of the Murder, Inc., defendants.

Life is six to five against.

—*Damon Runyon, "A Nice Price" (1934)*

Prologue
Naked City

New York at night is cruel, brutal, human, and
humorous. Come ready to be shocked.

—1941 Photo League Show, "Murder Is My Business"[1]

In 1940 and 1941, New Yorkers, especially, but Americans, generally,
were shocked, fascinated, and vastly entertained by a series of murder
trials in Brooklyn. Reporter Harry Feeney nicknamed the defendants
"Murder, Inc.," and the name stuck.[2] The trials were a sensation. Brooklyn's courthouse was packed for each of the trials; spectators alternately
gasped and guffawed at the outrageous defendants and witnesses, with
names like Kid Twist, Pittsburgh Phil, Happy, and the Dasher, and their
bizarre stories of mayhem and murder. Newspapers published hundreds
of stories about the trials and sometimes the Murder, Inc., stories even
pushed reports from the world war raging in Europe and Asia below the
newspapers' front-page folds. The shocking conclusion of the Murder,
Inc., story, in November 1941, won banner headlines across Gotham and
the country.

The Murder, Inc., story is part gangster history, part morality play. This
book addresses both, within the context of New York City during the
Roaring Twenties and the Great Depression. In this book, gangsters and
philosophers from Dutch Schulz and Lucky Luciano to Hannah Arendt
and Emmanuel Levinas jostle each other for space on a crowded stage.

Who or what was "Murder, Inc."? Murder, Inc., refers to a gang of
hoodlums, led by Abe Reles, that flourished in Brooklyn's Brownsville
neighborhood from 1931 until 1940. Reles and his gang, there were
maybe twenty or so full-time members of the gang, engaged in a whole
range of criminal activities, including murder. No one knows how many
people the gang killed; the best guess would be several hundred. Their

1

nickname, Murder, Inc., quickly took on a life of its own, and getting the story of Murder, Inc., straight can be very tricky. Journalists in 1940 and 1941 wrote, beneath screaming headlines, the first draft. Their stories are filled with eyewitness accounts and sometimes jumbled facts, sensational revelations, and regular exaggerations. The first attempt at a narrative history, E. E. Rice's *Murder, Inc.* (1949) consists mostly of gruesome photographs and wild claims. How many murders did Murder, Inc., commit? Maybe one thousand! Rice breathlessly answered. Maybe ten thousand! Rice thought of Murder, Inc., in the David and Goliath terms that Hollywood, later, would portray in its "syndicate" films.[3] On one hand, Rice explains, was the "Big Mob," secret and sinister, which created the "syndicate known as Murder, Inc.," a "totalitarian Combination." Opposing it stood the district attorney, vastly outnumbered but plucky and brave. According to Rice, "the instrument chosen by Providence to fight the Big Mob was Thomas E. Dewey [Manhattan's special prosecutor and district attorney] a juvenile district attorney."[4]

Actually, Burton Turkus, the Brooklyn assistant district attorney, prosecuted Murder, Inc.; he published his memoir of the case, *Murder, Inc.* (1951), just in time to take advantage of the surge in interest in gangsters triggered by the US Senate's Kefauver Investigations of 1950–51. Co-written with journalist Sid Feder, *Murder, Inc.* was a best seller. The only people who knew more than Burton Turkus about Murder, Inc., were the Murder, Inc., gangsters. Yet Turkus and Feder's account must be handled with caution, as historian Robert Lacey argues. Written in a hard-boiled detective style, structured as a battle to the death between the courageous lawmen and bestial predators, filled with dialogue that may be accurate or reconstructed or simply invented, *Murder, Inc.* is, as Lacey observes, "half documentary and half soap opera."[5]

Rich Cohen's *Tough Jews* (1998), part memoir, part hagiography, testifies to the continuing allure of the Murder, Inc., gangsters. Cohen's father and his father's friends (including television personality Larry King) grew up in Brooklyn in the days of the gangsters and had vivid memories of the tough guys in the black sedans. Cohen's mother's family operated a Brooklyn luncheonette frequented by mob guys. Cohen, of course, is fully aware of the viciousness of the hoodlums. When, long after the gangsters were dead, Cohen asked his grandmother about them, she responded, "[T]hey'll kill you, these men, they're not like you. They'll kill a boy like you." When Cohen assured his grandmother that the Brooklyn gangsters of her youth were long dead, she simply repeated, "[T]hey'll kill you."[6] And yet, for Cohen, the gangsters had an irresistible allure. Growing up in the wake of the Holocaust, Cohen yearned for stories about "tough Jews," and he found them in stories about New York's Jewish gangsters from the 1930s and 1940s. Cohen imagined the gangsters as "colorful, gun-toting action figures." If Brooklyn assistant district attorney Burton Turkus saw the gangsters as brutes, Cohen sees them, if not as heroes exactly, then as figures of power. Cohen writes of Abe Reles, the central figure in the Murder, Inc., story: "Reles emerged as a leader; [...] something in him demanded respect." Of Harry "Pittsburgh Phil" Strauss, Cohen says that "he was big, strong, reckless; he had a sense of fair play, of right and wrong, of justice. Still, he was a head case." And of Harry "Happy" Maione, an Italian American hoodlum allied with Reles and Strauss, he says that "Happy [...] was [...] charismatic as hell [...] he knew everyone in the neighborhood and helped everyone he did not have to hurt. He loved to be out among them, spending, talking, boasting, laughing."[7]

Radio, television, and the movies were fascinated by the Murder, Inc., story, and prosecutor Burton Turkus, after the investigations and trials had ended, hosted programs like *Crime Doesn't Pay* (1950–52) on radio and *Mr. Arsenic* (1952) on television.[8] Turkus's memoir, *Murder, Inc.,* was excerpted in *Look* magazine, in articles titled "36 Hours from Murder" and "The Mob Invades California."[9] Hollywood's "syndicate films" enacted Murder, Inc., themes; in *The Enforcer* (1951), for example, for which Burton Turkus acted as a consultant,[10] Humphrey Bogart stars as the crusading district attorney at war with the mob. Turkus was also a consultant for the 1960 film *Murder, Inc.,* in which Peter Falk plays the gangster Abe Reles and Harry Morgan plays Burt Turkus.

In 1940, when the Murder, Inc., story broke, the "gangster" was a fascinating newcomer to American popular culture. In the 1920s, to be sure, Chicago's Al Capone had become a celebrity, but only when Hollywood created the archetypal gangster, in the classic films *Little Caesar* (1931, with Edward G. Robinson and Glenda Farrell), *The Public Enemy* (1931, with James Cagney and Jean Harlow) and *Scarface* (1932, with Paul Muni and Ann Dvorak) did the "gangster" as a distinct cultural type emerge. As David Ruth writes, the media, and especially Hollywood, played a key role in "inventing the public enemy." According to Ruth,

[s]hortly after the First World War many Americans came to believe that rampant crime was a defining element of their society. Attention soon centered on the gangster, the paragon of modern criminality and eventually the subject of innumerable newspaper and magazine articles, scores of novels and plays, and more than a

hundred Hollywood films. The media gangster was an invention, much less an accurate reflection of reality than a projection created from various Americans' beliefs, concerns, and ideas about what would sell.[11]

With the appearance of the gangster film, real life and fantasy merged— movies modeled themselves on actual hoodlums and actual hoodlums went to the movies. "Murder, Inc." was simultaneously a criminological reality and a cultural phenomenon.

From the classic gangster films of the 1930s to *Guys and Dolls* (1950); from *The Godfather* (Mario Puzo's 1969 novel and Francis Ford Coppola's films, 1972, 1974, 1990), to *The Sopranos* (1999) and *Boardwalk Empire* (2010); from the rapper "Public Enemy" to the graphic novel *Brownsville* (2006),[12] gangland images and metaphors have profoundly shaped American culture. The phrase "Murder, Inc." has become a kind of free-floating meme. Sometimes it refers to the New York gangs of the 1930s and 1940s; sometimes to the underworld in general. In 1943, a young American bomber crewman named Kenneth Williams, from Charlotte, North Carolina, flying for the 351st Bomber Group, was shot down over Germany. Williams was wearing a bomber jacket with "Murder, Inc." painted on the back. His German captors crowed that they had seized a notorious "Chicago gangster."[13] In 1982, Bruce Springsteen recorded a brooding song he called "Murder, Inc." In the second verse, Springsteen sings,

Now you check over your shoulder everywhere that you go
Walkin' down the street there's eyes in every shadow
You better take a look around you (come on now)
That equipment you got's so outdated
You can't compete with Murder, Incorporated
Everywhere you look now, Murder, Incorporated.[14]

A rock-and-roll band, in 1991, called itself "Murder, Inc." In 1999, hip-hop entrepreneur Irv Gotti founded a record label that he called Murder, Inc. In the television political drama *The West Wing* (1999–2006), the audience learns, in the episode called "Holy Night" (2002), that the acerbic presidential speechwriter, Toby Ziegler, is bitterly estranged from his father because his father was a Brooklyn gangster—and a member of Murder, Inc.

Gangsters have inspired an enormous literature. First, there are mountains of police records, trial records, prison records, and accounts of public hearings, such as the famous Kefauver Hearings of the early 1950s. As valuable as these records are, they reflect, of course, the government's perspective, and the gangsters, in most cases, did their best to disguise their real activities from the government. The records, often full of frustrating holes, are typically a stew of criminal deceptions, detectives' laconic narratives, lawyers' arguments, judges' ponderous opinions, and politicians' clichés. Gangsters have always been tabloid fodder, and the racier newspapers regularly carried stories and photographs about hoodlums; although more restrained, the respectable newspapers covered crime as well, and the Murder, Inc., story appeared in both the tabloids and the broadsheets. The irresistible sensationalist impulse shapes many of the books in the gangster literature; many are essentially heated police procedurals, spiced with Mickey Spillane–esque tough-guy violence.

Gangsters and their friends and relations have produced a sizable memoir literature, although it must be treated cautiously. Peter Maas's *The Valachi Papers* (2003), for example, is an account of journalist Maas's encounters with Joe Valachi, who grew up in the New York gangs in the 1920s and 1930s, and then, in 1963, testified before a Senate committee investigating organized crime. *The Valachi Papers*, then, are not exactly Joe Valachi's papers; they are, instead, reporter Maas's summary of and comment on Valachi's testimony and conversations with Maas. *The Last Testament of Lucky Luciano* (1974), complied by Martin Gosch and Richard Hammer, claims to be a kind of Luciano autobiography, but as Luciano's biographer, Tim Newark, points out in his *Lucky Luciano. The Real and the Fake Gangster* (2010), accounts such as those of Gosch and Hammer are not always exactly accurate. On the other hand, there are a number of thoroughly researched, solidly documented biographies such as Newark's biography of Luciano; others include, for example, Robert Lacey, *Little Man. Meyer Lansky and the Gangster Life* (1991); Neil Hanson, *Monk Eastman* (2010); Patrick Downey, *Legs Diamond, Gangster* (2011); and David Pietrusza, *Rothstein* (2011).

Sociologists and historians have long studied crime, in general, and gangsters, in particular; good introductions to the gangster world and the moral dilemmas it triggers are Jack Katz, *Seductions of Crime. Moral and Sensual Attractions in Doing Evil* (1988); Thomas Reppetto, *American Mafia* (2004); and Selwyn Raab, *Five Families* (2006). The gangsters have been the subject, too, of some fine social and cultural history, such as Albert Fried, *The Rise and Fall of the Jewish Gangster in America* (1980); Jenna Weissmann Joselit, *Our Gang. Jewish Crime and the New York Jewish Community, 1900–1940* (1983); David Ruth, *Inventing the Public Enemy* (1996);

and Fred Gardaphé, *From Wise Guys to Wise Men. The Gangster and Italian American Masculinities* (2006).

The "golden age of gangsterism," the era from the beginning of Prohibition to the end of the Great Depression, has received a great deal of serious study. Among the basic narratives of the era are John Toland, *The Dillinger Days* (1995); Bryan Burrough, *Public Enemies* (2004); Patrick Downey, *Gangster City* (2004); and Marc Mappen, *Prohibition Gangsters. The Rise and Fall of a Bad Generation* (2013).

Gangsters have inspired fiction too, such as William Kennedy, *Legs* (1975); Mario Puzo, *The Godfather* (1983); Damon Runyon, *Guys and Dolls* (1992); and E. L. Doctorow, *Billy Bathgate* (2010)—but film has been the distinctly gangster genre. The critical literature on the gangster film is immense and includes, for example, Carlos Clarens, *Crime Movies* (1997); Jonathan Munby, *Public Enemies, Public Heroes: Screening the Gangster from "Little Caesar" to "Touch of Evil"* (1999); Fran Mason, *American Gangster Cinema* (2002); Jack Shadoian, *Dreams and Dead Ends. The American Gangster Film* (2003); and Alain Silver and James Ursini (eds.), *Gangster Film Reader* (2007).

Literature on the gangbusters, especially Fiorello La Guardia and Thomas Dewey, is just as rich. Stores about each filled the newspapers; each is the subject of thorough biographies, including Thomas Kessner, *Fiorello La Guardia* (1989); Alan Brodsky, *The Great Mayor. Fiorello La Guardia and the Making of the City of New York* (2003); and Richard Norton Smith, *Thomas E. Dewey and His Times* (1982).

What does *Murder, Inc., and the Moral Life* add to all this? Virtually everything written, or filmed, or sung, or acted about gangsters includes some reference to "morals"; talking about outlaws and crime without some reference to law and justice is impossible. Yet, in all this enormous gangster library, no single text explicitly and systematically relates the gangster phenomenon to contemporary moral thought. Doing so is this book's task.

This book, then, is both history and ethical reflection. It regularly mixes genres; it is a history text that explores ethical arguments and an ethics book rooted in one particular historical event. Its approach to ethical argument may be unfamiliar. The old warhorses of ethics—utilitarianism, deontology, social contract, and virtue theory—play at most a very small part in this discussion. Instead, this book relies on other ethical thinkers including, for instance, Emmanuel Levinas, Hannah Arendt, Amartya Sen, and Zygmunt Bauman. Moreover, the discussion does not rely on a single ethical perspective but examines Murder, Inc., from multiple points of view. As William James argued,

> there is really no more ground for supposing that all our demands can be accounted for by one universal underlying kind of motive than there is ground for supposing that all physical phenomena are cases of a single law. The elementary forces in ethics are as plural as those of physics are.[15]

This book both tells the story of Murder, Inc., and reflects on the morals[16] of that story. Each chapter addresses both "what" and "so what" questions; that is, each chapter both considers an aspect of the Murder, Inc., case and reflects on the ethical dimensions of that aspect of the case.

Hannah Arendt, writing in the shadow of Auschwitz, argued that what the ancient philosophers called the "mysterium iniquitatis," the mystery of iniquity, was the most important issue her generation had to face.[17] "The problem of evil," Susan Nieman writes, is not only an issue for the postwar generation; the problem of evil "is the guiding force of modern thought"[18] in general. Evil may be, Neiman writes, "demonic" and monstrous but also "banal" and shockingly common; "the greatest crimes," she continues, "can be committed by people less likely to arouse terror and awe than contempt and disgust."[19] Evil is not necessarily something cosmic; it can flourish locally, on street corners or down alleyways in places like, say, Brooklyn. To think about evil in the context of Murder, Inc., is an effort to invite thought to leave the academy and move into the neighborhoods, to encourage philosophy, as Neiman says, "to return to the place, closer to home, where philosophy arises."[20] The "mystery of evil," however, inspires reflection on the "mystery of good." Conscience, moral imagination, and compassion are, as Adam Smith thought, universal. Why, then, when some people's moral imaginations are so dead, do others' come alive?[21]

There is, also, the problem of "the wheat and the tares." A farmer, in Jesus's parable, sows wheat. But, somehow, tares spring up too. "Do you want us to pull up all the tares?" the farmhands ask the farmer. "No," the farmer replies, "because if you pull up the tares you might pull up the wheat. Let them grow up together until the harvest" (*Matt* 13:24–30). Good and evil grow up all entangled together; distinguishing between them at any one moment would be very hard. Good might seem harsh. Evil can be glamorous. The moral history of Murder, Inc., is complicated.

The first attempt at moral reflection on gangsters began with the gangster movies, and so Chapter 1 of this book, "Reel Gangsters: Mobsters and the Movies," examines the creation of the Hollywood gangster, his relationship to street-corner gangsters like those who became Murder, Inc., and, most important, the sort of moral reflection about gangsters that occurred in the first gangster movies.

Gangsterism, though was also a sociological phenomenon; there really were "real" gangsters, and Chapter 2, "Real Gangsters: Abe Reles and the Origins of Murder, Inc.," considers the social origins especially of the people who would become Murder, Inc., the social roots, that is, of evil.

In New York City, in the 1930s and 1940s, gangsterism was not only a social pathology; as Chapter 3, "Gangster City," explains, gangsterism became a political evil. Crime has been a chronic problem in American cities. In 1906, James Bryce noted in *The American Commonwealth*, that "the growth of the great cities [in the United States] has been among the most significant and least fortunate changes in the population [. . .] since 1787." Bryce added that "there is no denying that the government of cities is the one conspicuous failure of the United States."[22] Bryce grimly charged that American cities were plagued by a host of "evils," including "extravagance, corruption, and mismanagement."[23] Just two years before, in 1904, muckraker Lincoln Steffens, in *The Shame of the Cities*, had made a similarly sober argument. In America's great cities, Steffens claimed, public office was regularly used for private gain; citizens did not enjoy equal justice under law; instead, laws were routinely ignored. Bribery, special deals, kickbacks, and payoffs were everywhere the norm. By the era of Murder, Inc., New York City was captive to these sorts of political evils, and the story of Murder, Inc., is a key moment in the story of New York's dramatic struggle in the 1930s and 1940s to escape the gangsters' power.

In New York of the 1930s and early 1940s, if there were plenty of gangsters, there were also plenty of gangbusters. Chapter 4, "Fiorello La Guardia and the Cinema of Redemption," reflects on Mayor La Guardia's determination to root out the gangsters. Chapter 5, "Gangbuster: Thomas Dewey and Imperfect Justice," discusses the Thomas Dewey investigations of the mid-1930s and their effort to achieve some sort of rough justice in Gotham.

Murder, Inc., was born out of this struggle, and Chapter 6, "Murder, Inc.:'I Got Used to It,'" focuses on the Brooklyn gang's archetypal act— killing people. Chapter 7, "A Theater of Ethics: Mr. Arsenic and the Murder, Inc., Trials," examines especially the performative nature of the law's confrontation with the Brownsville gangsters. Chapter 8, "Ethics of Ambiguity: The Canary Could Sing but Couldn't Fly," considers the shocking end of the Murder, Inc., story, and the role that ambiguity plays in the moral imagination. The conclusion, "That Dangerous and Sad City of the Imagination," brings the Murder, Inc., story to its close.

A caution about sources: criminals tell lies. This account of Murder, Inc., should properly be peppered with "it seems" and "it is alleged" and so on, but such constant hemming and hawing is irritating and distracting. This preliminary caution will have to suffice: when dealing with gangsters, be suspicious.

And so we enter the orbit of Murder, Inc., a strange world located somewhere between Damon Runyon and Weegee.

Born in Kansas and raised in Colorado, Damon Runyon, at eighteen, served in the Spanish–American War. In 1911, he became a sportswriter for the *New York American* and quickly mastered a unique, colloquial, wise-guy, New York style. In the 1920s, sportswriter Runyon began publishing short stories staring figures from New York's demimonde with names such as "Harry the Horse" and "Nicely Nicely." Runyon's characters were gamblers and hustlers, petty criminals and hoodlums, figures from a modern *Three Penny Opera*. His stories are comic, his figures tricksters, and readers loved them. Sixteen of his stories were turned into films, including *Little Miss Marker* (1934), starring a very cute Shirley Temple, and *The Big Street* (1942), with a young Lucille Ball in one of her first dramatic roles. The hit Broadway musical *Guys and Dolls* (1950), later turned into a film, was based on Damon Runyon's stories. Outrageous and funny, not unlike the grotesque characters in the films of Joel and Ethan Coen, Runyon's comic gangsters provoke amazed laughter. They come from another, very strange, world; their speech is stilted and peppered with the oddest jargon; their suits with padded shoulders and their loud shirts and ties make them a kind of outré urban clown. There were times, during the Murder, Inc., trials, that people in the courtroom burst into laughter, almost as if some Runyon character, and not a brutal killer, were in the witness chair.[24]

But Weegee, too, reflects the noir world of Murder, Inc.

In 1941, New York's Photo League sponsored an exhibition of the photography of Arthur Fellig. Fellig was forty-two that year. Born in 1899 in what is now Ukraine, Fellig and his family were part of that vast wave of Jewish immigration that swept into New York around the turn of the century. Fellig's father came to New York first, in 1906, to prepare a place for his family; Arthur and the rest of the family arrived in 1910. Arthur Fellig grew up on New York's streets; when he was thirteen or fourteen, he dropped out of school. As a teenager, he did odd jobs, slept on park benches, sometimes in Penn Station. When he was eighteen, he became fascinated by photography. He found a job with a photography studio in Lower Manhattan and soon he was taking his own pictures. In the 1920s and 1930s, he scrambled to make a living as a freelance photographer, rushing from fire to crime scene to street festival looking for shots. Editors were amazed that somehow Fellig always knew just where to go, in the middle of the night, to get the best picture. It was as if, some said, he had a "Ouija Board." Maybe that is how Fellig got the nickname "Weegee."[25] Weegee's photographs appeared in all New York's raucous tabloids and sometimes even in the city's more respectable papers. By 1940, Weegee was the staff photographer for the newspaper *P.M.*

The title of Weegee's 1941 Photo League show was "Murder Is my Business." Materials announcing the show warned that "New York at night is cruel, brutal, human, and humorous. Come ready to be shocked."[26] The show was inspired by Murder, Inc. Weegee had been following gangsters for years. One of his better-known murder photographs was "Trunk in which a slain man was found." The August 5, 1936, *New York Post* story about the corpse in the trunk was titled "Gang Stabs B'klyn Man 48 Times." The *Post* reported that the victim had been stabbed repeatedly with an icepick and then stuffed into a trunk, which was then abandoned on a Brooklyn street. Almost certainly the killing was the work of Murder, Inc. Weegee's photograph would become famous. In the original version, Weegee himself is on the left of the frame, peering at the corpse in the trunk. When the photograph was first published, the corpse was airbrushed out of the picture, so Weegee is, oddly, staring into an empty trunk. In April 1937, *Life* magazine published a story about Weegee and included side-by-side images of the trunk without the corpse and the trunk with the corpse.

In 1939, Weegee published a photo of a check he had received from Time, Inc. The amount of the check was thirty-five dollars. In the explanation section below the check, some clerk at Time, Inc., had typed in "Two Murders." Weegee had sold a picture of two men killed in a gangland murder. He later explained: "A check from *Life*: Two murders, thirty-five dollars. *Life* magazine pays five dollars a bullet. One stiff had five bullets in him, the other had two."[27]

Weegee's photographs were pure tabloid—weird, shocking, and sometimes gruesome. He snapped pictures of accidents and fires, circus clowns and murdered hoodlums. Most were taken in the middle of the night when decent New Yorkers were safe in their beds. Weegee's images had strange lives. Often they were lifted from their original context and were freely floated through the media. A 1936 image titled "Corpse with a Revolver," of a murdered gangster, his fedora and revolver beside him,

Brooklyn Bridge and Lower Manhattan at night, c.1933–39. (New York City Municipal Archives)

appeared in tabloids, true-crime magazines, and on the cover of one of James M. Cain's novels.[28] Even something as simple as a picture of bundles of newspapers tumbled onto a street corner in the middle of the night, "Sunday Morning in Manhattan," undated—the papers bright white, throwing shadows into the slick blackness—seems vaguely sinister.

Weegee's pictures attracted a surprisingly wide audience. Some viewers simply liked the grim and garish. Others, perhaps, were attracted by scenes from a nocturnal New York that they knew was real but that they fearfully avoided. Weegee's pictures forced people to stop, look, maybe even think. Artists got interested in Weegee, and even Clement Greenberg, the stern critic of mass culture and the advocate of the avant-garde, allowed that photography had its place among the arts.[29] Ellen Handy writes that "Weegee emphatically eschewed picture postcard views and tourist attractions"; his work, she writes, "is defined by a searing chiaroscuro." What interests him is night, glare, and danger.[30] Thomas Crow argues that just as avant-garde artists, "from above," surprise and sometimes shock their audiences into thought, popular artists like Weegee can do the same "from below."[31]

In 1945, Weegee published a collection of his New York photographs that he called *Naked City*. *Naked City*, its dark images partly inspired by Murder, Inc., "emerged as the most widely known single-volume visual representation of the city." *Naked City* also "quickly became the most profitable photo-book in the history of American photography."[32] Weegee's brief essays were abrupt and laconic, and one caption especially summarized his experience of New York City in the era of Murder, Inc.: "People get bumped off [. . .] on the sidewalks of New York."[33]

Weegee's images urge us to think about "night, glare, and danger," gangsters and gangbusters and the noir universe of Murder, Inc. Martha Nussbaum writes that "a just society needs to try to understand the roots of human bad behavior. It is difficult to know how citizens' dignity and equality should be protected, if we do not know what we are up against."[34] Mary Midgely asks, how can we ever understand the good if we do not consider the bad? Sooner or later we must address what Midgely calls "wickedness"; unless, Midgely writes, "we are willing to grasp imaginatively how it works in the human heart, and particularly in our own hearts, we cannot understand it."[35] We must think about wickedness because, "simply by not thinking," Midgely warns, we "can do immeasurable harm."[36] But, then, we also ought to think about good; above all, we ought, to paraphrase James Thurber, to figure out, sometime before we die, what we are running from, and to, and why.[37] As gangster Dutch Schulz said, "this tough world ain't no place for dunces."[38]

1

Reel Gangsters—Mobsters and the Movies

> These fellows were like gods to me.
>
> —*Actor George Raft, remembering gangsters he'd known*[1]

On Sunday evening, July 22, 1934, John Dillinger, "Public Enemy Number One,"[2] went to the movies. His companions were Polly Hamilton and Anna Cumpănaş, who also called herself Anna Sage. Anna Sage was wearing a bright orange dress (she would become infamous, later, as "the lady red").[3] It was a hot day in Chicago; spending an hour in a movie theater would have been a nice way to cool off. Dillinger, Hamilton, and Sage picked the Biograph Theater on North Lincoln Avenue, in the Lincoln Park neighborhood. The Biograph was only a few blocks away from the site of the notorious 1929 St. Valentine's Day Massacre, in which Al Capone's hoodlums murdered seven of Bugsy Moran's hoodlums— but not Bugsy. Dillinger, Hamilton, and Sage were going to the Biograph to see *Manhattan Melodrama*, a gangster movie, starring Clarke Gable, Myrna Loy, and William Powell.

That John Dillinger would go to a gangster movie is, in retrospect, no surprise.[4] In 1934, gangster movies were the hot new genre in a very new and immensely popular form of mass entertainment. Each of the three pioneering gangster movies, *Scarface*, *Little Caesar*, and *The Public Enemy*, had been huge hits, and Hollywood eagerly rushed out spin-offs like *Manhattan Melodrama*. Reel gangsters in the movies and real gangsters on the street-corners were, in the films, engaged in a strange and vibrant dialogue. Reel gangsters, inspired by real gangsters like Al Capone, created the very type of the gangster, complete with distinctive look, swagger, slang, and costume. Although they may have inspired the movie gangsters, the real gangsters on the street corners were simultaneously shaped by the

13

movie gangsters they saw on the screen. This interplay between fiction and fact, between screen and street, engaged the movie viewer in precisely what this book attempts to do, that is, ethical reflection on the gangster experience. The first part of this chapter considers the ways reel gangsters incarnate real gangsters and endow their lives with a set of distinctive moral themes. The second part investigates the ways in which real gangsters on the street were swept up in the celebrity produced by the movie gangsters. Finally, this chapter argues that the very structure of gangster films propels viewers into the deeply ambiguous realm of the moral imagination, and so thinking about gangster movies is the best place to begin thinking about Murder, Inc., and the moral life.

Dillinger, Hamilton, and Sage walked up to the Biograph around 8:30 p.m., the time when the show was to begin. Once inside, Sage sat by herself. Dillinger and Hamilton sat together; Hamilton would later say that Dillinger seemed unusually affectionate that evening. Anna Sage was a madam who ran a brothel; Polly Hamilton worked for Sage. Dillinger was on the lam.

A bank robber and a killer, Dillinger thought he was safe staying with Anna Sage, but she betrayed him. She had secretly been in touch with the Federal Bureau of Investigation (FBI). She told them that she, Hamilton, and Dillinger were going to the movies that Sunday night and that she would be wearing a bright orange dress.

Inside, *Manhattan Melodrama* began. It would run about ninety-three minutes. Outside, grim looking men appeared out of nowhere. They silently stationed themselves in front of the Biograph, at its rear exits, and in the alley alongside. The Biograph's manager saw the men and got nervous; he thought they were gangsters and called the police. Around 10:20 p.m., two police cars roared up, and officers leaped out, guns in hand. "Police!" they shouted. "Put up your hands!"[5] The grim men around the Biograph shouted back, "FBI!" After a moment of chaos, the Chicago police backed away, and the FBI agents prepared their ambush. Their leader, Melvin Purvis, had been hunting Dillinger for months.

Manhattan Melodrama, directed by W. S. Van Dyke and written by Arthur Caesar, Oliver Garrett, and Joseph L. Mankiewicz, was an effort by Metro-Goldwyn-Mayer to cash in on the rage for gangster movies. D. W. Griffith's silent film *Musketeers of Pig Alley* (1912) is usually described as the very first gangster movie, and several other notable crime films had come after it, including Josef von Sternberg's *Underworld* (1927) and Lewis Milestone's *The Racket* (1928). The combination of Prohibition, bootleggers such as Legs Diamond and Dutch Schulz, Tommy guns, black sedans, the St. Valentine's Day Massacre in 1929, tabloid journalism, and, above all, the shockingly flamboyant Al Capone sparked movie-goers' enthusiasm for gangster films. Not everyone approved. As early as 1928, *The New Yorker* reported that "women's clubs and mother's clubs throughout the land are protesting the output of underworld pictures."[6]

Little Caesar (1931), *The Public Enemy* (1931), and *Scarface* (1932), though, were the three classic films that established the gangster genre. Gangster movies would be, like westerns, a distinctly American contribution to world cinema. The genre would replicate itself over the decades in a dozen subgenres and remain, despite periodic attempts at censorship, remarkably successful. A generation after *Little Caesar*, audiences flocked to Francis Ford Coppola's *Godfather* trilogy (1972, 1974, 1990), and a generation after that, millions of television viewers dedicated a portion of their lives to *The Sopranos* (1999–2007). Critics raved about *The Sopranos*; the *New York Times* called it possibly "the greatest work of American popular culture in the last quarter century."[7] In 2010, another hit television gangster series, *Boardwalk Empire*, succeeded *The Sopranos*.

Little Caesar, directed by Mervyn LeRoy, was adapted from a novel of the same name by William Burnett. At the box office, *Little Caesar* would have a huge impact.[8] *Little Caesar* starred Edward G. Robinson as Caesar Enrico "Rico" Bandello, a small-time crook who makes it big. The evil "Big Boy" (Sidney Blackmer), Rico's boss, is the film's Al Capone figure. This was Edward G. Robinson's breakout role, and his career, often playing a villain, skyrocketed after his performance in *Little Caesar*. For an audience to respond with fear and pity while watching Rico rise through daring and violence and then shockingly fall ("Mother of Mercy," Rico famously cries at the end of the movie, "is this the end of Rico?") was hard. Rico is "one of the first legitimate antiheroes in American cinema," Carlos Clarens writes. Producer Darryl Zanuck remarked that "[e]very other underworld picture has had a thug with a little bit of good in him. He reforms before the fade-out. This guy is no good at all. It'll go over big."[9] It went over big. According to Laurence Bergreen, Al Capone's biographer,

in New York, a crowd of 3,000 stormed a theater at Broadway and 47th Street, shattering glass and assaulting the box offices. The movie proved especially popular with children; a 1933 survey found that impressionable young boys from poor neighborhoods were prone to identify with the doomed Rico. As they watched it over and over, the boys absorbed a gangster lingo coined in Hollywood; expressions such as "You can dish it out, but you can't take it" and "take him for a ride" immediately entered the language.[10]

The Public Enemy was based on an unpublished novel by John Bright and Kubec Glasmon, entitled *Blood and Beer;* Bright and Glasmon claimed to be veterans of Chicago's Prohibition-era street battles. Tom Powers (James Cagney) and his brother, Mike (Donald Cook), grow up in the same house in the same neighborhood. Tom, a testosterone-fueled teenager, evolves from petty criminal to major gangster. Brother Mike stays on the straight and narrow. As Tom rises in crime, he drops his girlfriend, Kitty (Mae Clarke, and famously shoves a grapefruit half into her face), and falls for the ultimate gun moll, Gwen (Jean Harlow). Jack Shadoian notes that "*Little Caesar* was an unusually ascetic gangster hero. Tom Powers is the prototype of the high-living gangster, synonymous in the public mind with fast, fancy cars, easy money, loose women, boozing, swank nightclubs, and reckless, uninhibited activity."[11] But Tom is not all bad. His mother (Beryl Mercer) loves him, as does his brother, Mike. Tom brings money home to his mom, although Brother Mike indignantly rejects the dirty money. Tom is loyal to his partner, Matt (Edward Woods); at the end of the film, Tom is killed because he tries to avenge Matt's death. In the last grim scene of the movie, Tom's body is dumped at the family home.

Scarface, directed by Howard Hawks and Richard Rosson, was based on a 1929 novel by Armitage Trail. Trail's novel was inspired by the real Al Capone. Carlos Clarens writes that *Scarface* would become "perhaps the most famous crime film of its time."[12]

Paul Muni plays Tony Camonte, an Italian immigrant turned bootlegger. Ann Dvorak plays Tony's sister, Francesca. Tony murders his mob boss, takes over the gang, and becomes the underworld's chief. In the process, Tony turns into a monster. His relationship with Francesca is obsessive and downright pathological. Tony's distorted and exaggerated body language and facial expressions translate Tony into something inhuman; he becomes, as Fran Mason notes, "a thing rather than a person."[13] *Scarface* is both a gangster film and something like a monster film. At the same time, Tony is so "innocent" in his outrageous violence that he is almost, as Robin Wood writes, "comic."[14] In 1983, Brian De Palma would direct Al Pacino in a remake, famous for its maniacal violence, of *Scarface.*

All three films were smash hits. At the same time, they were only three of a tidal wave of gangster films. In 1931, for instance, "fifty-one gangster films reached the theaters, almost one per week."[15] All the films were shaped by the Roaring Twenties' fascination with the gangster; as Clarens notes, "the gangster was the romantic male figure of the period." Actors such as Edward G. Robinson, James Cagney, George Raft, and later Humphrey Bogart would rocket to fame, in large part, because of their associa-

Little boy studying a billboard in front of an unidentified movie house in New York; one of the films advertised is the gangster film "Murder at Dawn" (1932) starring Jack Mulhall. (New York City Municipal Archives)

tion with real gangsters. They would have, as Clarens says, a kind of "charisma endowed by crime."[16] The charisma began in the street, coursed through the movies, electrified the actors, and made them stars.

Even as the gangster movies exploded on screen, Hollywood was in the process of limiting what could be shown in the movies. Critics had complained about Hollywood's risqué films for years, and in 1922, the Motion Pictures Producers and Distributors Association (MPPDA)—Hollywood's trade association—had decided that the best way to avoid being policed by outsiders was to police itself. The MPPDA, later renamed the Motion Picture Association of America, asked President Warren Harding's postmaster general, Will H. Hays, to serve as its director. Hays was a firm Presbyterian and an Ohio Republican; he had been chair of the Republican National Committee and had managed Warren G. Harding's 1920 presidential campaign. Hays would run the Motion Picture Association from 1922 until 1945; his presence was so central that the association became known simply as the "Hays Office."

Critics had been after Hollywood all through the twenties, and Hays urged filmmakers to adopt a program of self-censorship. In 1930, just as the gangster film boom began, Hollywood adopted the "Motion Picture Production Code," designed to assure viewers that Hollywood films were family-friendly, wholesome entertainment. Popular enthusiasm for the new gangster films deeply worried some Americans. As Fran Mason points out, "religion, morality, and the work ethic are all absent from the gangster's life, as he embraces violence, power, consumption and technology without any check on his desires."[17] The Hays Office was concerned that audiences were "thrilled" rather than "horrified"[18] by the gangsters' exploits, and churches and other defenders of social morals loudly demanded that Hollywood live up to its own code. Mayor Anton Cermak banned *Scarface* from playing in Chicago.[19] Finally, in 1935, Hollywood declared a "moratorium" on the production of gangster films.

The impact of the code and the moratorium on the gangster genre is unclear. On one hand, Hollywood abandoned the increasingly wild excess typical of the "first cycle" of gangster films, especially *Scarface*. On the other hand, Hollywood, mindful of the genre's enormous profitability, began experimenting with slightly more palatable variations on the gangster theme. *Manhattan Melodrama* is one of the earliest "postcode" films. Its "Cain and Abel" structure splits the protagonist in half, between the "good" Jim Wade and the "bad" Blackie Gallagher. However, as bad as Blackie is, he has a good heart in him, and in a sense, he's a kind of outlaw police agent, "someone operating outside the law who does legitimate society's dirty work," a "gangster-as-policeman," a precursor of the "G-Men" who, despite being "government-men," look and act just like gangsters.[20]

To be sure, critics now complained about the caution of the postcode films. They were, critics charged, repetitious, generic, and so focused on personalities and relationships that they ignored social forces and public issues; these critics mocked what they called the "burbankization" of narrative.[21] However, Clarens argues that Hays, the code, and the moratorium probably did more good than harm:

> From the artistic point of view, Hay's influence was infinitely beneficial; not because it deterred some moviegoers from imitation but because it forced filmmakers to use subterfuge, ellipsis, and stylization, and to convey much of the forbidden through a system of visual hints. Ironically, Hays himself was godfather to the gangster hero that the films borrowed from the tabloids.[22]

Real gangsters continued to infuse life into the gangster genre. New York City's struggle against the gangsters, including the Dewey and Mur-

der, Inc., investigations, provided Hollywood with a cornucopia of characters and themes. Tim Newark reports that "several of the prostitute
witnesses [from the Thomas Dewey investigations] were invited to Hollywood to appear as themselves in movies rushed out to capitalize on the
publicity of the [Lucky Luciano] trial, including *Missing Witnesses* (1937)
and *Smashing Rackets* (1938)." Warner Brothers cast Bette Davis and
Humphrey Bogart as stars in the 1937 film *Marked Woman*, based on the
Dewey investigations.[23] *The Enforcer* (1951) and *Murder, Inc.* (1960) were
explicitly based on the Murder, Inc., story. Films ranging from, for example, *Counsel for Crime* (1937), about lawyers who defended gangsters; to
Racket Busters (1938), with a young Humphrey Bogart as a New York City
gangster; to the famous and controversial *On the Waterfront* (1954), written by Budd Schulberg, directed Elia Kazan, and starring Marlin Brando;
to *Lepke* (1975), in which Tony Curtis plays mobster Louis "Lepke" Buchalter, were all inspired by the La Guardia–era battle against organized
crime in New York City. So were the "syndicate films," in which citizens
discover that a vast criminal network actually dominates their city, and
their cousins, the "Last Just Man" films, in which a single brave citizen
or private eye, as in *The Phenix City Story* (1955), decides to do the right
thing and fight the syndicate, even though there seems to be no chance
of beating the monstrous criminal organization.[24]

At 10:30 p.m., on that warm evening of July 22, 1934, in the Biograph
Theater, *Manhattan Melodrama* ended, and the audience members clum-
sily got to their feet. John Dillinger put on his straw boater hat. Polly
Hamilton took his arm. Anna Sage followed behind.

Everything that happened next happened with such explosive fury
that afterward, no one could possibly say just what happened. (Philosopher Slavoj Žižek notes that if evil is violence, then the subjective experience of violence, for the victim and sometimes even for the perpe-
trator, becomes, because of the trauma involved, unspeakable. "There is
something inherently mystifying in a direct confrontation" with violence,
Žižek writes; "the overpowering horror of violent acts [. . .] prevents us
from thinking."[25] Perhaps this is why accounts of violence are so varied
and why we have recourse to indirect speech, to metaphors and filmic
images, when we wish to think about the unthinkable.) That Chicago
night, the brutal violence that the Hays Office wanted eliminated from
Hollywood gangster films erupted just outside, on the sidewalk, in real life.

FBI agent Melvin Purvis spotted Dillinger and quickly lit his cigar;
that was the sign to the other agents that Dillinger was in the crowd.
Dillinger seemed to sense something, he dropped Polly's arm, crouched,

suddenly reached into his pocket for a pistol, spun around, and bolted into the alley beside the Biograph. The FBI agents opened fire; a racket of gunfire rattled that sweltering Sunday night; the crowd froze in disbelief; Dillinger crashed to the ground bleeding profusely from the chest and head. The crowd panicked; several people, hit by ricochets or splinters of brick, screamed. The whole shootout lasted no more than a few seconds, although to the people there, it seemed like some long slow-motion sequence in a movie. Reporters flashed the story around the country. The next morning, from Manhattan to Miami, from Spokane to Sioux City to Bangor, everyone had to talk about it—they got Dillinger.[26] A real-life gangster shootout climaxed a fictional gangster movie.

If real-life gangsters like John Dillinger, and especially Al Capone, influenced the movies, did the movies influence the gangsters? John Dillinger went to at least one gangster movie; did Murder, Inc., go to the movies?

Here the evidence is murky; Abe Reles, Harry "Pittsburgh Phil" Strauss, Harry "Happy" Maione, Martin "Buggsy" Goldstein, and the other members of the Brownsville gang left no list of their favorite movies.

Yet, as H. Peter Steeves, argues, "identity [...] is always performative"; that is, who we *are* is profoundly shaped by the social roles we *play*. Scripts for these roles are socially constructed and are both reflected in and generated by the culture, including the mass culture, we inhabit.[27] If this is true, then to understand people like Kid Twist Reles, Pittsburgh Phil Strauss, Buggsy Goldstein, and Happy Maione, recognizing that their actions were, in some way, culturally mediated—that to some extent, they knew who they were because they saw themselves in the movies—is necessary.

There are striking echoes of the movies in the lives of the members of the Brownsville Murder, Inc., gang. Everyone in the gang wanted to "be somebody," just like Rico in Little Caesar. They wanted the "fast, fancy cars, easy money, loose women, boozing, swank nightclubs and reckless, uninhibited" life[28] that Tom Powers enjoys in The Public Enemy. "Everyone," Rich Cohen writes, "familiar with the Brooklyn boys was convinced that Edward G. Robinson based his film persona on Buggsy Goldstein, who had the same side-talking, duck-walking, tough-guy attitude as the movie star."[29] Or maybe Buggsy had seen Little Caesar too many times. Old and gray, exiled in Italy, living in Naples, at the center, rumor had it, of a drug-smuggling ring that would later become famous as the "French Connection,"[30] but otherwise retired, gangster Lucky Luciano, who had made his fortune in New York City in the 1920s and 1930s, began thinking about his legacy. Special prosecutor Tom Dewey, after one of NewYork's most sensational trials, had sent Luciano to prison in 1936. Luciano liked movies and had sketched out a screenplay about his life. The center of the drama pitted an innocent gambler (Luciano) who was set up by a corrupt district attorney (Tom Dewey). Luciano chatted about his film idea with movie producer Barnett Glassman. "Pity Humphrey Bogart is dead," Luciano mused. Bogart would have been just the actor to portray him, he thought. Of living actors, few tough guys were left—maybe George Raft or Marlon Brando would do.[31]

The media in general, not only the movies, loved gangsters—Will Hays wrote that "the gangster cycle [of the 1930s] was a natural because the gangster cult had been a main theme of journalism for a decade"[32]—and gangsters paid close attention to the media. Jack "Legs" Diamond, for example, was one of the most notorious New York City gangsters during the age of Murder, Inc. Legs Diamond was a thief and a bootlegger; Dutch Schulz (Arthur Flegenheimer) was his archrival. Patrick Downey, Diamond's biographer, notes that when the famous explorer, Dr. Herbert Spencer Dickey, was searching for the origin of the Orinoco River in South America, he and his team carried a short-wave radio with them. They could pick up the New York Times radio signal. Back in the United States, when reporters asked Dickey about the dangers he faced, he replied: "You people talk about the dangers of the jungle [. . .] do you know that the people down there, after hearing all about Al Capone and Legs Diamond over the radio, have an idea that the Americans are just a race of bloodthirsty bandits? They ask us about the dangers of life in the United States, just as you ask about the dangers of the jungle."[33] In 1931 alone, Legs Diamond was mentioned in the New York Times some 103 times, 19 times on the front page. New York's tabloids were crazy about him. Diamond got fan mail; people pleaded with him for his autograph; "surely he was," Downey writes, "the most photographed outlaw of his day." Not only did Diamond impress the media; the media also impressed Diamond. He "read everything they wrote about him," Downey notes; Diamond "even kept a scrapbook with newspaper clippings."[34] Long after his death, Legs Diamond inspired a movie, The Rise and Fall of Legs Diamond (1960); a novel, William Kennedy's Legs (1975);[35] a Broadway musical, Legs Diamond (1988); and even a 1980s Los Angeles rock-and-roll band, "Legs Diamond." When bootlegger extraordinaire Arthur Flegenheimer was asked why he preferred to be known as Dutch Schulz, he explained that "Arthur Flegenheimer" would not fit into the headlines.[36]

In July 1931, The New Yorker published a profile of Legs Diamond. The profile, written by Joel Sayre, who met with Diamond in his home in

Acra, New York, high up in the Catskill Mountains, north of New York City, was titled "Profile: Big Shot At." The title poked fun at Diamond's reputation for being shot repeatedly but, thus far, without fatal consequence. Sayre began, saying, "[T]oday, Legs Diamond is known throughout the world—in Melbourne, Cape Town, Shanghai. In London, they call him 'Cunning Jackie;' in Berlin, 'der Shack Diamant,' and many of his moronic and mendicant fellow-countrymen write him fan letters." But, Sayre writes, Legs Diamond is really just a burglar and thief, no real heir to Chicago's Al Capone or New York's super-gambler, Arnold Rothstein.

Legs Diamond had been a bodyguard for Arnold Rothstein, but, alas, something drove them violently apart. When Eddie Diamond, Legs's brother, developed tuberculosis and moved to Denver for his health, Rothstein "ordered two of his men, Eugene Moran and Frank Devlin, to follow. There was a slip somewhere, for when the pair arrived in Denver, the police immediately took their machine guns away." The Diamond brothers struck back, and their revenge was probably the cause of the "deaths of Devlin, Moran, Fatty Walsh, Morty Schubert, Harry Veasey, and Jack Waller, all members of the Rothstein Expeditionary Forces."

Sayre reported that Legs never really got back on his feet after the shootings, on July 13, 1929, of two men at his Hotsy-Totsy Club at 1721 Broadway. Both the police and the underworld went after Legs, who fled to the Catskills, where he fortified himself in his home in Acra. Diamond gave Sayre a tour. "He has certainly been pleasant to meet," Sayre reported,

> if he thought you were "legitimate" and were introduced by somebody he knew [. . .] he is handsome, with large brown eyes and black hair that is beginning to thin in front, and although he is always referred to as "the little racketeer," he is five feet ten and a half inches tall, and between shootings weighs about one hundred and forty-five. The only mark of hardness about his face is the little arrow of care always between his brows, even when he is laughing. Although his tailoring is good, for some strange reason an expanse of shirt is usually visible between his trousers and vest. He wears dark clothes, sober ties, letting his extravagances in color run to silk underwear and pajamas of Algerian red, Chinese gold, lovebird green, flame, turquoise, and coral, with elaborate designs, from primitive polka dots to the most complicated modern whorls and tangents.

Sayre did not think Diamond was the "typical" hoodlum: "he doesn't talk out of the side of his mouth; his grammar, save for a little trouble with personal pronouns in the objective case is good, and he still retains the phonetics and syntax of Philadelphia," where he spent his childhood. Sayre continued: "Aside from the newspapers, of which he is a careful reader (he has a large collection of clippings concerning his own exploits stored in empty stationary boxes) his literary taste runs mostly to the novels of Oliver Curwood, Zane Grey, and other authors of the bing-bing-bing school."

Sayre concluded grimly: Diamond's "future looks very black." Most likely, Sayre thought, Diamond, who had already been shot repeatedly, would end up with a "reputation of rather doubtful value as the clay pigeon of the underworld."[37]

The New Yorker kept up with Diamond for the next few weeks. In July 1931, in a "Talk of the Town" segment titled "Gangster at Home," *The New Yorker* reported in more detail about Diamond's home in Acra in the Catskills. Reporters had complained that Diamond was reluctant to show off the interior of his home. *The New Yorker* thought it knew the reason for his modesty:

> During Legs Diamond's latest spell in the public eye, you may have noticed that of all the photographs in the various newspapers of his home at Acra and its surroundings, there have been none of its interior. A gentleman who was prowling around there at the time reports that he knows the reason for this. It appears that Mrs. Diamond has a passion for various highly feminine knickknacks, particularly those spindly stuffed-satin French dolls which you tie into knots and leave lying around on the furniture. Mr. Diamond humors her in this, to the extent that the house is practically filled with the things. When the photographers came around he was going to give them the freedom of the house but it suddenly struck him that this was no way the interior of a gangster's fortress to look, full of dolls and all. He figured that pictures of them would make him seem ridiculous to the public. So there were no interior views.[38]

In August 1931, the "Talk of the Town" reported that the jury in a recent Diamond trial had been treated by the court to a night at one of New York's most popular shows, the *Third Little Show*, at a cost to the taxpayers, the shocked "Talk of the Town" reported, of seventy-seven dollars.[39]

Sayre's idea of the "typical hoodlum," who "talks out of the side of his mouth," sounds a lot like Edward G. Robinson or James Cagney. Hollywood, in particular, but the media in general, created a whole gangster persona, instantly recognizable and easy to adopt. The snap-brim fedora, the suit with the padded shoulders, the strut, the attitude, the fractured grammar, the bundle of money in the pocket, the gun in the shoulder holster bulging behind the double-breasted suit jacket—everyone knew what a gangster was supposed to look and sound like. As David Ruth convincingly argues, the archetypal gangster was a media creation.[40]

Abe Reles and the others certainly played their gangster roles well. The whole point of being a gangster was to be seen being a gangster. Of course, crimes had to be kept secret from the police, but the gangster strut and swagger were on display daily on the corner of Livonia and Saratoga Avenues in the heart of the Brownsville neighborhood in Brooklyn. Everyone in Brownsville, after 1931, knew that Abe Reles was the tough guy who had shot his way to power by killing his gang leader predecessor. On any day Reles, Strauss, Goldstein, Maione, and others could be found hanging around on the corner of Livonia and Saratoga in front of "Midnight Rose's" candy store. Rich Cohen writes that his grandmother ran a diner in Brownsville in the 1930s and that "gangsters were such a regular part of the clientele" that when Cohen's grandmother went into labor while working at the diner, "Abe Reles drove her to the hospital."[41] The police, of course, knew Reles and the others, too, and regularly picked them up on suspicion of this and that. Reles would swagger into the precinct station, smirk at the desk sergeant, jokingly give his occupation as "luncheonette operator" or "soda jerk,"[42] pull out an enormous wad of money, bail himself out, and swagger away. The whole performance was a mix of Edward G. Robinson and James Cagney. Reles was so well known that by the later 1930s, the New York Times would call him "Brooklyn's Public Enemy No. 1."[43]

Violence was central to the gangster performance both in the movies and on the street. On February 16, 1934, Reles and (most likely) Pittsburgh Phil Strauss drove into a gas station on East 98th Street in Brownsville. They honked at the attendant, Charles Battle, and demanded service. Battle told them to keep their shirts on and that he would get to them, or something like that. Whatever Battle said, Reles and Strauss exploded in fury. They leaped from their car, Strauss grabbed Battle and pinned his arms behind him; Reles began to pound Battle with his fists. Reles and Strauss dropped Battle, jumped in their car, and drove off. However, they were not done. They returned, jumped from the car, and, again, attacked a man they thought was Battle. The man was not Charles Battle, however; Battle had gone to the police and sworn out a complaint against Reles. The man Reles and Strauss attacked this time was another attendant, Alvin Snyder. There was a scuffle; Reles or Strauss pulled a knife; Snyder was stabbed to death. What had so infuriated Reles and Strauss? Maybe race was involved; both Battle and Snyder were African Americans. Certainly, respect was an issue; both Reles and Strauss flew into hysterics whenever they thought they were being disrespected.

There was not enough evidence to indict either Strauss or Reles for Snyder's murder, but there was enough—Charles Battle's complaint—to indict Reles, described by the *Times* as "well-known in the Brownsville section," for second-degree assault. In May 1934, the jury found Reles guilty but of third-degree, not second-degree, assault. The presiding judge, George Martin, was furious. Second-degree assault carried a prison term of seven years; third-degree assault carried only three years. Martin scolded the jury for virtually releasing Reles. Judge Martin then mocked Reles. "This fellow," Judge Martin said, "is brave enough to stab in the back or shoot a defenseless person and, with a gang supporting him, might punch or kick an invalid [. . .] He'd never stand up to a square man-to-man fight. He hasn't that kind of courage." Reles, outraged, shouted to his lawyer, "[T]ell that judge that I'd take on any cop with pistols or anything else!"[44] That sort of boast sounded like it had come straight from a Jimmy Cagney movie.

By the 1930s, the media and the gangster were inextricably mixed. Why had Joel Sayre, *The New Yorker* writer, assumed that Legs Diamond would speak out of the side of his mouth? Probably because that is how actor Jimmy Cagney spoke when he portrayed gangsters. Why did people assume Diamond was short? Maybe because early gangster actors, such as Edward G. Robinson, James Cagney, and George Raft, were short.

George Raft was a New Yorker who knew real gangsters, and when he went to Hollywood to become an actor he played gangsters. Raft, for example, played Rinaldo in *Scarface*. With Edward G. Robinson, Jimmy Cagney, and later, Humphrey Bogart, George Raft forged the archetype of the big-city gangster. Born in 1901 in the "Hell's Kitchen" section of Manhattan, Raft was only a few years older than Abe Reles. Raft became close friends with Owney Madden and Bugsy Siegel; some thought that Raft and Siegel looked enough alike to be brothers. Raft later reminisced:

> These fellows were like gods to me [. . .] They all had Dusenbergs and sixteen-cylinder Cadillacs and wherever they went there were police captains and politicians bowing to them, and I thought, "these fellows can't be doing anything wrong."[45]

Raft, as a fictional gangster, was slim and always immaculately dressed. He wore the finest jewelry, a snap-brim fedora, and flipped a coin while cracking wise. Raft gangsters were no gorillas. As tough as the Raft characters seemed, they were also lithe, tightly sprung, just a little nervous, like dancers; Raft began in show business as a song and dance man, just like James Cagney.

Dutch Schulz, the Beer Baron of the Bronx and Legs Diamond's arch-rival, never had a *New Yorker* profile done on him. Long after his death, though, Schulz inspired E. L. Doctorow's 1989 novel, *Billy Bathgate*, which, in 1991, became a movie of the same name starring Dustin Hoffman as Schulz. In the novel, a kid named Billy Bathgate, one of several "skinny kids with encrusted noses and green teeth," watches in awe as a La Salle coupé comes around the corner of 177th Street and Park Avenue. Billy and his friends know that the warehouse they are staring at is one of Dutch Schulz's beer drops, and they know that "in Mr. Schulz's mind his enterprise was an independent kingdom of his own law, not society's, and it was all the same to him whatever was legal or illegal."[46] A Buick Roadster follows the La Salle, and a Packard follows the Buick. All the skinny kids stand to stare. Dutch Schulz gets out of his car and looks at the kids. Billy, who happens to be showing off his juggling skills, looks at Schulz in astonishment, "to the effect of omigod it's him standing there." Billy keeps juggling; "the great man laughed and applauded, and glanced at the henchman beside him to encourage his appreciation, which duly came."[47] Schulz motions to Billy to come closer; he peels off a ten-dollar bill from a great wad of money, pats Billy's cheek, and rasps, "[A] capable boy." Schulz hands the ten-dollar bill to Billy, who stands in awe, "hearing the great gangster of my dreams."[48] Billy eventually becomes part of Dutch Schulz's gangster entourage. The historical Dutch Schulz becomes, in the novel, a figure in a fiction that reflects on real events, a fiction that becomes a movie about a fictional story about a real hoodlum.

Talking about Murder, Inc., or gangsters without discussing movies first is impossible because movies, and the wider media, created a vast stock of metaphors and images that made gangsters comprehensible both to gangsters and to everyone else. The "gangster" image moves and morphs, from immigrant New York neighborhoods to Hollywood to television to pop music. Sometimes, distinguishing what is culture and what is history is hard. During World War II, a young Chicago hoodlum named Sam Giancana, who would, over the years, rise to greater criminal things only to be murdered in 1975, was drafted. Selective Service officials asked Giancana his occupation. Giancana replied "I steal." Selective Service declared him a "psychopath," graded him 4–F—unfit for service, and released him. Film critic Carlos Clarens points out that the phrase, "I steal," is one of the famous lines from the 1932 hit film *I Am a Fugitive from a Chain Gang.*

Maybe Giancana was being honest; maybe he was being ironic; maybe he was just a wise guy; maybe he was citing the film. In the gangster universe, distinguishing fact from fiction, the streets from the movies, is very tricky.[49]

Later gangster epics would speculate about the relationship between the real gangster life and the movies, about the interaction between cultural scripts and the roles people play. The hugely successful television series *The Sopranos* (1999–2007) regularly reflects on both gangster life and gangster film. Both the series itself, in theme and style, and the fictional characters within the series, constantly reference *The Godfather*. Tony Soprano's favorite film (he is the fictional gang boss in the series) is *The Public Enemy*.[50]

Louis "Lepke" Buchalter was yet another notorious 1930s Manhattan gangster. Lepke and his allies terrorized the needle trades. To eliminate witnesses against him, Lepke would mobilize Abe Reles and his Brownsville gang, who would become known, then, as Murder, Inc. The government's hunt for Lepke became one of the media sensations of the late 1930s; Lepke would turn himself in to the best-known radio personality of the day, Walter Winchell. In 1939, the Federal Bureau of Investigation (FBI) described Lepke Buchalter, like this: Lepke's eyes were "alert and shifty." He has a "habit of passing change from one hand to the other." Lepke wore "a yellow gold ring on the small finger of his left hand. The ring is set with a large 'cats-eye' stone described as being palish [*sic*] blue in color similar to a Star Sapphire." He also wore "a very expensive and flashy yellow gold pocket watch set with emeralds and rubies." Lepke, the report concluded, "has a habit of looking at his watch every five minutes"; also, he "habitually wears snap-brim felt hats."[51] Reading the FBI's Lepke file, the image that emerges is not of a dowdy Manhattan hoodlum but, rather, that of a suave, if jittery, celluloid gangster who flips a coin while smirking at the camera, just like George Raft.

Gangster movies do many things. Americans have always loved outlaws, and urban gangsters are motorized versions of Wild West bandits. Some gangster films portray id unleashed, and their visualization of appetite, sex, and especially violence is, no doubt, another source of their popularity. Viewers can both enjoy excess and then, with the gangster's demise, primly repudiate it. Gangster films work through male fantasies and anxieties; the films often include searing critiques of corporate power and permit a kind of virtual radicalism; their insistent modernism—they are urban films, the protagonists deploy all the modern technologies, and indulge in all the modern vices—permits the films to mediate, display, criticize, and interpret modernism for viewers struggling to navigate the modern world. The early gangster films, as Jonathan Munby points out, literally give voice to urban immigrants who, before, had only limited roles in popular culture. Big-city immigrants and their children could finally see people like themselves not just in the gangsters but also in all the figures in the gangster movies.[52]

People see part of themselves in gangster films. "When we view gangster movies," Jack Shadoian writes, "it is our psyche we watch—displaced, dislocated, alien, yet familiar."[53] But, Shadoian adds, the gangster film's appeal is not only psychological. Yes, the gangster film "realizes our dreams, exposes our deepest psychic urges." Yet, the gangster film's

> imperative has been, as well, to stick close to the tawdry, unpleasant, ugly aspects of American life [. . .] The genre speaks not merely to our fascination/repulsion with aspects of our socioeconomic milieu that we prefer to shut our eyes to but also to our fascination/repulsion with the most haunting depths of ourselves [. . .] the gangster is a paradigm of the American dream.[54]

Gangster films, for all their tabloid inspiration, are also films about ideas. "The gangster film," Fran Mason writes, "became the site of opposing ideologies, one nostalgic evoking order, hierarchy, and discipline [. . .] the other foregrounding the excess and chaos of modernity (represented by the gang)."[55] According to Gwyn Symonds,

> [p]opular culture's fascination with organized crime, in which fictional and actual gangsters share an archetypal theatricality on the same media stage, bespeaks a recognition that the drama or the real life events in gangster lives of crime is inherently theatrical fodder, ripe for aesthetic recasting [. . .] The dramatic glamour of their stories, with larger than life characters and classic scenarios of greed, revenge, betrayal, power, survival, and execution, draws the public gaze and the creativity of storytellers.[56]

Most important, the gangster film, like all film, carries an ethical charge. According to Noël Carroll,

> The idea that certain movies might undermine common decency or morality is usually revived several times a year by this or that pundit [. . .] while, on the other hand, different films are often commended for improving moral understanding or advancing superior moral standards. If only because of their close connection to the emotions, films are apt to call forth an ethical response.[57]

Gangster movies are morality plays. Unlike any other film genre, gangster films typically turn the villain into the protagonist and that fundamentally alters the moviegoer's experience. Most plays and movies have villains who are antagonists to the hero-protagonist, and viewers identify emotionally with the hero-protagonist and not with the villain. Even if, as in tragedies, the hero is destroyed through his or her own hubris, audiences still do not identify with the villain; we may weep for Othello, but we do not like Iago.

But in many gangster movies, the villain is the protagonist, and that disrupts everything. To be sure, some gangster films follow a simple Manichaean formula and juxtapose the good-guy protagonists (the brave citizen, the plucky cop, the noble district attorney) against the villainous gangster. In classic gangster films, though, from *Little Caesar, The Public Enemy,* and *Scarface* to *The Godfather* and *The Sopranos*, the protagonist is the bad guy, and viewers are jerked into a very awkward position. At one moment, we are attracted to the villain-protagonist; the next moment, confronted with the villain-protagonist's cruelty and brutality, we are repulsed. Then we are repulsed by what attracts us, and even attracted by what repulsed us. Viewing a gangster movie is not easy.

This attraction and repulsion generate a kind of Brechtian "alienation-effect," an anti-Aristotelean phenomenon in which viewers are not so much invited to participate vicariously in the protagonist's life but, rather, are encouraged to detach from it periodically, think about it, and reorient themselves to it. This constant back and forth, engagement and disengagement, assessment and reassessment of what is admirable about the protagonist and what is not, and an orientation and reorientation of the viewer toward the film are fundamentally a form of moral reflection.

Gangster films force viewers to shift what Amartya Sen calls their "positionality."[58] We are all in our own skins; we all are in some geographical and biographical space; we all have a "position" from which we view the world. If we fail to recognize our "positionality" and mistake our "positionality" for "universality" and if we assume that our position is the only one possible, then we are not so much morally inspired as merely biased. If we possess all the moral answers we need, then we have no need for serious moral questions. If, however, we are unsure, if we confront a complex issue that permits no easy answers, if we encounter paradoxes and ambiguities that require us to act even in the face of doubt, then we need to free ourselves from what Sen calls our "positional confinement,"[59] shift our positionality, and view things not from the perspective of pat answers but of vital questions. By shifting the position of the protagonist, gangster

films require us to shift our positionality as well and thus to begin to reflect morally.

Such a shift of positionality does not mean a collapse into relativism. Instead, it means adopting the role of the "impersonal spectator"
that Adam Smith, and following Smith, Amartya Sen, think so central
to ethical reflection.[60] We need to free ourselves from our narrow "self,"
and cultivate the ability to view both others and even, perhaps especially,
ourselves, from the perspective of conscience, which is not identical with
"self." Indeed, we might even argue that this shift in positionality provokes
the kind of "conversion" Emmanuel Levinas discusses, in which we move
from unquestioned answers and primitive narcissism to an awareness of,
and sense of responsibility for, the "Other,"[61] even when the "Other" is
radically different from "me."

Ambiguity and doubt, not certainty and assurance, are at the heart of
moral reflection, and gangster films, in which the villain is the protagonist,
are nothing if not ambiguous. We are attracted to Rico, Tom Powers, and
Scarface but are shocked by them too. Part of us wishes we could enjoy
the gangster's life of excess, even while another part is appalled by the
gangster's total lack of restraint. The gangster protagonists are bad guys,
but we, nevertheless, care about them. In gangster films, while the normal
bad guys are often at least partly good, the normal good guys—the cops,
the lawyers, and those from high society—are often at least partly bad.
Sometimes, as in the "Cain and Abel" films (with one good brother and
one bad) and the "G-man" films (in which the cops wear snap-brim fe-
doras and trench coats and fire machine guns just like the gangsters), it is
hard to tell the crooks from the cops and the cops from the crooks.[62] Far
from defeating moral reflection, precisely this sort of experience provokes
moral reflection.

Robert Warshow described the film gangster as modern America's
"tragic hero";[63] like ancient tragedies, he continues, gangster movies provoke moral reflection. Gangsters inspired gangster films and gangster films
created the very idea of "gangster"; both, with extraordinary vitality and
urgency, invite us to think about good and evil, fate and choice, excess
and restraint, the subordination of people to money,[64] courage and cowardice, virtue and vice, corporations and rackets, the "gangster look" and
"gangster realities," modernity and its discontents, loyalty and betrayal,
masculinities and femininities, the city and its dangers, and what matters
and what does not. A voyage into the cinematic underworld fires our
moral imagination.

2
Real Gangsters
Abe Reles and the Origins of Murder, Inc.

> If you wanted someone to help you break a
> head, beat up a guy, break a strike, buy dope,
> set a fire, plan a robbery, or muscle a peddler,
> you could find him at Label's [Poolroom].
>
> —*Sammy Aaronson, remembering Brownsville*[1]

Behind the reel gangsters in the movies lurked the real gangsters in the neighborhoods. The movie gangster, as David Ruth reminds us, "was an invention" and was not "an accurate reflection of reality."[2] So what were real gangsters like? This chapter explores some of the things known about Murder, Inc.—the role that gangs played in New York City's immigrant life, the interplay between nature and nurture, and the clash between first- and second-generation immigrants. Yet, the members of Murder, Inc., were not quite what one might think. Murder, Inc., is full of surprises.

Murder, Inc., was a New York City Depression-era gang. The gang flourished in Brooklyn's Brownsville neighborhood from 1931 to 1940. Its leader was Abe "Kid Twist" Reles. Its members included Harry "Pittsburgh Phil" Strauss, Harry "Happy" Maione, Martin "Buggsy" Goldstein, and Frank "the Dasher" Abbandando. At its height, the gang included perhaps a score of active members and an equal number of neighborhood kids who hung around mobsters.

From the Irish "Dead Rabbits" in the 1850s to the "Sharks" and "Jets" of Leonard Bernstein's *West Side Story* (1957) and well beyond, gangs have been a staple of New York City immigrant life. At least since the nineteenth century, there had hardly been a poor neighborhood without a gang. Herbert Asbury, in his 1927 "informal history of the underworld," *The Gangs of New York*, is pretty harsh in his judgment of gang members: "in the main," Asbury writes, "the gangster was a stupid roughneck born in filth and squalor and reared amid vice and corruption."[3] Irving Howe, in his history of Jewish immigration to New York, is a bit more sympathetic. "Juvenile crime and hooliganism" were ubiquitous in Jewish immigrant neighborhoods Howe notes; by about 1900 or so, a "distinctive youth delinquency" had become a serious problem. Youth gangs had, by then, become one of several kinds of "improvised social forms" among teenagers. On one hand, Howe writes, were "the good and earnest boys, future reformers and professionals," who organized a myriad of educational and self-improvement clubs. "At the other extreme," according to Howe, "were the 'tough' gangs, made up of boys from six to twenty." These gangs were, Howe concludes, "rough schools of experiences," which "gave a certain structure to the interval between childhood and independence—half-illicit, half-fraternal agencies for the passage into adult life."[4]

In the 1890s, Theodore Roosevelt was thinking of becoming New York's streets commissioner; he would become, instead, New York's police commissioner. The problem with New York's streets, Roosevelt thought, was not simply garbage. The bigger problem was the "toughs," teenage boys who stood on street corners, harassed passersby, and constantly got into trouble. Roosevelt wrote to Jacob Riis, author of the shocking exposé of poverty in New York, *How the Other Half Lives* (1890), that while clean streets would be wonderful, "it would be a better thing to have our schools large enough to give ample accommodation to all who should be pupils and to provide them with proper playgrounds [. . .] to take the children off the streets so as to prevent them from growing up toughs."[5] Riis had angrily written that New York's vast slums were virtual factories for the manufacture of hoodlums. "That such conditions as were all about us should result in making 'toughs' was not strange," Riis argued.

> Rather, it would have been strange had anything else come of it. With the home corrupted by the tenement; the school doors closed against them where the swarms were densest and the children thrown upon the street, there to take their chance; with honest play interdicted, every natural right of the child turned into a means of oppression, a game of ball became a crime for which children were thrust into jail, indeed, shot down like dangerous criminals when running away from the policeman; with the lawlessness of the street added to the want of rule at home [. . .] it seemed as if we had set out to deliberately make trouble under which we groaned.[6]

In the early 1940s, sociologist William Foote Whyte completed his pioneering study of big city gangs, titled *Street Corner Society* (1943).[7] White's neighborhood hoodlums grew up mostly unsupervised in rough neighborhoods. They were not loners and quickly found other young men just like themselves with whom to associate. Gang members spontaneously sorted themselves out into a hierarchy, with one young man emerging as the boss and the others assuming the role of followers. The gangs waged turf wars against other gangs. Their antisocial behavior ranged from intimidation to vandalism to burglary and smuggling to homicide. Things had not changed much since the 1890s.

To be a member of a gang was to adopt what Assistant District Attorney Burton Turkus would call a kind of "social code."[8] To begin with, and to mark a kind of birth into the gang, just about everybody in a gang received a nickname. Sometimes Jewish and Italian gang members took on whole new names, often Irish or German names because the Irish and Germans were the earlier immigrant groups and had become more or less respectable. Francisco Castiglia, for example, became "Frank Costello." Sometimes a nickname was simply a diminutive of a surname. Irving Wechsler, for instance, took the name "Waxey Gordon." "Gordon" was nicely WASP-ish; "Waxey" may have referred to Wechsler's skilled pickpocket hands or may simply have been an abbreviation for Wechsler. Salvatore Lucania took the name "Charlie" as an all-purpose "American" sounding name and changed Lucania (with the feminine sounding *a*) to the more masculine Luciano. Dozens of stories exist about the origin of Luciano's nickname "Lucky." Maybe he was "Lucky" because he survived an assassination attempt, but maybe "Lucky" was just a shortened version of "Luciano." Some nicknames came from popular culture. In the 1920s and 1930s, *buggsy* meant "wild" and "crazy," like the cartoon character "Bugs Bunny." Many gang members were nicknamed "Bugs" or "Buggsy"—Benjamin "Bugsy" Siegel was the most famous. Vito Gurino was nicknamed "Socko," after the slang term for a punch or a fighter. Gurino boasted that he was the best shot in Brooklyn, that he practiced by shooting the heads off chickens, so, of course, he was nicknamed "Chickenhead" as well. Other nicknames were descriptive—Jack Diamond got the name "Legs" probably because of his quick getaways.

Most guys in Abe Reles's crowd had nicknames too. Harry Strauss was "Big Harry"—a reference not so much to his size as to his swagger. Strauss was also called "Pep," referring to his vigor, and "Pittsburgh Phil." There had once been a real "Pittsburgh Phil." His name was George E. Smith. Born outside Pittsburgh, Smith worked in Pittsburgh as a laborer but quickly demonstrated a genius for gambling. A pool shark in Chicago, he was known as "Pittsburgh Smith," to distinguish him from the

Abe Reles. (*Brooklyn Eagle*, Brooklyn Public Library)

other pool hustlers named Smith; why "Phil" was added to "Pittsburgh" is unclear. In any case, horse racing proved to be his specialty. In 1887, Pittsburgh Phil moved to New York and became, according to the *New York Times*, the "most remarkable and successful betting operator [...] ever." He was called a "plunger," or a spectacular loser, but the name was not accurate; Pittsburgh Phil the Plunger was normally a big winner. Around 1900, he was one of the most famous sporting men frequenting New York racetracks. Sadly, only in his forties, Phil developed tuberculosis, and he died in Asheville, North Carolina, in 1905. He was buried amid a "blinding snowstorm" in Pittsburgh's Uniondale Cemetery; an "immense crowd" attended the cemetery services, despite the blizzard. Journalist Edward W. Cole kept Phil's memory alive. In 1908, Cole published *Racing Maxims and Methods of Pittsburgh Phil*, which became must reading for racetrack bettors. In the 1930s, the name "Pittsburgh Phil" was still in the ether; a 1931 sports story in the *Brooklyn Eagle* referred to "an old maxim of Pittsburgh Phil," and in Damon Runyon's 1933 story "Broadway Complex" is a character named "Pittsburgh Phil."[9]

Harry Maione, who invariably wore a scowl was, of course, nicknamed "Happy." Martin Goldstein was another "Buggsy." Just how Frank Abbandando received the name "the Dasher" is not clear. According to one story, an assailant once chased Abbandando around a Brooklyn block, but Abbandando was a fast runner, so much so that he actually ended up chasing his chaser. A more mundane story says that Abbandando was such a speedy runner on a reform school baseball team that he earned the nickname "the Dasher." Sometimes nicknames recalled gangster history. Arthur Flegenheimer took the name "Dutch Schulz," the name of a leader of the old Frog Hollow Gang in the Bronx.[10] Abe Reles took the name "Kid Twist," in memory of Max Zweibach, a criminal killed in 1908.[11]

Nurture, of course, played a central role in the origins of the Brownsville gang. When, around 1900, Sam and Rose Reles crossed the Williamsburg Bridge from Lower Manhattan and entered the wide-open spaces of central Brooklyn, they must have felt like they had moved to the Promised Land within the Promised Land.[12] Sam and Rose had ridden that vast wave of Eastern European Jewish immigration all the way from Austria to New York City, only to find themselves trapped in the fetid slums of the Lower East Side. Their son, Abraham, was born there on May 10, 1906.[13] One way out of Manhattan's slums was to head east, and the young Reles family, like thousands of others, packed their few belongings, said so long to the Lower East Side, and headed across the East River, into the new housing developments sprawling across central Brooklyn. According to Irving Howe,

> [p]erhaps the most traveled route out of the East Side was to Brooklyn, especially the Brownsville, New Lots, and East New York sections. Brownsville was [. . .] regarded as a pastoral village in which 'Jews could live as in the old country, without any ruse or excessive worries' [. . .] By the early 1890s some four thousand Jews had settled in and near the Brownsville area; by 1905, about fifty thousand.[14]

Central and eastern Brooklyn had long been farmland; when it was first carved into separate properties in the early 1800s, people called it the "New Lots." By the 1860s, New Lots was home not just to farms but to a variety of small factories and to New York City's largest garbage dump as well. New Lots was lowland, and it flooded easily. Even worse, New Lots was, on bad days, downwind of the bone-boiling plants on Jamaica Bay, and the stench from the boiled bones was prodigious.[15] In 1858, William Suydam, an ambitious farmer in New Lots, divided some of his farmland into single-home lots with the hope of attracting New York City workers, but his development scheme went bust. In 1861, Charles Brown, a real estate developer, snapped up Suydam's properties; began putting up rows of small, boxy one- and two-story homes; renamed the place Brownsville; and started recruiting buyers. Brown succeeded where Suydam failed, and by 1883, some 250 modest homes filled Brooklyn's Brownsville. Entrepreneurs built factories, too, and constructed company housing for their workers—Brownsville became a distinctly working-class neighborhood. Then, after the Williamsburg Bridge between Manhattan and Brooklyn went up in 1903, the human flood into Brownsville began. Fleeing tenements, looking for work beyond Manhattan's sweatshops, thousands of Jewish and Italian immigrants headed for central Brooklyn, and Brownsville, congested, noisy, full of hardworking poor people, became a clone of the Lower East Side.

Pitkin Avenue was Brownsville's Fifth Avenue, a main thoroughfare with lots of stores. Four blocks south, under the El tracks, Saratoga and Livonia Avenues crossed. On the corner where they crossed was Gold's convenience store; in New York, convenience stores were called "candy stores." Rose Gold ran the store; because it was open twenty-four hours, locals nicknamed it "Midnight Rose's." To the guys who hung out on the corner of Saratoga and Livonia, it was The Corner. Midnight Rose's would become, according to Burton Turkus, the "assembly room and dispatch bureau of killers—the office of the mob."[16]

Alfred Kazin, who would become one of America's premier literary critics, grew up in Brownsville, and he remembered "raw patches of
unused city land all around us filled with monument works where they
cut and stored tombstones"; he remembered Brownsville as "dead land,
neither city nor country."[17] Playgrounds were scarce; the neighborhood's
only park, Betsy Head Park, was not finished until 1914 and was inevitably packed with people. Schools, shops, miniature factories, auto garages,
tiny two-story tar-paper-roofed homes, and crowded tenements were
all on top of each other helter-skelter. By 1920, when Abe Reles was a
teenager, 85 percent of the people in the neighborhood were Jewish,[18]
just about all of them first- or second-generation immigrants; most of rest
were first- or second-generation Italian immigrants.

Brownsville's Jews were an unusual crowd. Poor immigrants, they were
not unlettered peasants. Jews had fled Russia and Eastern Europe after the
1880s not simply because they were poor but also because they were Jews,
and as Jews, the targets for the homicidal pogroms inspired by the tsarist
state. Laborers fled to America, and so did entrepreneurs. Schoolteachers
fled, and so did rabbis, doctors, poets, musicians, carpenters, criminals, and
saints. Because they all left just about everything behind, they all were
poor. They were Jewish. But beyond that, they were divided by a thousand differences. Eastern Europe's Jews had been amid an extraordinary
cultural renaissance when the pogroms hit at the end of the nineteenth
century. Some Jewish intellectuals thought of themselves as Russians,
took an active part in late tsarist Russia's turbulent politics, and wrote
and thought in Russian. Some tried to revive classical Hebrew; others
defended Yiddish. Religiously, there were Orthodox, Conservative, and
Reform Jews, even atheist Jews. Politically, there were conservatives and
liberals, authoritarians and democrats. Zionists insisted that Jews had a distinct nationality and, therefore, desperately needed their own nation-state.
Bundists argued, to the contrary, that social class and social justice were
the key issues, not national identity.[19] Anarchists, socialists, and commu-
nists fought among each other even as all called for revolution. All of
them, it seemed, moved to Brownsville. Sol Hurok, who was raised in
Brownsville and became one of New York's leading music impresarios,
recalled that in the early years of the twentieth century,

> Brownsville was a steaming microcosm of cultures in the heart of
> Brooklyn, alive with intellectual striving and artistic hungers. In
> meeting rooms above the crowded stores, the air shook with furi-
> ously happy arguments. There was never any lack of audiences for

speakers, for concerts [...] In those days music was not big business—but music thrived in Brownsville.[20]

Brownsville was not much to look at. Tenements were typically in
tough shape; the little frame houses and stores were dowdy; sewers backed
up, sidewalks were broken, and there was trash in the streets. William
Poster, who grew up in Brownsville at the same time as Abe Reles, remembered Brownsville this way:

I heard the constant din of sirens, police whistles, fire engines. A
huge six-block square of junk shops, tinsmithies, stables, garages,
and miscellaneous small enterprises surrounded [the] main arteries.
How it all rang and clattered and buzzed and smelled! There wasn't
a quiet square yard in the whole district.[21]

In 1920, when Abe Reles was fourteen, about 100,854 people lived in
the Brownsville neighborhood.[22] For all its faults, it was a better neighborhood compared to some in New York. Wendell Pritchett, Brownsville's
historian writes,

In Henry Roth's novel, *Call It Sleep*, the Schearl family is forced
by economic circumstances to move from Brownsville back to the
Lower East Side, and David, the main character, experiences the
terror of poverty for the first time. In contrast to their new neighborhood, Brownsville was idyllic.[23]

But Brownsville was not safe. In 1939, its juvenile delinquency rate
was 25 percent higher than the rest of Brooklyn's.[24] A person could not
walk down Rockaway Avenue at night without be hassled by some gang
of teenage boys. William Poster remembered about his fellow Brownsville
teenagers: "We were content with being what everyone else reviled, and
ardently desired to be even rougher, tougher, dirtier, more ill-mannered,
more uncompromisingly opposed to every kind of law, order, and au-
thority."[25] Novels set in Brownsville from the 1920s to the 1940s, such as
Henry Roth's *Call It Sleep*, Irving Shulman's *Amboy Dukes*, and Arthur
Granit's *In the Time of Peaches*, highlight "the chaotic life of the streets and
constant confrontations between local youths."[26] Granit remembered that
in those days, "it was nothing unusual to have a body shot up and thrown
in some alleyway."[27]

Brownsville was a hard place in which to live, but the vast majority
of people who lived in Brownsville were not gangsters, so nurturing and
environment were not necessarily key reasons why young men became

hoodlums. Nature was perhaps even more important than nurture. Once, Abe Reles was asked what made a criminal a criminal. Reles thoughtfully replied, "[Y]ou have got to have criminal tendencies in you."[28] Brownsville's William Poster writes,

[w]holly without roots in the Jewish past, many of the second generation were, if not hostile, indifferent to their parents' way of life. "This explosive tension made it possible," wrote Professor Morris R. Cohen, "for the same family to produce saints and sinners, philosophers and gunmen."[29]

During the Murder, Inc., investigations, reporters from the *Jewish Daily Forward* interviewed some of the gangsters' family and friends, and over and over, this is what they heard: "All the children are doing well, married, earning an honest living. Only he! That one! He was different! He got into trouble in school! He got into bad company. We tried this, we tried that, but it did not help!"[30] Louis "Lepke" Buchalter, the Manhattan gangster who dominated the garment district and who worked regularly with Abe Reles and the others, had a brother who was a dentist, another who was a pharmacist, and stepbrother who was a rabbi; only Lepke ended up a criminal.[31]

Some teenage boys in tough neighborhoods always, it seemed, got into trouble. Across New York, plenty of girls and women got into trouble with the law too; workers in the illegal sex industry were mostly women, and some brothel madams exercised considerable power. In Harlem, Stephanie St. Clair was the "Queen of the Numbers Racket"—she's been portrayed by Novella Nelson in the film *Cotton Club* (1984), by Cicely Tyson in *Hoodlum* (1997), and by Fulani Haynes in a play by Katherine Butler Jones, *409 Edgecombe Avenue: The House on Sugar Hill* (2007)—but for most women, the gangster life simply wasn't an option. Women could, of course, be gangsters' partners or wives. Evelyn Mittelman, the "Kiss of Death Girl," was Pittsburgh Phil Strauss's sweetheart. *The New Yorker* explained that "when Evelyn Mittelman was seventeen, she was insulted by her beloved, one Hymie Miller, and Hymie was shot dead by a rival." A later lover, Robert Furer, was shot dead by Solomon Goldstein. Goldstein, in turn, "was beaten up by Pittsburgh Phil Strauss and taken on a one-way ride to Sullivan County." *The New Yorker* continued:

It must have been nervous work going around with Evelyn, dangerous and tedious to talk to her. She was far too touchy to be the ideal companion; we are glad she never came into our life [. . .] we

admire Miss Mittelman for her insistence on the proprieties, but we
can't help feeling that she has set a dangerous example. Let standards
as high as hers infect the fashionable world, and even the Stork Club
won't be safe.[32]

According to some reports, Mittelman, in addition to her romances, was
also a courier for the mob.[33]

Prosecutor Burton Turkus was struck by the roles played by the Brownsville gangsters' wives and companions, such as Abe Reles's wife, Rose;
Buggsy Goldstein's wife, Beatrice; and others. Turkus's investigators constantly asked, "[W]hat have these bums got that gets these dolls?" Turkus's
guess was that "the girls would glamourize the gorillas to themselves [. . .]
many of the girl friends started as kids, awestruck by the neighborhood
big shots."[34]

Occasionally, the wives and girlfriends participated in Murder, Inc.,
business. In October 1935, Louis "Pretty" Amberg was murdered by persons unknown. His body was driven to Brooklyn and left in a car, which
was doused with gasoline. The local gangsters decided to let one of the
women in the neighborhood toss the match that would ignite the car.
Assistant District Attorney Turkus mocked the event as "Ladies Night in
Murder, Inc." and referred to the woman who threw the match as "Miss
Murder, Inc." He reported that later, in the neighborhood, she had the
nickname "Hot Foot" and "Hot Tomato."[35]

Still, teenage boys became gangsters even while their sisters and brothers became teachers, factory workers, and city employees. Why did some
turn out so bad when others turned out so good? Hollywood called this
the "Cain and Abel" motif. *Angels with Dirty Faces* (1938) was one of
Hollywood's best-known attempts to think about this. In *Angels*, Rocky
(Jimmy Cagney) and Jerry (Pat O'Brien) were best friends. They grew
up in the same Lower East Side neighborhood, knew all the same people,
and struggled with the same poverty. Each, as teenagers, made choices, and
each choice forged another link in a fateful chain. Rocky began to hang
out with the neighborhood gangs and became a criminal and a killer. Jerry
became a priest who returned to the old neighborhood and struggled to
save the next generation of teenage boys from the gangs. The fateful decision for each was to join, as Rocky did, the local gang, or to resist the
gang, as Jerry did.[36] Personal psychology obviously was crucial—Rocky
was fired by an incendiary mix of testosterone and adrenalin; his hunger
for things and status was insatiable; he needed both risk and violence.
Maybe Brownsville's teenage criminals became addicted to the adrena-

line rush they craved; Jack Katz has written that the thrill of crime can be astonishingly seductive.[37] Maybe some kids just never made it beyond adolescence; writing about Meyer Lansky and his hoodlum friends, Robert Lacey notes that "there is a sense in which criminals never grow up."[38]

Generational conflict combined with nurture and nature to create gangsters. William Poster was struck by the huge generation gap between immigrant parents and their sons in Brownsville where he grew up in the 1920s. "Relations between children and parents reached an extreme of imbalance," Poster wrote, "not only among the Jews, but also in all of America that was going, at different rates, through a prolonged crisis of transplantation in which scarcely anyone had more than an inkling of what is to be preserved or destroyed."[39] Muckraker Lincoln Steffens was also struck by the huge gap between immigrant parents and their children in the early years of the twentieth century. He remembered:

> We saw it everywhere, all the time [. . .] responding to a reported suicide, we would pass a synagogue where a score or more of boys were sitting hatless in their old clothes, smoking cigarettes on the steps outside, and their fathers, all dressed in black, with their high hats, uncut beards and temple curls, were going into the synagogue, tearing their hair and rending their garments [. . .] Their sons were rebels against the law of Moses; they were lost souls, lost to God, the family, and to Israel of old.[40]

Sammy Aaronson ran an amateur boxing gym in Brownsville in the 1920s, when Abe Reles was a kid, and Aaronson knew young Reles. "Brownsville," in those days, Aaronson thought, "was a breeding ground of crime." This is how it worked, he explained:

> Kids began a sort of spring training course for thugs when they were nine or ten years old. The insidious pattern was pretty standard. It was followed by every kid in Brownsville who went wrong. The first step was raiding penny candy and gum machines in the subway stations and corner stores. After a few months swiping pennies, the kids would start hopping wagons to steal fruit or vegetables. They would do that for a long time, maybe three years or so, before moving up to muscling pushcart peddlers, which came next.

After that, by the time he was a teenager, the kid was shaking down neighborhood storeowners, stealing and fencing things, and maybe killing people. Of Abe Reles, Aaronson said, "[H]e had a good family background." Aaronson continued: "[H]is parents were nice, gentle people, but they couldn't handle the kid. They knew he was going with a tough crowd but they were helpless to stop him." As a teenager, Reles worked out in Aaronson's gym. Aaronson took a liking to him. "I don't think that Reles wanted to be a thug. A push in the right direction at the right time would have made all the difference."[41]

By ages fourteen and fifteen, in the early 1920s, Reles was already cutting school, hanging out on the street with other teenagers like Buggsy Goldstein and Pittsburgh Phil Strauss, and getting into trouble. In the 1920s, Reles, Goldstein, and Strauss began hanging out at places like Louis Capone's coffee shop a few blocks north of Brownsville. No, Capone would inevitably explain, he was no kin of the famous Al Capone. But Louis Capone did know people. Tough guys would swagger into Capone's coffee shop to talk business, and tough kids like Reles, Goldstein, and Strauss would hover in the background and gawk.

Sometimes, Reles, Goldstein, Strauss, and the others would hang around Label's poolroom on Sutter Avenue. According to Sammy Aaronson,

[i]f you wanted someone to help you break a head, beat up a guy, break a strike, buy dope, set a fire, plan a robbery, or muscle a peddler, you could find him at Label's.

Of course, Aaronson said, the police knew all about Label's, but they weren't interested. "Many of the cops around Label's," Aaronson recalled, "knew what was going on, but they never interfered. I've seen guys dragged out of Label's screaming while a cop stood on the corner and looked the other way. I've watched a cop on the street and a hood in a car talk for twenty minutes with a victim rolled up in plain sight in the back seat, but the cop didn't ever do anything about it."[42]

Abe Reles grew up in Brownsville, which, when he was a kid, "had the highest rates of assaults, robberies, and total crime in Brooklyn."[43] He dropped out of school and worked as a laborer in a warehouse. When he was sixteen, he and a companion attacked the warehouse watchman and stole a whole truckload of dolls. By the time he was twenty-one, in 1927, he had "started racketeering" seriously; he was arrested six times before 1928.[44] By then, he had become, according to Burton Turkus, "a loathsome hoodlum" with a "warped intellect."[45]

Reles's fellow gang members had life stories very similar to his. Harry "Happy" Maione was first arrested when he was sixteen, in 1924; he was charged with assault and battery, but the charge was dismissed. Arrested for burglary in the following year, he was sentenced to eight months in jail. During his criminal career, from 1924 to 1940, Maione would be arrested thirty-four times. Frank Abbandando was first arrested when he was twelve, in 1921, and charged with "juvenile delinquency"; he was shipped off to a Catholic reform school. When he violated his parole in 1923, aged fourteen, he was shipped back. By 1940, Abbandando was arrested some twenty-one times. Martin "Buggsy" Goldstein was first arrested at age seventeen, in 1922, charged with petty larceny. Over the next few years, he would be charged with, among other things, unlawful entry, felonious assault, and assault and robbery. By 1940, Goldstein had been arrested thirty-eight times. Emmanuel "Mendy" Weiss, one of Lepke Buchalter's lieutenants, was first arrested at age seventeen, in 1923, and charged with unlawful possession of a revolver. As for Lepke Buchalter, he was first arrested at age fifteen, in 1912, and charged with "juvenile delinquency." By 1940, Buchalter had been arrested sixteen times.[46]

Harry "Pittsburgh Phil" Strauss underwent a psychiatric evaluation during the Murder, Inc., trials, and a summary of the results, compiled by Joseph Hayden, the investigating probation officer, provides a striking portrait of one of Murder, Inc.'s key figures.

Harry Strauss was born "in Russia" on or about July 29, 1909. His parents were Jacob and Yetta Ostrosky, who immigrated to New York City in 1914 and changed their family name to Strauss. The Strauss family settled into the Lower East Side; eventually there were five children—Harry, Fannie, Hymen, Alex, and Sam. Jacob Strauss was a harness maker and worked for the city's Department of Street Cleaning.

Jacob, Yetta, and their five children moved constantly, first around the Lower East Side and then up to the Bronx. Young Harry regularly changed schools. His report cards indicated conduct ranging from B to C and his schoolwork ranging from C to D. His third-grade report card noted that little Harry was "not proficient in anything." He dropped out of school when he was fifteen.

Harry had no strong relationship with his father, Jacob. Harry was one of five children, and in any case, Jacob was killed in an industrial accident in 1917 or 1918, when Harry Strauss was eight or nine years old. Yetta later remarried. Harry's relationship with his mother was tumultuous. Strauss told friends that his mother "beat him frequently" because he would not "bring home money." His mother, however, told psychiatrists that Harry would "beat her" if "his meals weren't cooked right."

"There is no evidence that [Strauss] was ever gainfully employed," the report continues. His life after age fifteen, when he dropped out of school and lived on his own, "remains a secret." He was first arrested in 1927

when he was eighteen and was charged with felonious assault and unlawful possession of a revolver; the charges were dismissed. In 1928, he was
arrested three different times and charged with robbery, assault, and auto
theft; the charges were dismissed. For the rest of his life, Strauss would be
arrested for something or other almost every year. In each case, charges
would be dismissed for lack of evidence.

He first appeared in Brownsville in 1928, when he was nineteen. "He
was known to pool room and street corner habitues there as a house
burglar of no particular importance." In April 1928, he was involved
in his first known violence. Strauss had a friend named Henry Kravitz. That April, Strauss and Kravitz met Kravitz's brother, "Slim," in a
poolroom on Livonia Avenue. Strauss angrily accused Slim Kravitz of
stealing a pearl-handled pistol from him. Strauss and Slim Kravitz got
into a furious argument; Strauss threatened to kill Kravitz, who dared
him to. Strauss pulled out another pistol and shot Kravitz at point-blank
range. Strauss went into hiding, assisted by Harry "Happy" Maione. Slim
Kravitz recovered. Neither Henry nor Slim Kravitz would tell the police anything.

Strauss never married; his "closest female associate" was "one Evelyn
Mittelman." Strauss stayed in Brownsville and, after 1928, worked with
Happy Maione, Abe Reles, and others. He was part owner of a garage at
the corner of Hinsdale Street and Belmont Avenue in Brooklyn. Some-
times, Strauss's younger brother, Alex, would work with Harry; Alex
Strauss would develop a police record almost as long as Harry's.

Between 1928 and his arrest in 1940, Harry Strauss would participate
in "no fewer than twenty-eight gangland murders." He not only killed
people in the normal ways—with guns and/or knives or by strangula-
tion—but "he is credited by police and by some of his former confeder-
ates with being the deviser and most conspicuous user of many of the bizarre instruments of torture and death with which gangdom has shocked
the public in recent years." Among other things, Strauss would tie victims
up in contorted knots and then stab them repeatedly with an ice pick.
He, Reles, and the others participated in auto theft, burglary, assaults, robberies, fencing stolen goods, distribution of illegal drugs, and just about
any "illegal activity from which a revenue could be derived." However,
sometimes, Strauss's actions seemed "prompted by nothing more than a
sheer sadistic wantonness."

Strauss liked "prize fights and crap games." According to some reports,
he traveled periodically to places like Miami "and other resorts, always
living in a lavish scale." Strauss

always strove for sartorial elegance and a certain personal fastidiousness, which was marred only by a nasty habit of indiscriminate spitting. His faculty for appearing always the dapper and disdainful dandy without visible means of support once aroused the wrath of the Police Commissioner of the City of New York. By his associates he was given the sobriquet of "Pittsburgh Phil" (after the notorious gambler of that name) in recognition both of the suave, well-groomed exterior that hid the ruthless criminal within and also of the fact the he once spent some time in Pittsburgh where he managed to get arrested at least once.

The psychiatrists who examined Strauss found no evidence of mental illness. The probation officer's report described him as "a cruel, ruthless, and hardened killer."[47]

But if the gangsters' stories sound familiar, Murder, Inc., itself, was full of surprises.

Murder, Inc.? One might assume that Brownsville's Murder, Inc., was some sort of Mafia, Italian immigrant gang. It was not. Abe Reles, Harry Strauss, Martin Goldstein were all children of Jewish immigrants. This time was, in fact, a "golden age" for Jewish hoodlums: Meyer Lansky, Benjamin "Bugsy" Siegel, Lepke Buchalter, and Dutch Schultz were all children of Jewish immigrants. Harry Maione and Frank Abbandando were second-generation Italian Americans, and the Brownsville gang accepted Albert Anastasia, another Italian American, as a kind of overlord; Anastasia, in turn, was allied to both Charlie Luciano, an Italian, and Lepke Buchalter and Meyer Lansky. There were, indeed, ethnic gangs in New York in the interwar years, but the most striking thing about them was not simply their ethnicity but also their immigrant status. Italians and Jews had been among the leading immigrant groups around the turn of the century; Italians and Jews typically made up the gangsters in the 1920s and 1930s, though there were still occasional Irishmen, like Legs Diamond, Vincent "Mad Dog" Coll, or Brownsville's Seymour "Blue Jaw" Magoon, in the gangs. All the gangs cooperated with each other, waged war on each other, and betrayed each other, regardless of shared ethnicity. Jews would ally with Italians to wage war on Italians and Jews. Although some gangs were ethnically homogeneous, other gangs, like Reles's Brownsville gang, were ethnically ecumenical: Reles, Goldstein, and Strauss were Jewish; Abbandando and Maione were Italian; Seymour Magoon was Irish. The district attorney who prosecuted them, William O'Dwyer, was Irish; his assistant for homicide, Burton Turkus, was Jewish.

Gangsters? We might imagine that gangsters are members of a tight clan, a kind of urban tribe, led by a cunning patriarch. We might think of the gangsters as, in this sense, somehow "premodern." The classic portrayal of the premodern gang is in Francis Ford Coppola's epic film *The Godfather—Part I* (1972). The Corleone gang is led by a wise and generous, if ferocious, patriarch who, for all his *terribilità,* is a "man of honor." The gang is rooted in Don Corleone's extended family, which is ethnically homogeneous, as well. A real gangster in the movie is a Mafioso, a member of a complex Sicilian family, a family that is not just close, but closed to outsiders. The image is hard to shake; discussions of, for example, *The Sopranos* often assume that this is what a New York gang was like.[48] The image is partly true, of course. There were Italian gangs in New York City and elsewhere by, say, 1890; sometimes, they were exclusively Sicilian; often, they also included siblings, cousins, and in-laws. From this perspective, the gangs were premodern, patriarchal, tribal transplants to urban villages in the big cities, where they forged petty neighborhood kingdoms and waged feudal wars against their neighbors.

This premodern model of the neighborhood gang is irrelevant to Murder, Inc. The Brownsville gang was not led by an old-world patriarch; it was led by Abe Reles, a brutal twentysomething. The gang sometimes included brothers and cousins, but membership had nothing to do with kinship. Murder, Inc., had no initiation ceremonies and no tribal code of honor. Nothing about Murder, Inc., was premodern.

Burton Turkus was convinced that the gangs he knew most definitely were "modern," not "premodern." The gangs were mixes of ethnicities, especially second-generation Jewish and Italian immigrants. They were capitalist, profit-maximizing enterprises, and carefully organized into multiple, hierarchically arranged levels; they were led by sinister men in silk suits who insisted that they were "just businessmen." The gangs were mirror images of corporate America; they were rationally structured, stable, ruthlessly efficient, moneymaking machines. Turkus insisted that "there actually existed in America an organized underworld [. . .] a government-within-government [. . .] just as real as any fifth column of totalitarianism";[49] this parallel, underground state was, Turkus argued, an immense parallel economy, a supercorporation. Organized crime, Turkus wrote, "was—and it is today—big business, with all the appurtenances of big business."[50] "The boss" was the gang's chief executive officer, and killings were according to "contract." By the 1930s, no investigation of organized crime was complete without a detailed wire diagram of the criminal organization being investigated that showed the corporate-like

criminal chain of command. Burton Turkus thought of NewYork's gangs
in these terms; organized crime, to Turkus, was an "unbelievable industry"
organized "along the same corporate lines as a chain of grocery stores."[51]
Historian Marc Mappen points out that this sort of thinking had already
become popular in the 1920s, when "the term 'gang' was replaced by
'syndicate' or 'combination.'"[52]

Accounts of the 1930s gangsters often assume this criminal-corporation
metaphor. In 1940, Joseph Freeman, in *The Nation,* breathlessly reported
that Murder, Inc.,

> is a nation-wide, highly organized business which operates major
> rackets from coast to coast, trains its personnel, has its own code
> of conduct, and kills on contract. It is a grotesque caricature of
> American big business, and its ramifications are almost as manifold:
> labor unions, politics, industry, all covertly recognize the racketeer
> as a functionary of American society[53]

Lepke Buchalter's biographer, Paul Kavieff, writes that

> Murder, Inc. operated smoothly, profitably, and with astonishing effi-
> ciency. There had never been anything like it [...] It was a government
> within a government; it was a suprapolice force [...] the members of
> the mob were incredible men [...] Murder, Inc. was [...] the enforce-
> ment branch of the Supreme Court of the underworld."[54]

Hollywood portrayed this obsession with bureaucratically organized
evil in hundreds of "syndicate" films. In "syndicate" films like *The Phenix
City Story* (1955) and *The Brothers Rico* (1957), naive Americans suddenly
discovered, to their horror, that they were in the grip of a vast criminal
corporation.[55] In the 1950s, this general fear of the gangster corporation
merged with fear of the international communist conspiracy and memories of the Nazis' homicidal bureaucracies; the Kefauver organized crime
hearings paralleled the McCarthy anticommunist investigations, and together they created a kind of paranoid epic in which lonely citizens confront a monstrously evil criminal corporation.[56]

There is, of course, truth in this "modern" image of Prohibition- and
Depression-era organized crime. Lucky Luciano himself had, after all,
talked about organizing brothels along the lines of A&P supermarkets.
Frank Costello and Meyer Lansky were gambling entrepreneurs whose
great goal in life was to make a fortune. Lansky would always insist that
whether as a bootlegger or a gambler, he was a businessman, not a hoodlum. Lansky, like Costello, disliked violence. "It's always much better not

to shoot if you can help it," Lansky liked to say; "it's better to use reason—
or if that fails, threats."[57] Speaking about his bootlegger days with Bugsy
Siegel, Lansky said, "We were in business like the Ford Motor Company.
Shooting and killing was an inefficient way of doing business. Ford salesmen didn't shoot Chevrolet salesmen. They tried to outbid them."[58]

Yet, as Robert Lacey, Lansky's biographer, explains, the gangs really
were not corporate enterprises at all. Arnold Rothstein, "the Brain," was
one of the key organizers of New York's gangs, and Rothstein, according
to his lawyer, "the great mouthpiece," William Fallon was "a man who
dwell[ed] in doorways [. . .] a gray rat, waiting for his cheese." What was
remarkable about Rothstein's "organization," Lacey writes, was precisely
its lack of organization. "The essence of organized crime as perfected by
Arnold Rothstein," according to Lacey, "was not structural organization as
the conventional world knew it. It was, rather, the absence of structure [. . .]
this was not the integrated empire of a czar or a J. P. Morgan. Such com-
parisons failed to grasp the secrecy and nimbleness essential for success in
organized crime." Lacey concludes by rejecting what he calls two "myths"
about the Prohibition and Depression-era gangs. First, they were not pre-
dominately Italian, and they were not units of some monolithic "mafia."
True, there were Italians in the gangs; there were Jews, Irishmen, and
even the odd Englishman (Owney Madden), too. Poverty and immigrant
status were far more useful predictors of gang affiliation than simply ethnicity. Second, the gangs were not tidily structured quasi-corporations.
They were, to the contrary, fluid, constantly morphing, loose affiliations
of "gray rats [. . .] unconfined by structure," each gangster and temporary
gangster-partnership "free to scavenge for themselves and to pursue profit
as opportunity and their aptitudes led them."[59]

Certainly, this freedom to scavenge was true of Brownsville's "gray
rats." The Brownsville gang and most other contemporary gangs were not
so much "premodern" or "modern" as they were "postmodern." New
York's gangs were not stable, coherently structured, goal-setting, rationally governed quasi-corporations. They were, instead, shape-shifting, ka-
leidoscopic, often temporary alliances among people who acted as often
on impulse as according to plan. The gangs certainly had hierarchies
and gangsters were intensely status conscious, but the hierarchies themselves were fluid. In Brownsville, the young "bat boys" like Dukey Maffetore, Pretty Levine, and Blue Jaw Magoon deferred to the higher-status
gangsters like Buggsy Goldstein, Pittsburgh Phil Strauss, and Kid Twist
Reles. Reles, Strauss, and Goldstein, in turn, deferred to Albert Anastasia;
Anastasia deferred to Manhattan gangsters like Lucky Luciano and Frank

Lineup. (*Left to right*) Harry "Pittsburgh Phil" Strauss, Harry "Happy" Maione, Frank "the Dasher" Abbandando. (City University of New York, John Jay College, Lloyd Sealy Library, Special Collections)

Costello. Yet these networks were kinetic and unstable. In Brownsville, Meyer Shapiro was the neighborhood boss until Abe Reles killed him. Reles then insisted that he was the boss; however, Strauss, Goldstein, and Maione were never fully subservient to him. Maione, in fact, had his own East New York gang, with members like Frank Abbandando and Vito Gurino, and Maione thought of himself not as Reles's subordinate but as Reles's temporary ally. "Albert A.," as Anastasia was called, stayed out of Brownsville's business so long as he got his share of the loot. When he communicated with the Brownsville gang, Anastasia rarely followed any predictable chain of command. Sometimes he spoke with Reles, sometimes with Strauss, sometimes with Louis Capone, who then spoke with Reles or Strauss. Ethnically, the Brownsville gang was postnational; Strauss, Reles, Goldstein, and Levine were of Eastern European Jewish background, although none was religiously observant. Maione, Abbandando, and Gurino were Italian Americans; they spoke some Italian and enjoyed Italian cooking, but knew nothing about Italian politics or culture. Seymour Magoon was Irish, though he had no real tie to Ireland. All were, in fact, American, though none ever expressed any particular American patriotism. Their fluid structures and postnational identities gave the La Guardia era gangs a decidedly "postmodern" quality, which made them extraordinarily difficult to eradicate. Remove a leader, and another pops up; fracture this gang, and its pieces reconfigure into other gangs; squeeze off this source of income, and the gangs find another.

If it makes sense to refer to Murder, Inc., as in some ways "postmodern," can we then speak of a kind of "postmodern" malice typical of Murder, Inc.? But are moral categories not timeless? Is evil not just evil, regardless of whether it is premodern, modern, or postmodern? One might well argue that the evil done by Murder, Inc., was essentially the same as the evil done by the Spanish Inquisition or, for that matter, Nero. Harm is harm. Yet, in several striking ways, the evil done by the Brownsville gang has a distinctly postmodern quality.

The very concept of "postmodernity," of course, is itself contentious. Robert Pippin, for example, argues that what is vaguely called "postmodern" actually is a "continuation of late modern concerns."[60] Still, if we accept the concept of "postmodernism" at least as a hypothesis and agree with Steven Connor that postmodernism has its own particular "ethical possibility"[61] and if we recognize, as well, that postmodernism arose in part as an attempt to rediscover the ethical in everything from the social sciences to literary criticism,[62] then perhaps we can, however tentatively, try to think about Murder, Inc., and its malevolence from a postmodern point of view.

Postmodernism is fascinated by the play of images and the ways in which images and the media that transmit them mediate virtually every encounter we have with reality. At its most extreme, some postmodernists might even deny that there is any "reality" at all and that, instead, what we now have, in our postmodern condition, are images and images of images, spectacles and illusions, all of them turned into commodities to be consumed; this is the sort of argument explored by Jean Baudrillard.[63]

Certainly, it is true that "the gangster" as a cultural type was created by Hollywood, and in film after film, images of "the gangster" circulated across the country. It also appears true that if Hollywood was inspired by real gangsters, real gangsters were inspired at least, in part, by the movies and the media. The Murder, Inc., story was translated from the street back into film in dozens of 1950s movies. The very name "Murder, Inc." was a media invention. The Brownsville mobsters never called themselves that, although thanks to the newspapers, "Murder, Inc." is what they became. Most important, Murder, Inc., met its end in 1940 and 1941 in a series of judicial spectacles, all of them reabsorbed into the voracious media. Murder, Inc., certainly must be understood within what Chris Hedges calls the postmodern "Empire of Illusions."[64] Moreover, according to postmodernism, all is image, and sooner or later, image turns into entertainment—issues become images radically simplified into caricature, and the wave of images stimulates desire, provides a kind of voyeuristic pleasure, and diverts attention from more serious matters. In the postmodern world, we "amuse ourselves to death," as Neil Postman writes.[65] In 1940 and 1941, the gruesome deeds of the Brownsville gang became a vastly entertaining public spectacle in the Murder, Inc., trials; prosecutor Burt Turkus turned the trials into a best seller; Turkus's best seller became the basis of the 1960 film, *Murder, Inc.* The progression from street-corner killings to an entertainment film was complete. Whatever ethical commentary we might make about Murder, Inc., whatever thoughts we might have about the malice of the Brownsville gang, have to take into account this ecology of mass-produced, commoditized, and endlessly repeated image, spectacle, and entertainment.

Commodification, Fredric Jameson argues, is the key concept in late capitalism, and late capitalism's aesthetic, postmodernism. Capitalism not only produces objects of desire to be bought, sold, hoarded, and consumed—commodities—but late capitalism also accelerates the obsession with commodities and turns everything imaginable into a commodity—religion, sexuality, even human beings. Jameson agrees with Guy Debord's "remarkable formulation of the image as 'the final form of commodity reification.'"[66] This obsession with the commodities of late capitalism—with all the "stuff" that so impressed actor George Raft: the "Duesenberg cars," and fancy clothes, and beautiful women (themselves become objects to be possessed)—are typical of the Hollywood gangster. Having stuff—the instant gratification by having stuff, and feeling human because of having stuff, because people are stuff—is part of the "American Dream," heightened to the point of caricature in the movie gangster. Abe Reles,

Harry Strauss, and the other members of the Brownsville gang were just as obsessed with stuff, money, and sex, as their movie counterparts. The Brownsville gang and the gangsters in general, though, took commodification a step further; part of their trade was to turn persons into objects, into dead things. The extent to which this act, the act of killing, satisfied desire, is the topic for a later chapter. It is enough to say, here, that Reles and the others lived in the world of commodities, were obsessed with getting the money needed to get the commodities, and would certainly kill anyone who threatened to take away the money they needed to obtain the commodities they desired.

Certainly the most famous aspect of postmodernism is its vehement repudiation of all "metanarratives." This is the claim Jean-François Lyotard made in *The Postmodern Condition* (1979). In a rapidly globalizing, increasingly pluralist, heterogeneous, and diverse world, any claim to be *the one true story* must be treated with skepticism. This "hermeneutics of suspicion" can lead in many different directions; it may lead to openness and tolerance, but as critics of postmodernism charge, it may lead to nihilism. Indeed, according to critics, a pervasive nihilism is the distinctive temptation of the postmodern condition. If modernism brought with it the death of God, then postmodernism, in some guises at least, reflects the death of humanity; it expresses "the end of all attempts to discover ultimate 'origins' or a certain method, or to revolutionize human consciousness."[67]

The Murder, Inc., killers were postmodern nihilists. Some were of Jewish heritage and even, on occasion, honored Jewish traditions, but the Jewish killers in no way reflected Judaism. The Italian killers were nominally Catholic, but nothing about their behavior is "Catholic." No longer Jews or Italians from the Old Country, but not quite fitting fully into "normal" American life, the Brownsville killers had no particular religious or ethnic identity. They did not kill because of their religious or political convictions; they did not stand for any cause or belong to any movement; they did not execute enemies in the name of justice. There was no "there" in the there of the Murder, Inc., criminals. Instead, the kind of nihilism that is one possibility of postmodernism was on full display on the corner of Livonia and Saratoga. Eventually, the sheer destructiveness of the gang would destroy the gang itself.

"Otherness," that is, alterity, is a basic postmodern category. Emmanuel Levinas argues that the encounter with the Other is the very foundation of the possibility of morality.[68] One's relationship to the Other is, then, the touchstone of one's morality. Jacques Derrida argues that "Western thought" is deeply flawed because typically, he thinks, "Western thought" leaves little room for the Other as genuinely Other. As John McGowan explains, "for Derrida, the fear of difference, of the other, is a crucial constitutive feature of all totalizing systems, while the addiction to totalization in thought is what he calls 'Western metaphysics' or the 'philosophy of the same.'"[69] Murder, Inc., was also very conscious of the Other. For Murder, Inc., "Other" meant "Target." Outsiders of any sort—rival gang members, neighbors, women, the police, anyone not in the gang—was treated with contempt, at least, and with homicidal rage, at most. Anyone within the gang who threatened the gang in any way, if only by not sharing the booty, would be killed. For Levinas, compassion for the Other engenders morality; for Murder, Inc., the destruction of the Other was imperative.

Thinking about Murder, Inc., requires considering the possibility that Murder, Inc., is emblematic in some ways of the postmodern condition. Thinking of the Murder, Inc., gang in postmodern terms by no means exhausts the gang's ethos. But considering image and spectacle, commodification, nihilism, and Otherness—central postmodern categories—suggests that these 1930s' Brooklyn hoodlums enacted themes that their descendants would only begin to take seriously long after the Brownsville gang's leaders had gone to their electric deaths in Sing Sing.

3
Gangster City

Rudolph Halley, Chief Counsel for the
Kefauver Commission: "Well, aren't these
people we have been talking about what you
would call racket boys?"

Willie Moretti (New Jersey mobster): "Well, I
don't know if you would call it rackets."

Halley: "How would you put it?"

Moretti: "Jeez, everything is a racket today
[. . .] everybody has a racket of their own."

—*Testimony during the Kefauver Committee's
investigation of organized crime, 1951*[1]

During the Jazz Age, New York City became what Patrick Downey
calls a "Gangster City."[2] New York not only had gangs, but the gangs
also very nearly had the city. The gangs accelerated the transformation of
New York from a flawed but vital democracy into something dangerous
and sinister. Nothing about democracy is inevitable. As Francis Fukuyama
writes, political orders can decay, and even prosperous democracies can
fail.[3] Gangsterism is both a symptom and a cause of this collapse. Gangsterism is a social, economic, and political phenomenon, but it also carries
a distinctive ethos, and this ethos, what prosecutor Turkus called the gangsters' "social code,"[4] is a virus that kills democracies. In the 1920s and
early 1930s, in America's largest and most vibrant city, democracy very
nearly died. This gangster social code is complex; it identifies masculinity
with violence; it values gang solidarity over citizenship, cunning over
generosity, excess over restraint. Above all, as the movies, especially the
later *noir* movies demonstrated, the gangster ethos reflects a virulent com-

54

modity poisoning. Women, friends, killings, even the gangsters themselves are "thingified."[5] Murder, Inc.'s specialty was turning living things into dead things. The consequences for New York City were dire. This chapter offers, first, a brief tour of gangland's political economy, of which the Brownsville gang was a small but ambitious part. Then, the most shocking expression of this political economy, the public violence that seemed to endemic to New York in the Roaring Twenties and Great Depression, is considered. Finally, the gangster code, the ethos of commodification, and that code's grim consequences for Gotham become the focus.

On December 7, 1929, Ciro Terranova hosted a spectacular party. Terranova was New York's "artichoke king." When he was five, his parents brought him and his siblings from Sicily to New York. In New York's immigrant slums, Ciro and his brothers spent their days with their older half brother, Giuseppe Morello, who had immigrated to New York from Corleone, Sicily. By 1900, Giuseppe Morello; his friend Ignazio Lupo; Morello's half-brothers, the Terranovas, and their allies, owned the neighborhoods around 107th Street in Harlem. The Morello gang was involved in the usual run of bandit activities, ranging from counterfeiting to murder. When Morello and Lupo went off to prison, the Terranovas took over the gang; by the 1940s, the Morello–Terranova gang would be absorbed into Vito Genovese's crime family.

In the 1920s, Ciro Terranova cornered the market in artichokes. Italian immigrants loved artichokes; artichokes were sold at only a few markets in the city; Terranova and his friends appeared at the markets, threatened to kill the artichoke sellers if they did not pay off the Terranovas; the artichoke sellers paid, shrugged, and simply raised the price of their artichokes.

In the 1920s, Terranova made it a point to know everyone in the neighborhood, especially politicians; he happily contributed to their election campaigns and the politicians happily did him favors. So, on December 7, 1929, to celebrate one of these friendships, Ciro Terranova and the Tepecano Democratic Club hosted a dinner at the Roman Gardens, in the Bronx, to honor city magistrate Albert Vitale. The dinner was a lavish affair; judges, lawyers, politicians, police detectives, and mobsters all showed up to honor both Vitale and their host, Ciro Terranova.

The party was rolling along; a comedian had everyone in stitches, when, out of nowhere, seven masked men waving guns stormed in. Pointing their weapons at the guests, the gunmen demanded money, weapons, and police badges. They even snatched the service revolver of police detective Arthur Johnson. Their sacks full, the bandits ran off. Outraged, Terranova

Lineup. Abe Reles (*left*), Martin ("Buggsy") Goldstein (*right*). (City University of New York, John Jay College, Lloyd Sealy Library, Special Collections)

suspected that the bandits were not just ordinary crooks; they had been sent, he was sure, by one of his archrivals, Joe Masseria, who was on the eve of the bloody Castellamarese War against Salvatore Maranzano. The point of the raid was not theft; the point of the raid was to embarrass Terranova. The newspapers, of course, gleefully reported the story; politicians expressed their shock; Terranova claimed that he had become a "scapegoat" in the hoopla that followed; Mayor Jimmy Walker said that Terranova had gotten the wrong animal: he was not a "goat"; he was a "jackass."[6]

For many New Yorkers, the Terranova party stickup was grim evidence that their city had been taken over by mobsters. Hoodlums like Terranova; politicians, especially from Tammany Hall; cops and lawyers and judges were all entangled with each other in a dense, corrupt bargain. Everyone in the city was on the take; bribes, kickbacks, insider deals, and payoffs lubricated everyday life; only the gullible trusted anyone; everyone who knew New York understood that the cops, lawyers, and politicians were in the mobsters' pockets.

The problem was that some New Yorkers felt very strongly that certain practices were vicious public nuisances, but other New Yorkers thought of them as innocent diversions. Those who disliked the practices were able to make them illegal; those who wanted to enjoy them gladly paid any entrepreneur bold enough to flout the law and provide them. The bold entrepreneurs were the mobsters. The three key vices in question were gambling, prostitution, and intoxication. Some New Yorkers were determined to restrict them; others were just as determined to enjoy them; the mobsters made their money by providing them.

New Yorkers loved to gamble; they would bet on just about anything, and someone had to run the games. Gambling, however, was illegal. Whoever ran the games had to run the risk of colliding with the law; gangsters were willing to run the risk. Every neighborhood had craps games, poker games, and bookies who took bets on horse races. Everybody played the numbers game. Pick some random source—Babe Ruth's batting average, the total purse at the Saratoga Race Track, the day and time of a coworker's baby's birth—and get everyone to place a bet on his or her favorite number. Whoever guessed the right number would win the pot, after, of course, whoever ran the game got a cut. Some neighborhoods pooled their pots, increasing the volume of play, the size of the pot, and the profits for the game's organizers. Hoodlums in the neighborhoods demanded a percentage of the pots; by the 1930s, the numbers racket (also called the policy racket) was a remarkably complex citywide illegal operation. For example, according to one estimate, the gross play in Harlem's numbers banks in 1931 was around $35,000 per day. Winners would get about $7,700 of the total play, leaving a tidy profit of about $27,300 per day, just in Harlem.[7]

Meyer Lansky liked to tell the story of his introduction to gambling. He was just a kid, maybe thirteen or fourteen. He had a freakish gift for numbers, and he had made it a point to study the craps games all along Grand Street, where he and his family lived on the Lower East Side. He easily calculated the odds of a particular number rolling out on the dice, and he was sure he would be a winner. One Friday evening, Lansky's mother handed him a pot of stew—"cholent," a traditional Sabbath meal—and a nickel. He was to take the pot of stew down to the baker and ask the baker to warm it in his oven; the nickel was the baker's payment. Walking down Grand Street with the cholent and the nickel, young Lansky spotted a craps game underway. He watched a shooter step up and win again and again. Lansky decided to try. He rolled the dice and instantly lost his nickel. He trudged home with the cold cholent and confessed. He also figured out what went wrong. The game was rigged. The shooter before him was the shill, whose job it was to entice the unwitting mark into the game. The dice were loaded. Lansky learned a lesson: "[T]here's no such thing as a lucky gambler," he would later say. "[T]here are only winners and losers. The winners are those who control the game."[8]

Arnold Rothstein, another mathematical wizard, was, until his untimely death in 1928, New York's gambling king. A passionate gambler, Rothstein helped organize games all over town. Rothstein ran a casino in Manhattan's red-light "Tenderloin" entertainment district, which ran from 20th Street up to about 40th Street, between Fifth and Seventh Avenues, and Rothstein's casino was everyone's favorite place to play. In 1920, Rothstein was at the center of baseball's White Sox World Series scandal, although Rothstein insisted that he had nothing to do with "fixing" the World Series and no one was able to pin anything on him.[9]

Rothstein, fabulously rich, was plagued by petty thieves who wanted to pick his pockets, more ambitious thieves who stole winnings from his bookies and gamblers, and dangerous thieves who periodically threatened to kidnap him. He could hardly ask the police for protection, so he arranged for his own security. Inside Lindy's Restaurant on Broadway, or wherever Rothstein went, an entourage of twenty-somethings, tough-guys with attitude and swagger surrounded him. At one time or another, Legs Diamond, Dutch Schultz, and Lucky Luciano worked for "Mr. Rothstein."[10] Luciano later said about Rothstein,

Frank Costello. (City University of New York, John Jay College, Lloyd Sealy Library, Special Collections)

He taught me how to dress, how not to wear loud things but to have good taste; he taught me how to use knives and forks and things like that at the dinner table, about holdin' a door open for a girl, or helpin' her sit down by holdin' the chair. If Arnold had lived a little longer he could've made me pretty elegant.[11]

Frank Costello was another serious gambler. Costello and his partners took over a large share of Rothstein's gambling operations after Rothstein's sudden death.[12] Costello ran games, invested in casinos, organized bookies, and, in the early 1930s, expanded into slot machines. Costello and his partners provided machines to a sales force of aggressive young men who encouraged local stores and bars to accept the slots. In Brownsville, one way Abe Reles, Harry Strauss, and the others made a living was by finding homes for Costello's slot machines. Reles or Strauss would arrange for some kid in the neighborhood to tend a handful of slots; the kid would go shop to shop and bar to bar and collect the sacks of coins from the machines; the more enterprising kids would find store owners or bar owners who had not yet accepted the machines and encourage them—sometimes by means of a brick through the window—to set up a slot machine. When some New Yorkers began to complain about the slot machines, Costello organized the Mills Novelty Company to manufacture slots that would dispense candy (as well as money) to the winner. The machines were "candy machines," Costello insisted, not gambling machines. By 1931, Costello and company had thousands of slot machines installed all across New York City, generating hundreds of thousands of dollars in profits.

Commercial sex was almost as profitable as gambling. A single woman might, on her own, try to earn some money by exchanging sex for cash, but very quickly she would be accosted by some neighborhood thug who would demand a share of her profits; if she did not pay, she would be beaten or killed. Prostitutes not only had to pay off their pimp (or "booker," as they were called in the 1930s); prostitution was also indoor work, and they had to pay off the madam who ran the brothel where they plied their trade. Invariably, they had to pay off the neighborhood cops too, and the local lawyers, judges, and politicians who, if not paid off, would order them all arrested and fined. Of course, whichever gang ran the neighborhood where the prostitute worked would demand a share of her wages as well.

Johnny Torrio was the gangster who organized New York's sex industry. Torrio grew up on the Lower East Side, dropped out of school, shot craps, played pool, and quickly came to the attention of gang leader Paolo Vacca-relli, known as "Paulie Kelly." Paulie Kelly's "Five Points Gang" dominated Manhattan's Sixth Ward. Shopkeepers, saloon owners, and street peddlers all paid taxes to Paulie Kelly—if they failed to pay, the penalties were ter-rifying—and so, too, did all the Sixth Ward's thieves, fences, bookies, and gamblers. Paulie Kelly was the king of the Sixth Ward; politicians, especially Tammany Hall Democrats, who wanted to raise money or get out the vote to win an election, had no choice but to rely on Kelly. Kelly, in turn, ex-pected favors from the politicians—a blind eye from the cops on the beat, dismissals by judges, and, above all, a share in the boodle—city contracts, jobs, payments—controlled by the politicians. Paulie Kelly was quickly im-pressed by Johnny Torrio's hustle and brains. According to Luciano,

> Johnny was a guy who could always look around corners, just like Meyer Lansky. One time, I even told him that the barrel of his gun was curved, and he laughed at that, but he didn't deny it.[13]

Torrio and his allies went from booker to booker, from brothel to brothel, and demanded tribute. If the bookers, madams, and prostitutes would cooperate, Torrio would set up a kind of insurance system to bribe the cops and judges and to provide lawyers when needed. Torrio would provide security, too, and regularize the tax system; as it was, any thug needing money would go after bookers and madams and prostitutes, most of whom were virtually defenseless. Torrio promised to protect everyone and charge a regular and predictable fee. Of course, anyone who refused Torrio's generous offer would suffer gruesome consequences. However, Torrio was all about money, not violence. He constructed the classic set of concentric circles—on the outside, hundreds of hardworking prostitutes, who passed a sizable share of their pay to their madams and bookers; the bookers who passed along part of their profits to a much smaller circle of Torrio's collectors; and, in the center of it all, Johnny Torrio. He would later go off to wild Chicago to work with his uncle, the flamboyant gambler and brothel owner Big Jim Colosimo. Torrio brought to Chicago with him a young hoodlum named Al Capone.

However, Prohibition was the biggest thing that ever happened to the gangs. Prohibition, which went into effect on midnight January 16, 1920, made the gangsters rich. Anyone cunning enough to smuggle liquor into the speakeasies could become a millionaire overnight. Arnold Rothstein, Frank Costello, Charlie Luciano, Dutch Schulz, Legs Diamond, and scores of others became shockingly rich by bootlegging. Money cascaded onto the mobsters. Consider just Frank Costello. In the 1920s, Costello joined forces with "Big Bill" Dwyer, an Irishman who began as a longshoreman, got involved in the rackets, and leaped into bootlegging. During Prohibition, according to one of Costello's biographers, "federal investigators estimate the [Dwyer–Costello] combine brought in forty million dollars' worth of alcohol a year, and during that time, they were the only importers never to lose even a truckload of whiskey to hijackers."[14] By the 1930s, gangsters were into everything. Besides gambling, prostitution, and illegal liquor, gangsters were mercenaries in New York's seemingly interminable labor wars (that's how Lepke Buchalter got started). They all extorted "taxes" from all the little businesses in their neighborhoods, a regular source of profit for Abe Reles and his Brownsville gang. In the early twentieth century, on the Lower East Side, for example, Max Zweibach, the original "Kid Twist," would storm into a bar or a craps game and shout, "I want fifty dollars. What, you're not going to cough up? I'll shoot up your ——— place!" Paid off, he would stuff his money in his pocket and shout, as he strutted out, "I'll see you again in about a month!"[15] Things had not changed much a generation later. In the fall of 1933, one hoodlum was charged with wrecking a laundry because the laundry owner would not pay up; a restaurant owner and his wife were beaten, maybe by Abe Reles and Buggsy Goldstein, because they too failed to pay; routine cases, both were dismissed for lack of evidence.[16]

Mobsters ran enormously profitable short-term micro-loan businesses, otherwise known as loan-sharking; everyone, it seemed "had money out on the street." Anthony "Dukey" Maffetore, one of the "kids" on The Corner in Brownsville, tried, during one Murder, Inc., trial, to explain how the loan shark business worked. Big Harry, that is, Harry Strauss, gave Maffetore some money to put out on the street. Pretty Levine was Maffetore's partner. A guy they called "Izzy" collected payments for them. You loaned out $5 on Sunday and collected $6 the following Saturday. One of the lawyers asked, "A five-dollar investment brings you, if it is kept moving, no less than $50 a year profit?" Maffetore replied that yes, that was it. The attorney responded, "[O]ne thousand per cent [. . .]," at which point the judge interrupted: "That means a capital of $1000 would bring in $10,000 in profit in a year." Maffetore agreed that loan-sharking was very profitable.[17]

Hoodlums stole goods, fenced stolen goods, and smuggled and sold illegal drugs. Out on the street, it was busy, busy, busy.

No one knows the exact scale of the gangsters' economic enterprises, but the evidence suggests that the scale was enormous. Because gangsters controlled so many choke points in New York's economy, every New Yorker, in effect, paid a tax to the criminals. Lepke Buchalter controlled the trucks carrying produce into New York and clothing back out; the trucking companies paid Lepke off and passed along the costs to their customers. Ciro Terranova controlled artichokes. Joseph "Socks" Lanza and his people dominated the Fulton Fish Market; if you were in the fish business, you paid off Socks Lanza. According to the 1931 Seabury investigation of political corruption in New York,

> Every fisherman bringing his haul into New York has to pay tribute to dock his boat, and in default of payment he was unable to unload his cargo; the wholesaler had to pay tribute to get his fish from the dock to his counter in the market and if he failed to pay, no amount of money could secure him the necessary porterage; the retailer had to pay to have the fish carried from the wholesale counter to his wagon. If he failed to do so, he was not only unable to hire labor, but his stock was sprayed with kerosene oil and ruined. Moreover, while he was arranging to have his fish carried from the wholesaler's counter to his wagon, he [paid] to prevent his wagon from being destroyed or disabled.[18]

On the night he was fatally shot, October 23, 1935, Dutch Schulz and his aides were in Newark's Palace Chop House reviewing their books. Schulz's mathematical genius Otto "Abbadabba" Berman reported that in the previous six weeks Schulz's numbers banks had taken in $827,253.43, and paid out $313,711.99 in winnings, for a six-week profit for the Schulz organization of $513,545.44. By one estimate, the whole Schulz operation, ranging from numbers to extortion, netted some $20 million per year, with no taxes of course[19]—at a time when the annual per capita income in the United States was much less than $1,000, when it was big money for a worker in New York to earn $1.00 an hour.[20] In 1936, the newspapers regularly reported that New York's prostitution industry, allegedly run by Lucky Luciano, grossed at least $10 million per year, maybe much more.[21] In 1941, in the middle of the Murder, Inc., trials, the *New York Times* reported that Abe Reles and company generated from loan-sharking alone something like $1 million per year, most of which, the paper reported, went to bribes for police officers, lawyers, judges, and politicians.[22] The Seabury investigation of the early 1930s; the Dewey investigations of the mid-1930s, and the Murder, Inc., investigation and trials demonstrated that the underworld was awash in an ocean of cash, and no one paid any taxes. Prosecutor Thomas Dewey would argue that gangsters, in effect, imposed a 20 percent tax on every New Yorker and every business transaction in New York, and because of that a tremendous amount of money flowed into a very small number of very dirty hands.[23]

Violence, of course, was integral to the gangsters' business; in *The Lineup* (1958) the killer, "Dancer" (Eli Wallach) says, "[Y]ou don't understand the criminal's need for violence."[24] Because their immensely profitable businesses were outside the law, gangsters settled business disputes outside the law, sometimes by negotiation, sometimes by violence. Jazz Age and Depression-era New York was a big city; on a per capita basis, New York probably was no more dangerous than Chicago or Los Angeles. But the regular explosions of violence, especially when they killed innocent passersby, demonstrated to New Yorkers just how dangerous and powerful the city's underworld was.

In 1922, for example, Giuseppe "Joe the Boss" Masseria fought a bitter battle against his archrival Umberto Valenti. On August 11, 1922, Masseria agreed to have some of his people meet at a restaurant with some of Valenti's people. The restaurant was on the corner of 12th Street and Second Avenue. They were to meet for lunch; the city streets were crowded. Masseria's people arrived early; as soon as Valenti's people arrived, Masseria's gunmen opened fire. Panicked bystanders screamed, and everyone dove for cover. In the chaos, a street sweeper, Joseph Schepis, and an eight-year-old girl, Agnes Egglineger, were wounded; as Agnes fell to the pavement, she screamed, "I'm hurt, Mama!" Valenti, desperate to escape, jumped onto the running board of a taxi and sped away. One of the Masseria gunmen "planted himself in the street and fired shot after shot," the *Times* reported,

> taking careful aim each time until his revolver was empty. "It was the coolest thing I ever saw," said Jack Kahane, 19. "People were shrieking and running in all directions, and this fellow calmly fired shot after shot. He did not move until he had emptied his weapon."

One of the shots hit Valenti in the chest, and he tumbled off the cab's running board, dead. According to legend, the cool gunman was Lucky Luciano.[25]

In 1931, Dutch Schulz and Vincent "the Mick" Coll went to war. Coll would not stop hijacking Schulz's beer trucks; Schulz demanded that Coll be killed. In the fighting, some twenty gunmen were shot to death.[26] On July 28, 1931, in Harlem, Coll attempted to kidnap Joey Rao, one of Dutch Schulz's thugs. Coll and several men drove up to Rao's Helmar Social Club on East 107th Street between Second and Third Avenues, and spotted Rao outside. Coll and others leapt from their car and opened fire. Rao survived, but five children were hit. Samuel Divino, five years old, and Florence d'Amello, fourteen, suffered minor wounds. Michael Bevilacqua, three years old, "was shot twice in the back while lying in his white wicker baby carriage," and Salvatore Vengalli, seven years old, was struck by five shotgun pellets; both Bevilacqua and Salvatore Vengalli survived. Michael Vengalli, five, Salvatore's little brother, was not so lucky; little Michael was killed. New Yorkers were horrified. Governor Franklin Roosevelt called Michael's killing "a damnable outrage." Mayor Jimmy Walker called Coll a "mad dog." The shooting had happened around 6:30 p.m. on a Tuesday; the area was "thronged" with people, and "out of each shabby five-story tenement leaned many men and women," but, though everyone agreed that maybe sixty shots had been fired, no one wanted to testify. Newspapers, the American Legion, and the Police Benevolent Association offered rewards to anyone who could help the police. Detectives figured that the shootout was part of the Coll–Schulz war and that Coll was one of the gunmen. Police tracked Vincent Coll down and charged him with Vengalli's murder. Because there were no witnesses, the case collapsed, and Coll was released.[27]

Not a month after Michael Vengalli's murder, a spectacular gun battle erupted in the Bronx. August 21, 1931, was payday at the Mendoza Fur and Dyeing Works on 712 East 133rd Street. Just as the car with the cash payroll arrived, another car filled with gunmen roared up. The gunmen killed the police officer guarding the payroll, Walter Webb; snatched up the sacks of money; and tore off toward Manhattan. Another police officer on a motorcycle gave chase, and he was quickly joined by a police car with a detective on the running board. The fleeing bandits fired at the police, and the police returned fire; at least a hundred shots were exchanged. Along the twelve-mile route, civilians screamed and dove for cover; at least twelve were wounded. Suddenly a family car was trapped between gunmen and police. In the car were firefighter John Lopez, his wife, Matilda, and their toddler, four-year old Gloria. Their car was riddled with bullets; Matilda was not hit; John was slightly wounded; little Gloria was shot in the head and killed instantly. The battle finally ended in northern Manhattan, at Broadway and Dyckman Street. The three gunmen—Martin Bachorik, nineteen; John Brecht, twenty-five; Herbert Hasse, twenty-seven—were shot to death. They had been armed with automatic weapons and "dum-dum" bullets. Again New Yorkers were shocked. At least a thousand people, including the parents of Michael Vengalli, attended little Gloria's funeral. Classmates sent flowers; six police officers served as her pallbearers.[28]

Meanwhile, the Coll–Schulz war raged on. On February 1, 1932, gunmen, most likely sent by Schulz, fired on Coll and friends. Coll escaped, but two of his men and a woman bystander were killed.[29] The war finally ended at 12:30 a.m. on February 8, 1932. Coll was in a telephone booth in the London Chemist's drug store, on the corner of Eighth Avenue and 23rd Street in Manhattan. According to one version of what happened, Coll was on the telephone speaking with gangster Owney Madden, threatening to kidnap Madden's brother-in-law unless he came up with $50,000. Madden kept Coll talking; a friendly police officer helped Schulz's men trace the call. A man rushed into the store with a tommy gun and said to the civilians in the store, "All right, everybody, keep cool now and you won't get hurt." Coll was still on the telephone, in the telephone booth. The gunman shot Coll to pieces and ran out. Coll's funeral, on February 11, 1932, was a gaudy affair. Dutch Schulz sent a wreath with a ribbon that said "From the Boys."[30]

Meanwhile, at the very same time, in 1930 and 1931, the Castellammarese War raged across New York, the most violent explosion Italian gangs had ever endured.[31] Several dozen people at least, probably many more, were killed in the gun battles between rival gangs. The single most famous event in the war was the assassination of gang leader Giuseppe "Joe the Boss" Masseria, arranged by Charlie "Lucky" Luciano.

On April 15, 1931, Charlie Luciano asked to meet with Masseria. Luciano was, by this time, one of Masseria's top lieutenants. Luciano wanted to talk about business and about the war. Masseria, according to later accounts, drove his "steel-armored sedan, a massive car with plate glass an inch thick in all its windows" [32] to the Nuovo Villa Tammaro restaurant on West 15th Street on Coney Island. Masseria met Luciano there around noon. Other men came and went; eventually, Masseria and Luciano were alone. They played a friendly card game as they talked. Around 2:00 p.m., Luciano excused himself and went to the restroom.

Suddenly, several armed men burst into the restaurant; they opened fire on Joe the Boss and shot him dead. The killers rushed back outside and into a waiting car. When the gunfire ended, Luciano quietly emerged from the restroom and waited while the hysterical restaurant staff called the police. When the police arrived, Luciano said to them no, he knew nothing about what had happened. A photograph of Masseria's bullet-riddled body quickly appeared in the newspapers; in his dead and bloody hand, Masseria held an ace of spades (the *Times* reported that it was the "ace of diamonds").[33] Whether he really had been holding the card or whether a creative news photographer placed it there, no one knows. However, the photograph became an icon of New York's violent gangland; although it had nothing to do with Murder, Inc., a close-up of the bloody hand with the card became the cover image of the 2003 paperback edition of Turkus and Feder's *Murder, Inc.*

Just who the assassins were remained a mystery. One guess is that they were Vito Genovese, Albert Anastasia, Joe Adonis, and Bugsy Siegel.[34] Luciano, of course, had organized the assassination. Masseria's murder would become a kind of archetypal gangster moment, re-created, with variations, in a variety of films, notably in *The Godfather—Part I*, when young Michael Corleone goes to a restroom, retrieves a pistol, returns to the table at which he had been dining with enemies of his father, and shoots them dead.

With Masseria dead, Salvatore Maranzano claimed to be the boss of all the Italian gangs. On September 10, 1931, Maranzano himself was assassinated, mostly like on the orders of Lucky Luciano.[35] Several dozen of Maranzano's gunmen were also killed[36] (an event that inspired the concluding scene of *The Godfather—Part I*).

By 1932, things had calmed down in the underworld, although random killings still regularly occurred. For example, on May 16, 1932, James Alascia, a "petty racketeer" according to the *Times*, was walking along Forsythe Street in Lower Manhattan. It was midday, passersby were strolling along, and children were playing. Suddenly, a gunman stepped from a tenement at 186 Forsythe and began shooting at Alascia. "Stray bullets slightly wounded two passersby and whistled over the heads of a large number of children at play," the *Times* reported. The gunman ran off and was never caught; Alascia died of his wounds. He had been involved in narcotics; perhaps that was the reason for the shooting. Alascia had also been implicated in Maranzano's killing; maybe the shooting was an act of revenge.[37]

And where were the cops, and judges, and politicians in all this? To many New Yorkers, it seemed like they were all at Ciro Terranova's party. Cops, lawyers, judges, politicians, they all seemed on the take.

Criminals with money had infested New York's civic life for years. In 1892, for example, the social reformer and Presbyterian preacher, Charles Parkhurst, had charged that crime was out of control in New York because the criminals virtually owned the police department and the politicians. For a few dollars, the cop on the beat looked the other way when a crime was committed; for a few dollars more, lawyers, politicians, and judges would make sure the criminal never suffered any punishment for any crime. "In its municipal life," Parkhurst thundered, "our city is damnably rotten." Everyone in the legal and political system was on the take; everyone had a hand out. "Your average policeman," Parkhurst charged, "is not going to disturb a criminal, if the criminal has means. It is the universal opinion of those who have studied longest and most deeply into the municipal criminality of this city that every crime has its price."[38] New York was the perfect market economy—everything was for sale. Theodore Roosevelt struggled to change all this during his two tumultuous years as police commissioner, from 1895 to 1897, but when Roosevelt left, corruption soon got back to normal.

On November 6, 1907, an ambitious young man named Fiorello La Guardia was appointed an interpreter at Ellis Island, in New York; twenty-five years old, La Guardia was proficient in English, Croatian, Italian, and German. His parents were Italian immigrants; his mother, Irene, came from a Jewish Italian family in Trieste; his father, Achille, came from Foggia. Achille was a musician, and in America had become a bandmaster in the US Army. Fiorello had been born in New York City but grew up on army posts in the Old West; he always thought of Prescott, Arizona, as one of his homes. His parents and their children eventually returned to Italy, and young Fiorello got a job with the US consular service. In 1906, he returned to New York City, sure that his future was in America. He decided to become a lawyer and go into politics, but to make ends meet, he went to work for the Immigration Service.

The years before World War I were boom times for immigration to
New York. Thousands arrived weekly, Ellis Island was swamped, and Manhattan swarmed with immigrants, especially Italians, Jews, and Eastern
Europeans. In 1907, when La Guardia began working for the Immigration Service, 1.3 million immigrants came to New York; Ellis Island was
set up to process five thousand immigrants daily, but sometimes as many
as twelve thousand arrived per day.[39] La Guardia's job was not only to
translate for the immigrants but also to take them into the city to try to
get them settled somewhere. La Guardia earned his law degree from New
York University, in 1910; his first clients were immigrants.

Young La Guardia learned some very hard lessons about immigrant
life. When he took an immigrant couple to City Hall to help them get
married, for instance, he, and they, had to put up with bureaucrats' incompetence, contempt, and lewd jokes; inevitably, some minor politician
slid his hand out and demanded a small bribe just to fill out the proper
paperwork. Practicing in night court, lawyer La Guardia learned that at
the street level, courts had nothing to do with justice and everything to
do with winks and nods, favors and payoffs. Everyone was on the take,
and everything was for sale. Cops on the take would run in prostitutes
who would grudgingly pay off the cops, lawyers, and judges and then
include the costs in higher fees for the johns. The payoffs found their
way up and down the secret world of neighborhood politicians, cops on
the corner, saloon keepers, and tough guys in the shadows. That was how
it all worked. Everyone was tempted, just about everyone had a hand in
all that easy money. One of La Guardia's supervisors in the Immigration
Service once told him, "You can get experience on this job [. . .] or you
can make a great deal of money. I don't think you'll take the money. But
remember, the test is if you hesitate. Unless you say 'no' right off, the first
time an offer comes your way, you're gone."[40]

By the 1930s in New York, gangsters were ubiquitous. They were on
the street corners of every tough neighborhood; they were in the political
clubhouses, in the unions, on the boards of businesses. They performed
their distinctive roles with brio. Abe Reles, according to the *New York
Times*, was a "flashy, blustery, little gang boss."[41] He was, the *Times* reported,
"a short, coarse-featured man, given to swaggering and bullying [. . .] with
flashy clothes setting off his heavy jowls, cheap jewelry attracting the eye
to his pudgy fingers [. . .] Reles likes to round out the picture of himself
by frequent displays of bills of large denominations, preferably $1000."[42]
Happy Maione, Reles's partner, ran a flower shop; in 1935, asked by reporters what sorts of arrangements he liked best, Maione smirked and said,

"[M]y specialty is making funeral pieces."[43] In 1940, Brooklyn's newly elected district attorney, Bill O'Dwyer, vowed to end the wave of gangland killings that had plagued the borough. When reporters asked Maione about O'Dwyer's vow, Maione retorted, "[W]ho does O'Dwyer think he is? Tell him I'll drop packages all over Brooklyn."[44] By "package," Maione meant, "corpse." A *Times* reporter noted that Happy Maione, while on trial, demonstrated his tough guy disdain by "frequently rubbing his finger-nails on his coat sleeve and observing their sheen in the reflected light of the court room."[45] Julie Catalano, one of the Reles's gang's "kids" who testified during the Murder, Inc., trials, was a "belligerent" witness, "snapping out his answers in loud, racy slang."[46]

Gangsters were in show business; they owned the Cotton Club and the Copacabana. Lucky Luciano had an apartment in the Waldorf-Astoria; Frank Costello had an apartment on Central Park West. Costello seemed to know every Tammany Hall politician in the city; Dutch Schulz was Tammy leader Jimmy Hines' best friend. The cops and the crooks knew each other well. In 1931, for example, amid his ferocious war against former ally Vincent "the Mick" (and "Mad Dog") Coll, a furious Dutch Schulz burst into a Bronx police precinct. "Look," Schulz shouted at the detectives, "I want the Mick killed. He's driving me out of my mind. I'll give a house in Westchester to any of you guys who knocks him off." One detective, Fred Schaedel, who grew up in Schulz's old neighborhood and knew Schulz's first name was really Arthur, said, "Arthur, do you know what the hell you're saying? You know you're in the Morrison station?" To which Schulz replied, "I know where I am [. . .] I've been here before. I just came in to tell ya I'll pay good to any cop that kills the Mick."[47] In 1932, at the Democratic National Convention in Chicago—the convention that nominated Franklin Roosevelt for president—Lucky Luciano shared a room in Chicago with one delegate; Frank Costello shared a room with another.[48]

Meyer Lansky may have been the first to note that organized crime was "like the Ford Motor Company."[49] Reporter Harry Feeney, who worked for the *New York World-Telegram*, certainly was struck by the enormous wealth and power of the gangsters. Early in 1940, Assistant District Attorney Burton Turkus explained the activities of the Brownsville "Combination" to Feeney. Feeney was astonished. "It's just like Bethlehem Steel," Feeney exclaimed; "it has a board of directors, a treasurer [. . .] and runs like a big syndicate."[50] Feeney would coin the term "Murder, Inc." to describe the Brownsville gang. A generation later, the fictional gangster, Hyman Roth, in *The Godfather—Part II*, was quite right when he remarked to Michael Corleone, "Michael, we're bigger than U.S. Steel."

Lineup: Martin "Buggsy" Goldstein, Seymour "Blue Jaw" Magoon, and a gang associate, Irving Shapiro. (City University of New York, John Jay College, Lloyd Sealy Library, Special Collections)

In 1904, Lincoln Steffens published a collection of his exposés of American politics titled *The Shame of the Cities*. Classic pieces of Progressive Era muckraking reporting, Steffens's articles examined municipal government in St. Louis, Minneapolis, Pittsburgh, Philadelphia, Chicago, and New York. Steffens was appalled. The cities Steffens studied were plagued by shoddy infrastructure, failing schools, vast slums, disease, and grinding poverty. In some cases, hardworking city officials simply could not keep up with urban growth driven by waves of immigration. In others cases, city officials were simply disorganized and incompetent. However, Steffens's investigations unearthed a much more sinister problem. Taxpayers were required by law to pay their city taxes, city taxes were to be used for the public good, and every taxpayer penny was to be scrupulously accounted for, but in fact, city officials were stealing every penny they could find. Public money was being stolen on a massive scale; public officials were using their offices for private enrichment. Whole networks of thieves had grown up around city halls. Crooked purchasing officers directed city contracts to friends who returned the favor with kickbacks to the purchasing officers. Police officers and judges were selling their services to the highest bidder. Theft, gambling, and prostitution flourished because the people involved in those things bought off the police, judges, and politicians. Meanwhile, city services fell into decay.

Boss Tweed's "classic question," Steffens wrote in "The Shamelessness of St. Louis" (1903), "'What are you going to do about it?' is the most humiliating challenge ever delivered by the One Man to the Many." Steffens continued:

But it was pertinent. It was the question then; it is the question now. Will the people rule? That is what it means. Is democracy possible? The accounts of financial corruption in St. Louis and of police corruption in Minneapolis raised the same question. They were inquiries into American municipal democracy, and, so far as they went, they were pretty complete answers. The people wouldn't rule.[51]

What was at stake in the shame of the cities, then, was nothing less than democracy. And democracy, Steffens worried, was in grave danger.

The cause of this threat to democracy was corruption, but what caused the corruption? City government was in danger, according to Steffens, because "politics is business. That's the matter with it [. . .] the commercial spirit is the spirit of profit, not patriotism; of credit, not honor; of individual gain, not national prosperity; of trade and dickering, not principle."[52] Politics had become commercialized; the market had absorbed the polis, and the consequences were disastrous.

New York's gangsters famously insisted that they were "just businessmen," and in a sense, they were quite right. In a city where the market ruled, where everything was for sale, where everything had a price, where everything from sex to illegal alcohol to stolen goods to votes in an election to the cop on the beat to the judge on the bench to the politician in the legislature could be bought and sold, then those who bought and sold these commodities, who some might call gangsters, were really, in a way, just businessmen.

Is it wrong for the market to absorb everything, for everything to be for sale? Long before Adam Smith, scores of thinkers had puzzled over the relationship among the market, the polis, and the wider culture. In the twentieth century, in a late-capitalist, market-driven consumer society, it would appear that market forces are inexorable and benevolent. Money, of course, is America's lifeblood, from sports to politics to health care. In both the Afghanistan and Iraq wars of the early twenty-first century, the US military increasingly relied on private, for-profit contractors. By the late twentieth century, American universities, too, had largely become auxiliaries of the market. Of course, David Kirp writes, universities have always worried about revenues, but, he adds, "what *is* new, and troubling, is the raw power that money directly exerts over so many aspects of higher education."[53] But, Kirp asks, "if health care, museums, even churches have been caught up in, and reshaped by intensive competitive pressures, why should higher education be any different?"[54] Higher education should be different, Kirp argues, because higher education has values quite distinct from market values and to confuse these two ethical domains is pernicious. Kirp writes, "'There is a place for the market,' as economist Arthur Okun wrote some years ago, 'but the market must be kept in its place.'" Kirp continues:

> Embedded in the very idea of the university [. . .] are values that the market does not honor: the belief in a community of scholars and not a confederacy of self-seekers; in the idea of openness and not ownership; in the professor as a pursuer of truth and not an entrepreneur; in the student as an acolyte whose preferences are to be formed, not a consumer whose preferences are to be satisfied.[55]

Michael Sandel makes a similar argument. Sandel's argument includes a lesser point and a greater point. The lesser point is that while free markets may well be benevolent, sometimes what appears to be a free market is not really free. For example, New York's businessmen gangsters were not really "free marketeers"; monopolies created by violence were the source of their profits; they are more rightly described as "monopolists," not "entrepreneurs." But, and this is Sandel's major point, even if a market were genuinely free, it is not appropriate everywhere. Markets are all about buying, selling, and consuming commodities, including commoditized services, but in some domains of human life, these market activities are entirely inappropriate. "Are there," Sandel asks, "certain virtues and higher goods that markets do not honor and money cannot buy?"[56] Are there some things that are not for sale? Sandel's answer is yes; persons and families and religious services and justice, for example, all are, or should be, beyond price. Sandel's thinking is much like Steffens's. Sandel writes, "Since marketizing social practices may corrupt or degrade the norms that define them, we need to ask what non-market norms we want to protect from market intrusion [...] we need a public debate about the moral limits of markets."[57]

The "commodity," an object manufactured, bought, sold, and consumed, is the keystone of the market. The total market threatens to transform everything and everyone into a commodity. The gangster movies enact this relentless commodification of life, especially in the 1940s *film noir* gangster movies. In *film noir*, even people and their identities become commodities. According to Fran Mason,

[m]odernity's development of a culture of the commodity and the exteriorization of the self through the commodification of identity can be identified in the figure of the *femme fatale* whose concern with money and objects of value creates her as an objectified embodiment of the cultural pervasion of the commodity. It is also implied in *film noir* that masculine integrity is under threat from the commodity.

To "be a man" means to hoard and consume objects, but some "objects," such as the *femme fatale*, can be dangerous. Even worse, in *film noir,* the criminal's masculine identity becomes located not in the person but in the objects the person accumulates. Identity itself is transformed into a thing to "have." Mason sees this commodification in *noir* films like *Double Indemnity* (1944) and *Kiss Me Deadly* (1955) as confirmation of Fredric Jameson's comments about "'waning of affect' [...] in which the private self of emotion and intellect is displaced by an exteriorized identity that is more concerned with spectacle and display than with psychological, moral, or emotional responses to, and relationships with society." The female body is "fetishized"; "there is an emptying out of male identity as the masculine self becomes externalized, dissipated into the clothes the male body wears and the commodities it utilizes."[58]

Fred Gardaphé explores the relationship among gangsters, masculinity, ethnic identity, and cultural representation in *From Wise Guys to Wise Men*. Gardaphé is concerned with "the gangster as an artistic device" and not the "actual thug belonging to a group of organized criminals." The fictional gangster is a complex figure with a long history; among his many roles was to serve as a mode of being a man, a road map for the directions taken by variants of masculinity in America, and as a model for moving from poverty or the working class to the middle or upper class, and therefore as a trope for signifying the gain of cultural power through class mobility.[59]

The fictional gangster was transgressive, powerful, and dangerous, but, Gardaphé argues, has largely exhausted his possibilities: "as a model for masculinity, I believe the gangster is exhausted [. . .] I believe the notion of what it means to be a man, in Italian-American or any other ethnic American culture, will change from the violent type of the traditional wiseguy into the more mature figure of the wise man," free from the "culture of death" and able to "cultivate alternative ways of living."[60]

This "culture of death" is precisely what Murder, Inc., represented. Murder, Inc., earned its name in part because it had "commoditized" murder. Central to its, and gangsterism's, ethos is the principle that "everything is a thing," that is, "everything is a commodity and every commodity is for sale," and that to be a person is to be a man, and to be a man means possessing, consuming, and, indeed, becoming a commodity. This principle fundamentally degrades persons and equally degrades democracy's higher goods; democracy and the total market are incompatible. People like Fiorello La Guardia and Thomas Dewey, who were determined to rescue democracy in New York, had to craft an ethos radically different from that of the gangsters. To rescue democracy, they had to articulate some fundamentally different ethos, to find some way to convince New Yorkers that "some things are beyond price."

4
Fiorello La Guardia and the Cinema of Redemption

> I want it clearly understood that no bunch
> of racketeers, thugs, and punks are going to
> intimidate you, as long as I am the Mayor of
> the City of New York!
>
> —*Fiorello La Guardia, 1935*[1]

In December 1935, the mayor of New York—Fiorello La Guardia—declared war on the artichoke king—Ciro Terranova. Elected New York's mayor in November 1933 as a Progressive Republican and bipartisan Fusion candidate, La Guardia vowed to launch a host of democratic reforms. At the top of his list was his promise to run the hoodlums out of town. La Guardia had a visceral hatred of gangsters. As a boy, growing up in Arizona, La Guardia had been the target of vicious anti-immigrant and anti-Italian prejudice. He was a "wop," a "dago," and for the rest of his life he responded furiously to these sorts of slurs. That some Italians would behave in ways that seemed to him to invite mockery and attack made him just as angry. As mayor, he would ban Italian organ-grinders from the city's streets; all they did, he thought, was perpetuate an unwelcome stereotype. Viewing *Little Caesar* made him mad. The movie was just one more attack, he complained, on Italian immigrants; a spokesman for the motion picture industry retorted that actually La Guardia was mad because the villainous Rico (Edward G. Robinson) looked an awful lot like La Guardia![2] La Guardia's campaign against the underworld was part of a decade-long struggle in New York between gangsters and gangbusters that began with the Seabury hearings in the early 1930s, continued through the Dewey investigations of the mid-1930s, and culminated in the Murder, Inc., trials of 1940–41. La Guardia neither began nor concluded the war against the gangsters, but his enthusiastic participation in it was crucial. No one enacted the campaign against the hoodlums with

75

as much vigor as the "Little Flower." La Guardia did not simply oppose the gangs; he offered a compelling ethical alternative to the gangsters' "social code." This chapter outlines La Guardia's attack on the gangs and argues that to understand La Guardia's ethics, going back to the movies, not to the gangster movies but to what film critic Sam Girgus calls "the cinema of redemption," is necessary.[3] La Guardia translated the "cinema of redemption" from movie screens to the streets of New York.

New Yorkers, especially New Yorkers of Italian heritage, loved artichokes. Artichokes, however, were pricey. Everyone knew why. Gangsters, notably Ciro Terranova and his crowd, had taken over the artichoke market. The mobsters shook down the artichoke dealers; the dealers paid off the mobsters and passed the higher prices along to their customers. In the Roaring Twenties, when people had jobs, the high prices were bearable; in the pit of the Great Depression, when money was very tight, the high price of artichokes was infuriating. But what could anyone do? No one wanted to risk a run-in with gangsters.

In November 1933, New Yorkers elected Fiorello La Guardia their mayor. Short, stocky, perpetually rumpled, and belligerent, with an unruly shock of black hair, La Guardia, at age fifty, had endured a rough and tumble political career. Born in New York, but raised in Arizona, he liked to think of himself as a cowboy. The son of Italian immigrants—his father, Achille, became a bandmaster in the US Army; his mother, Irene, was of Jewish Italian heritage; though La Guardia thought of himself as a Christian and Italian, he always had strong Jewish ties and was proud of his fluency in Yiddish. Army bandmaster Achille La Guardia fell violently ill in 1898 after, his son always insisted, eating tainted meat sold to the US Army by criminal meatpackers during the Spanish–American War. Achille left the army, and the La Guardia family moved back to Italy. Fiorello, who had a flair for languages, found work as a translator and administrator for the American consular service. He returned to New York, completed law school at New York University, and plunged into politics. New York's Tammany Democrats were, in La Guardia's opinion, hopelessly corrupt, so he became a Republican, though as a Progressive, he was never popular among conservative Republicans. In his youth, the Republican Party had a strong progressive wing, but after World War I, the Republicans turned rightward, and La Guardia typically found himself at odds with both parties. Elected to Congress from Italian Harlem, La Guardia voted to declare war on Germany in 1917 and promptly enlisted in the army. Sent to Italy as an air corps officer, La Guardia flew combat missions as a bomber crewman and, at war's end, left the army with the rank of major.

Reelected to Congress in 1918, La Guardia resigned his seat in 1919 and got himself elected president of the New York City Board of Aldermen. His two years with the board were tumultuous; in 1922, he returned to Congress. For the next decade, he was an obscure if vibrant progressive congressman, defender of the poor and nemesis of the rich. In 1929, he ran for New York mayor and lost to everyone's favorite, Jimmy Walker. In 1932, the Republican La Guardia lost his congressional seat in the Franklin Roosevelt–led Democratic landslide. However, in November 1933, La Guardia was elected mayor and would be reelected in 1937 and yet again to a third term in 1941.

In 1935, with artichoke prices sky-high—the press guessed that Ciro Terranova's artichoke racket grossed something like $1 million each year[4]—La Guardia decided to attack Terranova.

According to city law, the mayor could, in some cases, also serve as a magistrate. La Guardia announced that, sitting as a magistrate, he had found the artichoke cartel a public nuisance. On December 21, 1935, just before dawn, in the freezing darkness, La Guardia and a flying squad of police suddenly appeared at the Bronx's biggest produce market. La Guardia climbed onto the back of a flatbed truck and signaled to the police; two police officers with bugles sounded a stirring reveille. La Guardia, in his shrill combat voice, announced that as mayor and magistrate, he hereby declared the artichoke market temporarily closed. To the men and women who sold the artichokes, La Guardia shouted,

> I want to make it clear that the merchants and workers of the Bronx market are honest and hard-working citizens [. . .] I want it clearly understood that no bunch of racketeers, thugs, and punks are going to intimidate you as long as I am mayor of New York!

The market workers cheered.[5] The artichoke sale ban lasted only a few days; once Terranova's people were driven out and the prices brought back down, sales resumed. La Guardia launched a similar raid on the city's biggest fish market, putting gangsters like "Socks" Lanza and Albert Marinelli temporarily out of the fish business.[6] The New York Times commented later that "there is always an element of the theatrical about the mayor." In this case, he deployed his theatrical skills to demonstrate his determination "to drive the racketeer out of New York."[7]

Fiorello La Guardia provided New Yorkers with the alternative to the gangsters' total market. He embodied what Sam Girgus calls a "cinema of redemption,"[8] a cinema that expresses, as Girgus explains, the distinctive ethics of Emmanuel Levinas. La Guardia—cinema of redemption—and

Mayor Fiorello La Guardia tossing confiscated weapons into the Atlantic. (La Guardia
and Wagner Archives, La Guardia Community College, City University of New York)

Levinas would be central to New York's redemption; just how this triad
worked takes some explaining.

The road to redemption began with the Seabury hearings.

Ciro Terranova's outrageous party of 1929 and the unsolved murder
of gambler Arnold Rothstein that preceded it in 1928 were, for reform-
minded New Yorkers, the last straws.[9] They demanded that New York's
governor, Franklin Roosevelt, do something. Roosevelt and the state
legislature set up a commission of inquiry, chaired by state senator Samuel
Hofstadter. Governor Roosevelt and the commission asked Judge Samuel Seabury to be the chief investigator. The commission quickly became
known as the Seabury hearings.

When he began his inquiries, Judge Samuel Seabury, fifty-seven, was
the very personification of New York respectability. Descended from and
named after Bishop Samuel Seabury, America's first Episcopal bishop,
Judge Seabury's father was a theologian and expert in church law; his

mother, Alice Van Wyck Baere, was a descendant of one of New York's oldest and most prominent Dutch families. Seabury began his life as a lawyer in 1893, and immediately became a young activist in good government circles. He and his allies, like Theodore Roosevelt, demanded limits on lobbyists; strict reduction of patronage; and a merit-based, non-partisan civil service. A Progressive Republican, Seabury denounced the corruption of Tammany Democrats. Determined to do something about New York's poverty, slums, crumbling streets and buildings, poor schools, exploited workers, and violent crime, Seabury was the darling of all sorts of reform societies. He ran for a judgeship in 1899, but was defeated by a Tammany candidate; in 1901, only twenty-eight, he was elected to a ten-year term as a city court judge. Seabury ran as a Citizens Union–Fusion candidate, and represented a wide range of independent, Progressive Republican, and independent Democratic voters. In 1901, the year Seabury was elected judge, the Citizens Union also elected reformer Seth Low as mayor. Son of a prosperous merchant; married to Anne Wroe Scollay, daughter of a US Supreme Court justice; and heir to a long political genealogy—Low's grandfather had been Brooklyn's mayor, back when Brooklyn was an independent city—Seth Low had himself been elected Brooklyn's mayor in 1881 and had played a key role in the construction of the Brooklyn Bridge. In 1890, Low was chosen to be president of Columbia College. Low moved the school from midtown Manhattan up to Morningside Heights and reorganized it into Columbia University.

Low first ran for mayor of New York in 1897 but lost. In 1901, running as a Progressive Republican, Fusion, and Citizens Union candidate, he won. Mark Twain campaigned for him. In 1902, Low became the second mayor of the newly united greater New York. Low launched a whole host of reforms—he moved scores of city jobs to the merit-based civil service list, he tried to root out corruption in the police department, and he expanded and reformed the city's public schools—but New York was not quite in the mood for reform. In 1903, Low was defeated in his race for reelection by Tammany Democrat George B. McClellan, Jr., son of the famous Civil War general.[10]

As for Judge Seabury, in 1905, he ran for a seat on the New York Supreme Court but lost; in 1906, again on a Reform Fusion ticket, uniting Republicans, progressives, and independent Democrats, he ran and won. In 1913, he ran for a seat on New York's Court of Appeals but lost; in 1914, he won.

To Seabury, political decay was no abstract issue. It took on a very personal face in 1912, when Seabury became involved in one of New York's great police scandals, the notorious Charles Becker affair.

Charles Becker was a lieutenant in the New York Police Department. A big, powerful, intimidating figure, Becker was everyone's image of the heroic street cop. But Becker was dirty. He demanded payoffs from everyone he came in touch with—gamblers, brothel madams, and miscellaneous hoodlums—and shared the money with a network of other cops and politicians. In 1912, an outraged bookie named Herman Rosenthal had had enough. Furious with constantly being shaken down by one police officer after another, Rosenthal complained to Joseph Pulitzer's scandal sheet, the *New York World*. The *World* alleged that Lieutenant Becker was a central figure in an enormous New York Police Department extortion ring. Two days after the *World* broke the story, Rosenthal stepped out of the Hotel Metropole on 43rd Street near Times Square and was shot to death by a team of gunmen. Only a few days before the shooting, Manhattan's district attorney, Charles Whitman, had made an appointment to interview Rosenthal about Lieutenant Becker and corrupt police. Whitman was convinced that Becker was somehow behind Rosenthal's murder.

Whitman tried Becker for murder in 1912, and the trial of a New York police officer for a gangland-style murder dominated the headlines for months. Becker was convicted, but on appeal, his conviction was overturned.

In 1914, Whitman tried Becker again—before Judge Samuel Seabury. Becker was convicted again, and on July 30, 1915, Becker was electrocuted to death in Sing Sing prison (the execution was bungled; it took something like nine minutes to kill Becker).[11]

In 1916, Seabury, with the encouragement of New York's independents and progressives, decided to run for governor. Unfortunately for Seabury, the incumbent governor and former prosecutor, Charles Whitman, was an ally of Theodore Roosevelt. Roosevelt urged Progressives to vote for Whitman, not Seabury. Seabury, outraged by what he perceived to be Roosevelt's betrayal, angrily called Roosevelt a "blatherskite" and retreated to his law office, vowing to quit politics forever. However, he did not really quit. Instead, he transformed himself from perennial candidate into political sage. He knew all of New York's lawyers and judges and everyone in the city's reform circles; with his white hair, solemn manner, and lawyerly costume, Judge Seabury personified Establishment New York's good-government ideal.

In 1930, the Seabury hearings cautiously began. Seabury and his investigators looked only at New York City's magistrates and what they uncovered led to the dismissal of two magistrates, the resignation of three

more, and the flight of one. The cumulative impact of what Seabury uncovered, the depth and breadth of corruption in New York's judicial system, so shocked both the public and the state, that the state legislature
created a new special committee to investigate not just the magistrates
but New York City's whole government as well, and Governor Roosevelt
appointed Seabury the committee's the special counsel.[12]

In 1931, Seabury's real investigation began, and his key target was the
mayor of New York, Jimmy Walker.

Jimmy Walker was the perfect Jazz Age mayor for Roaring Twenties
New York. A fiercely loyal Tammany Democrat, a friend to everyone, an
amateur songwriter (he had one hit—"Will You Love Me in December
like You Do in May?"), Jimmy, or "Beau James" as the press called him,
was a snappy dresser and greeted everyone with a ready smile. He knew
how politics worked, he knew how to make deals, and he knew not to
rock the boat. After a long career in the state legislature, Walker easily defeated Fiorello La Guardia in the 1929 mayoral election.

In his relentlessly methodical investigations, Judge Seabury unearthed
what everyone suspected. The web linking Tammany Hall politicians, police officers, city officials, and gangsters was thick and dense. Seabury discovered, for example, that several of New York's sheriffs were hopelessly
corrupt. Metropolitan New York includes five different counties—New
York County (Manhattan), Kings County (Brooklyn), Bronx County
(the Bronx), Richmond County (Staten Island) and Queens County
(Queens)—and each county had a county sheriff. In just about each
county, the sheriff and his officials operated a network of payoffs, kickbacks, and special deals. New York County Sheriff Tom Farley, for instance, admitted that yes, he did have something like $100,000 stashed in
a "tin box." Seabury badgered Farley about how that much money found
its way into his little tin box; Farley murmured that it must have been a
kind of "magic" tin box. The Kings County registrar of deeds admitted
that he had "borrowed" something like $510,000 over several years, but
he could not quite remember from whom.[13]

The most dramatic moment in the Seabury investigation occurred in
the spring of 1932. Seabury questioned Mayor Walker himself; the very
incarnation of good government reform confronted the very personification of Tammany Hall. No one ever proved that Jimmy Walker had
exactly committed a crime, but given the immense corruption Seabury
had exposed, it was clear that something dramatic had to be done. Governor Roosevelt had a tense meeting with Mayor Walker. On September 1,
1932, Mayor Walker resigned and fled to Europe to avoid prosecution.[14]

Following Mayor Walker's resignation, Joseph McKee, another Tammany politician, finished Walker's term as mayor. However, after three years of Seabury's shocking revelations, and with the Jazz Age drowned by the Great Depression, New Yorkers again turned toward reform. In the November 1933 election, Walker's old rival, Fiorello La Guardia, blessed by Samuel Seabury himself, became the hope of New York reformers. La Guardia won a multiparty election with some 40 percent of the vote. He was sworn in as New York's ninety-ninth mayor on January 1, 1934, by Judge Samuel Seabury.

Central to La Guardia's agenda was waging war on organized crime.

La Guardia was no political innocent; critics would regularly charge him with being somehow in cahoots with the criminals. He fully understood the rough side of New York politics. Tammany had won elections for generations by intimidating voters, threatening rivals, stuffing ballot boxes, and disrupting speeches, and, in his three victorious campaigns for mayor, in 1933, 1937, and 1941, La Guardia was determined to fight fire with fire. Ernest Cuneo was a young lawyer who volunteered to help with the La Guardia campaigns. Before one speech, La Guardia whispered to Cuneo, "Ernest [...] they're going to pull the fire alarm when I speak tonight." La Guardia ordered Cuneo to stand guard near the fire alarm: "[O]ver to the alarm box," La Guardia ordered Cuneo, "and punch anybody in the eye who comes near it!"[15]

Later, La Guardia gave Cuneo an even more daunting assignment. La Guardia wanted Cuneo to be a poll watcher and make sure Tammany thugs did not disrupt voting. Cuneo vowed to call the cops if he spotted anyone tampering with the voting process.

"No," La Guardia said. "We don't want arrests; we want votes. If they rush the machine, knock them away from it. Then cast as many votes for me as they stole. You hear? Vote until they knock you out!" La Guardia continued: "I've given you a post of honor. Ernest, it's dangerous [...] They might shoot you. You could be killed."

Shaken, Cuneo said he would carry a gun. "No," La Guardia said, "you can't have a gun. I'd sooner see you dead than tried for murder."

So, Cuneo, who actually would rather have been tried for murder than killed defending a ballot box, went off to his post. He spotted a Tammany guy passing out money to likely voters. Two police officers lurked about, but Cuneo had no idea whether they were honest or on the take. Soon, other Tammany guys came into the polling station. One actually walked up to a voting booth and began to raise the curtain so he could see how the voter was voting. The two police officers looked the other way.

Cuneo knew his duty. "I belted him on the jaw with everything I had," Cuneo remembered.

He went flying into the machine and collapsed to the floor. All hell broke loose. The two cops jumped me [. . .] [one] cop yelled that I was under arrest. I said *he* was [. . .] The cop and I had just broken apart, still arresting each other when a huge limousine hurtled to a screaming stop at the curb. Men tumbled out of it and came running into the store. This is it, I thought. I just stood there, waiting for the bullets [. . .] "Now and at the hour of our death, Amen" came fleetingly to mind [. . .] Seven men rushed in, their right hands in their pockets. *But* they wore great big La Guardia buttons in their lapels! They formed a semicircle around me, facing the cops, and just stood there, crouched [. . .] Now another black car roared up and out jumped Fiorello [. . .] he burst in shouting "Attaboy, Ernest, give 'em hell!"[16]

There were rumors that Joe Adonis, one of Brooklyn's leading gangsters, had, for his own reasons, decided to support La Guardia in 1933. There were other rumors that Vito Marcantonio, La Guardia's young aide, had mobster friends.[17] La Guardia, though, he hated gangsters. Lucky Luciano and the others never understood why. Luciano said, "I just couldn't understand the guy [. . .] When we offered to make him rich he wouldn't even listen."[18]

Throughout his mayoralty, La Guardia denounced the mobsters. Charles Garrett notes that "from his first day in the Mayor's office, La Guardia, reinforced by his passionate hatred for crime, made war upon the underworld with all the power at his command."[19] He once told a police Holy Name Society gathering,

Out where I was raised [. . .] we didn't have much of a police department. We had a Sheriff and a few deputies. We kept no locks on our doors, but robberies were unknown. Our Sheriff was quick on the trigger, if you know what I mean. Roughnecks call you "cops" and me a "wop" [. . .] If gangsters speak well of the Police Department, it's a sign there is something wrong in the department.

La Guardia concluded his remarks by warning gangsters that they had better get out of town.[20]

In 1934, the first year he was mayor, in the summer, La Guardia attended a dance contest in Central Park. Things began getting pretty rowdy; as he always did, La Guardia took personal command of the police

and managed to calm the crowd. Leaving Central Park, he spotted a dis-
traught woman who had become separated from her family. La Guardia
hurried over to the woman; she was an Italian immigrant, so La Guardia
spoke with her in Italian. He took her to the local precinct and told a
lieutenant to take charge. The lieutenant did not recognize the new mayor
and demanded to know just who the hell La Guardia thought he was. La
Guardia responded: "Personally, Lieutenant, I am a person of no importance, but—the job I happen to hold is Mayor of the City of NewYork—
and damn you Lieutenant, I want to see my police force function!"[21]

La Guardia's first choice to make his police force function was General
John O'Ryan. As police commissioner, O'Ryan was more concerned
about spit and polish than chasing crooks and La Guardia quickly replaced
him with Lewis J. Valentine. Valentine would prove to be La Guardia's key
ally in his war against the gangs.

Valentine had been on the NewYork Police Department since 1903,
and he was an honest cop. He was as blunt as his nightstick. His parents,
he wrote, taught him "honesty above all"; his first police mentor was
"Honest Dan" Costigan, who impressed on young Valentine that a police
officer's job was to protect the citizenry and stay clean. Valentine would
develop a ferocious hatred for both the hoodlums who thought they
could scare him and the politicians who thought they could buy him.[22]
Like all NewYork kids, Valentine knew about gangs; more than once he
had gotten into fistfights with gang members. "When I became a rookie
cop," he later wrote,

> I thanked myself for having learned to use my fists well as a boy.
> Cracking jaws and flattening noses was the only effective means of
> impressing law and order upon cheap hoodlums. To me they have
> always been bums, from those young hooligans who toppled over
> the chimneys of abandoned houses on passing cops as I pounded my
> beat to the suave and murderous gangsters of a later day who tried
> to pull City Hall over my head.[23]

Valentine had had a rough career during the long years when Tammany politicians ran the city. He had been promoted—everyone agreed
that he was a "cop's cop"—but he would not be bought; he disliked
most politicians, so he was periodically reassigned to Siberias in the outer
boroughs.

The NewYorker published a three-part profile of Police Commissioner
Valentine in 1936. Jack Alexander, *The NewYorker*'s writer, told his readers that

Police Commissioner Lewis J. Valentine. (New York City Municipal Archives)

Lewis J. Valentine is a restless man. He gives the impression of always being tightly wound up, like a clock spring. He is taciturn and talkative by turns; when he talks at length he is always articulate and often robustious and inelegant. His face is roughhewn and has an unflagging muscular intentness.[24]

Born and raised in Brooklyn, Valentine, *The New Yorker* reported, had worked as a laborer and then had joined the force. Over three decades, he experienced both promotions and bureaucratic exiles. In 1934, La Guardia charged him with remaking the New York Police Department.

Early in his tenure, Valentine met with his detectives. He put them on warning. "I'll have no shirkers in squad rooms," he said,

listening to the radio and reading newspapers when they should be out fighting crime. And don't wait until crimes are reported to you. Go out and prevent them. If you slow up, if you are out of step, if you are not producing, you are on your way out.[25]

He backed up his warning with stern discipline. During his first six years as commissioner, Valentine fired three hundred officers, formally rebuked four thousand, and fined eight thousand.[26]

One of Valentine's first measures, *The New Yorker* reported, was to revive the department's "strong-arm squad," detectives whose mission was to harass hoodlums. "I want the gangster to tip his hat to the cop," Valentine told his detectives. "There'll be promotions for the men who kick these gorillas around and bring them in."[27]

In November 1934, Police Commissioner Valentine attended a routine morning lineup of suspects arrested the day before. As usual, a score or more of top detectives attended. Valentine normally dressed very simply, in a plain civilian suit, but he had just bought a rather nice Chesterfield topcoat. He hung the coat on a peg and, with the detectives, began to view the lineup. One man in the lineup caught his eye. He was a "jaunty Brooklyn hoodlum,"[28] "lean" and "narrow-eyed."[29] One of the detectives pointed to the hoodlum's fine topcoat and whispered to Valentine, "[L]ook at that bum. He's got a coat exactly like yours!"[30] Valentine, that day, was in a grim "don't-touch-me" frame of mind.[31] He pointed to the young man with the smirk and the brand new Chesterfield topcoat and blew his stack.

The young man was Pittsburgh Phil Strauss. He had been brought in on suspicion of stabbing to death gas station attendant Alvin Snyder. According to the *New York Times,*

Strauss bore an easy pose in his smartly cut Chesterfield overcoat with velvet collar. His blue suit was pressed to razor sharpness and a new blue shirt, held fast by a tie to match, was snug around his neck. A new pearl-gray fedora was canted over one eye at a jaunty angle.

Just the sight of Strauss infuriated Commissioner Valentine. To his assembled detectives, Valentine shouted,

> This man is a pal of Abe Reles [...] You men are handicapped when you face men like this. When you meet such men draw quickly and shoot accurately. Look at him—he's the best dressed man in this room. Yet he's never worked a day in his life. When you meet men like Strauss, don't be afraid to 'muss 'em up. Men like him should be mussed up. Blood should be smeared all over his velvet collar. Instead, he looks as though he just came out of the barber shop.

According to the *Times*, Strauss shifted nervously on the stage from one foot to another, looked at the ceiling, and tugged at the brim of his fedora. Valentine continued:

> You men will be supported by me no matter what you do, if what you do is justified [...] Make it disagreeable for these men. Drive them out of the city. Teach them to fear arrest. Make them fear you. Don't treat them lightly. And take this message back to your associates. Make [the thugs] learn that this town is no place for muscle men or racketeers [...] The sooner we get rid of the gangster, the better [...] On the other hand, no police brutality will be tolerated. The decent, hard-working people should be, and will be, protected, but it should be the crooks who are carried out in boxes, not the cops.

According to the *Times,* when Valentine finished, "his face was flushed with anger."[32]

Civil libertarians were horrified. Mayor La Guardia himself had long been a critic of police power and had defended the rights of trade unionists, immigrant advocates, and citizens, in general, to organize, assemble, and peacefully protest without being hassled by the authorities. But when it came to the gangsters, La Guardia vociferously supported his police commissioner.[33]

Over the next several years, La Guardia and Valentine launched a series of dramatic raids on the underworld. Both were convinced, for example, that bookies, as well as Frank Costello's slot machines, were a public nuisance. La Guardia had little patience for the poorly paid worker who lost his money to bookies or slot machines. He had nothing but contempt for impoverished workers who insisted that they were "honor bound" to pay off their debts to crooks. La Guardia snorted, "[H]ere's a boob, with kids that are hungry. Does he use his last two bucks to buy them food? No, this boob pays it over to some tinhorn bookie because his honor— his honor—is involved. Huh! Some honor. Some boob."[34] In New York, in the 1930s, there were thousands of slot machines in bars, corner stores, and groceries, and they brought in, tax free, something like $500,000 per day. In 1932, the slot machine business, run by Frank Costello, grossed something like $37 million.[35]

The slots robbed workers; worse, bar owners and restaurateurs were threatened if they did not install them. Profits from the slots financed a host of other illegal activities. Commissioner Valentine called them "mechanical pickpockets."[36] Their legal status was a bit confusing; Costello had rigged the machines so they also dispensed candy, and his lawyers insisted that the machines were candy machines (that happened to dispense coins too), not gambling machines. State law prohibited gambling devices, but were these candy-dispensing machines really gambling devices as defined by state law? La Guardia had no intention of awaiting the lawyers' opinions. La Guardia announced that in his capacity as a city magistrate, he'd declared the slots a public nuisance and demanded that they be removed from the city. Commissioner Valentine's police happily rounded them up. In October 1934, 1,155 were loaded onto barges. Mayor La Guardia, with reporters' cameras clicking, clambered aboard one barge, sledgehammer in hand, and proceeded to pound the slots to bits. The photograph of La Guardia swinging his sledge at the slots appeared all around the country.[37] He would do the same with illegal guns rounded up by the police; images of La Guardia tossing shotguns and machine guns into the ocean made all the papers.

In August 1935, Dutch Schulz was put on trial for federal tax evasion. His lawyers convinced the judge to change the trial's venue from New York City, where, Schulz's lawyers complained, Dutch would never get a fair trial, to the little town of Malone, in upstate New York. Schulz was acquitted. Mayor La Guardia heatedly announced that Schulz "won't be a resident of New York City. There is no place for him here." Schulz, with, as the *Times* said, "characteristic bravado," responded: "So, there isn't room for me in New York. Well, I'm going there." But Schulz didn't. La Guardia, Valentine, and Special Prosecutor Tom Dewey showered Schulz with court orders and subpoenas; to play it safe, Schulz holed up in New Jersey.

Meanwhile, La Guardia and Valentine ordered the police to focus on Lucky Luciano, Meyer Lansky, Bugsy Siegel, Lepke Buchalter, and their gangs. When six jewel thieves turned up in a police precinct looking as if, according to La Guardia's biographer, Thomas Kessner, "their faces had been used to drill the hole through the wall leading to the heist," La Guardia had no sympathy for them. The mayor said, "[W]hen six gangsters meet six policemen and the gangsters are mussed up, it's just too bad for them. We have no room in the Police Department for sissies."[38]

La Guardia's campaign against the gangsters, however, relied on a weapon much more powerful than Commissioner Valentine's strong-arm squad. La Guardia personified an ethical vision for New York far more compelling than the gangsters' "social code." La Guardia understood that hope and compassion really are far more powerful than fear and violence.

Why did La Guardia confront the gangsters? He was a politician, of course, with long experience in neighborhood politics both in Greenwich Village and in Italian Harlem. He knew that some people admired mobsters, but he also knew that many others feared them. Going after the artichoke king was a shrewd and popular exercise in political theater.

Personal identity played as big a role as political calculation did in La Guardia's intense dislike of hoodlums. La Guardia was the son of Italian immigrants when Italian immigrants were not exactly welcome in the United States, the son of a Jewish mother when anti-Semitism was rampant. He was the short kid in the tall kids' playground. Growing up in Arizona, he identified with the Indians and Mexican immigrants who were regularly the target of appalling abuse. His favorite readings were weeks-old copies of Joseph Pulitzer's *New York World* in which good guys battle the forces of evil.[39] La Guardia was sure that his father's early death was caused by his father's consumption of rotten meat sold to the army during the Spanish–American War by criminal meat packers. Once launched in politics, La Guardia was the belligerent defender of the little guy, the lonely immigrant, the unemployed, the harassed worker.

La Guardia was a showman, a master of political theater. His long career in New York City politics generated scores of stories and everyone who knew him had some anecdote about him.

Being called a "wop" infuriated him. In 1920, for example, La Guardia was the newly elected president of New York's Board of Aldermen, second only to the mayor in the city's political hierarchy. He advocated a whole host of reforms. He called for an improved sanitation system, cheaper mass transit, subsidized public housing, a more progressive city tax, and

greater investment in public schools.[40] His nemesis was the Democratic
city comptroller, Charles Craig. Ferocious arguments between La Guardia
and Craig quickly punctuated meetings of the Board of Aldermen. At one
meeting, Craig urged the mayor to "hit that little wop over the head with
the gavel." At another meeting, when LaGuardia insisted on debating a
proposal Craig opposed, Craig threatened to give La Guardia "what he deserved." La Guardia lunged at Craig; Craig's secretary grabbed La Guardia;
La Guardia shouted to the secretary, "You try to start anything with me and
you'll go out of that window, you bootlicking valet!" The secretary shouted
back that, at least, "I'm no wop!" As other aldermen grabbed La Guardia,
he shrieked at the secretary, "What's that you say?! What's that you say?!"[41]

Years later, when La Guardia was mayor, a New York alderman, during
a city council meeting, attacked his generous aid for the unemployed; the
alderman indignantly claimed that, why, he had heard that even prostitutes
were getting unemployment benefits! La Guardia dramatically jumped to
his feet and shouted, "I thought that question was settled two thousand
years ago, but I see I was wrong! Mr. Sergeant at Arms, clear the room!
Clear the room! So this big bum can throw the first stone!"[42]

Novelist Fannie Hurst called La Guardia a "blazing rebel" who was
"always about to explode in indignation against social injustice."[43]

La Guardia advocated a robust sense of "citizenship." Citizenship means
much more than simply residence in a certain place. Following Aristotle,
Hannah Arendt argues that the distinctive thing about human beings is
that they are creatures "who live in a polis." A polis, however, is neither
a family nor a tribe. A polis is a unique space, a kind of theater, a pecu-
liarly "human artifice,"[44] in which strangers, "others," can interact freely,
as equals, and deploy rhetoric and logic to deliberate about their common
good. Freedom, equality, and plurality are the essential qualities of this
human artifice. "Freedom is exclusively located in the political realm,"[45]
not in the household, tribe, or market. Ideally, some participants in the
political realm are not freer than others; all are equally free and equally
able to participate in deliberations about the common good. "The *polis*,"
Arendt writes, "was distinguished from the household in that it knew only
equals."[46] "Plurality," moreover, "is [. . .] the [. . .] *sine qua non* [. . .] of [. . .]
the public realm. Hence the attempt to do away with this plurality is always
tantamount to the abolition of the public realm itself."[47]

La Guardia shared this deeply egalitarian ideal of citizenship. Citizens
are inherently equal. La Guardia was hostile to most hierarchies, such as
hierarchies based on lineage. Once, during his first term, he responded this
way to a worried voter's concern about his genealogy:

I am sure you are quite mistaken in the genealogy of my family. I have never had time to look this matter up myself. In fact, the only member of our family that I know who has a real pedigree is our little Scotch Terrier known as Mac, who is a son of McIntosh, who is a son of Dundee, who is a son of Glasgow, but with all of that is only a son of a bitch. Very truly yours, Fiorello La Guardia.[48]

He was hostile to hierarchies based on class as well. For example, when he was mayor, a wealthy constituent wrote him to complain that the police regularly ticketed her limousine. Many cities, she pointed out, had special "courtesy cards" that one could put on one's limo's windshield, and police would be instructed never to ticket limos with courtesy cards. How might she obtain such a courtesy card, she asked the mayor. La Guardia replied, "Mrs. La Guardia, Mrs. Vanderbilt and Mrs. O'Flaherty are treated all alike and get the same privileges. The only Courtesy Card we have for parking is that for parking baby carriages in our beautiful and well-kept playgrounds. How many such cards can I send you?"[49]

Once, Mayor La Guardia heard that people in line for relief were being bullied by the very people who were supposed to help them. La Guardia rushed to the scene and elbowed his way to the front of the line. As biographer William Manners tells the story,

> [a] man tried to stop him, but La Guardia hurled him to one side, and gave another the same treatment. Then a third man—a cigar in his mouth, a derby on his head—tried to block him. With two swings, La Guardia knocked the cigar from his mouth and the derby from his head. "Take off your hat when you speak to a citizen!" La Guardia shouted.[50]

La Guardia expressed this robust sense of citizenship from the very beginning. On January 1, 1934, in his inaugural address, La Guardia spoke in general terms of his agenda, of the need to get New York's financial house in order, of the need to combat the Great Depression. He spoke of his coming administration as an "experiment."[51] He concluded his address with a reference to the classical political tradition with its powerful sense of the citizen. Citing the "Oath of the Young Men of Athens," La Guardia said, "We will never bring disgrace to this, our city, by any act of dishonesty or cowardice nor ever desert our suffering comrades in the ranks."[52]

Meyer Lansky's biographer writes that the essence of the gangster ethic was the conviction that New Yorkers lived in "a city where everything was for sale."[53] La Guardia's notion of citizenship meant that all citizens, regardless of their wealth or poverty, regardless of class or race or ethnic origin, were inherently equal and that some things, like equal citizenship, were beyond price. La Guardia's "citizen" was the antidote to Meyer Lansky's "gangster."

However, La Guardia's alternative to gangsterism was not only political; it was also cinematic. With his squeaky voice, disheveled hair, rumpled suits, and fierce egalitarianism, La Guardia was actually a familiar figure in the 1930s; he was a real live version of Jefferson Smith, the fictional Mr. Smith who went to Washington.

Frank Capra's *Mr. Smith Goes to Washington* (1939), starring Jimmy Stewart as Jefferson Smith, is a classic New Deal–era film. Capra's films are often dismissed as "Capracorn," sentimental, naïve, and melodramatic.[54] Yet as Sam Girgus argues, there is much more to Capra's films than patriotic pathos. Capra's films, Girgus insists, enact the moral thought of Emmanuel Levinas, and this Levinasian sensibility gives Capra's films a remarkable moral intensity.

The French philosopher Emmanuel Levinas insists that ethics, what Plato cryptically called the "good beyond being," is the foundation of philosophy. All other branches of philosophy—metaphysics, epistemology, aesthetics—flow from ethics. My ethical imagination is first awakened, Levinas thinks, when I am confronted by death. One day I awaken to the painful realization that I am not all that there is, that it's really not all about me, that like every other human being I come from nowhere and return to nowhere. Such an experience can trigger panic, blaming, and aggression, as I scramble to protect my besieged ego. But such an experience can, if I learn to let go of my ego, also be liberating. I can, like Ebenezer Scrooge, awake after terrifying dreams and climb above my own ego; I can learn to extend my self-esteem and self-compassion beyond my narrow self. This awakening carries me off into a different sort of time, a special kind of time that is not simply one moment after another but a different, separate, "diachronic" time in which some things become very important. The thing that becomes most important is my sudden awareness that my world is inhabited by more than just me, that there are Others there too. Beyond me is the Other, and my esteem and compassion now can extend to the Other. This new and special time is marked by a sudden awareness of the Other, an awakening to relationships that include but are not centered on me, an experience of compassion for the Other and an acute sense of responsibility to and for the Other. The Other, meanwhile, remains genuinely other and not simply a replication of "me." The birth of the ethical, triggered by an encounter with death, characterized by a compassionate turn toward the Other, marks my own redemption. This movement above and beyond my narrow ego translates me into the realm of the good and the world of hope.[55]

In *Mr. Smith Goes to Washington,* Sam Girgus argues, the fictional Jefferson Smith undergoes a Levinasian ethical transformation. Smith goes on a journey that ends in redemption. Americans love redemption films; the "cinema of redemption" is as distinctive of American film as the western or the gangster film. Smith initially fails in Washington and undergoes a kind of death and rebirth on the steps of the Lincoln Memorial, during which time seems to stop and Smith seems to enter another nontemporal, nonspatial dimension; at the moment of conversion, time and space are "unhinged." His egoism "drained," the fictional Smith senses another dimension to life; he can imagine "a world accessible to hope." But, crucially, this is not some narcissistic event but precisely its opposite. Smith is not just personally converted; his conversion moves him beyond himself to the Other.[56] By engaging the Other, Smith creates a "world." The "country bumpkin" is converted, by confronting despair and death, into an ethical hero, called to "defeat the evil of the Goliath of great power in the service of greed."[57] Transformed himself, Mr. Smith can now transform the nation.

Fiorello La Guardia was Jefferson Smith. Partly, of course, there is the accident of resemblance. La Guardia, like Smith, was just an ordinary citizen, an ordinary person with no wealth, no pedigree, and no social status. La Guardia and Smith signaled their "just an average person" identity with their wrinkled suits, uncombed hair, and unaffected diction. Both looked, acted, and sounded just like someone next door.

More important, La Guardia went through a Levinasian awakening much like that of Jefferson Smith.

In 1921, a series of near-mortal blows almost destroyed La Guardia. His political career seemed to be careening to a fatal crash. Hostile to Tammany Democrats, but never really embraced by Republicans, La Guardia constantly had to scramble to cobble together a fusion alliance among scattered progressives. In 1919, he had given up his safe congressional seat to become president of New York City's Board of Aldermen, with the hope that he would be well positioned to run for New York mayor. His tenure as president had been tumultuous; he had made much of political New York angry with him. No one wanted him to be mayor. There was no guarantee that he would win another congressional seat. Then, in May 1921, catastrophe struck. La Guardia's eleven-month-old daughter and only child, Fioretta, contracted spinal meningitis and died on May 9. At the very same time, La Guardia's wife, Thea Almerigotti, was battling tuberculosis. Thea, aged twenty-six, died on November 29, 1921. In something like six months, La Guardia had buried his child and his wife. It about killed him.

Somehow he found his way through. Amid these disasters, reporter Zoe Beckley of the *New York Evening Mail* interviewed him and asked about his vision for the city. New York City's government spent about a million dollars a day; could La Guardia think of a better way to spend that much money? "Could I? Could I?!" La Guardia exclaimed.

Say! First I would tear out about five square miles of filthy tenements, so that fewer would be infected by tuberculosis like that beautiful girl of mine, my wife who died—and my baby—I would establish "lungs" in crowded neighborhoods—a breathing park here, another there, based on the population. Milk stations next! One wherever needed, where pure cheap milk could be bought for babies and mothers to learn how to take care of them [...] I would keep every child in school to the eighth grade at least, well fed and in health. Then we could provide widows' pensions [...] I would provide more music and beauty for the people, more parks and more light and air and all the things the framers of the Constitution meant when they put in the phrase "Life, Liberty, and the Pursuit of Happiness" [...] a million a day spent in New York! And what do we buy *for the people?!*"[58]

The interview marks an extraordinary transition, from death to hope, from La Guardia's private suffering to concern for the millions of others in New York. Simon Critchley, writing about Levinas's ethics, argues that the "anarchic" and disruptive "meta-political ethical moment," the moment of awakening and conversion, "provides the motivational force or propulsion into political action." Ethics and politics are inextricably tied. "Politics without ethics is blind," Critchley writes, but "ethics without politics is empty."[59] La Guardia's biographer, Thomas Kessner, writes that La Guardia's politics were fueled by a sense of "civic possibility"; La Guardia himself would speak about bringing a "new politics"[60] to New York. Levinas insisted that hope was integral to ethics; La Guardia brought hope to gangster-ridden Gotham.

To be sure, one might object that La Guardia's, and Jefferson Smith's compassionate approach to public issues is quite out of place.

In 1914, La Guardia ran for Congress and lost. His Republican mentors managed to get him named a deputy to the New York State attorney general. The job was routine; the attorney general had lots of such depu-ties across the state, but La Guardia took his job very seriously. He worked assiduously to enforce New York's laws, and he was taken aback, once, when his opponent in the courtroom, defending a client from state law, was the very politician who had authored the law in the first place, Jimmy Walker. How could Walker work in the legislature to get a law passed—and then, in the courtroom, work to undermine that very law? Walker, who flourished in the sea of political winks and nods, was shocked too—by La Guardia's naiveté. "Fiorello, when are you going to wise up?" Walker asked La Guardia. "Why do you suppose we introduce bills? We intro-duce them sometimes just to kill them. Other times we even have to pass a bill. Why are you in the Attorney General's office? You're not going to stay there all your life. You make your connections now, and later on you can pick up a lot of dough defending cases you are now prosecuting [. . .] What are you in politics for, for love?"[61]

Jimmy Walker was not the only one suspicious of love in politics. Han-nah Arendt, for example, argues that love is appropriate in the family and among kin and friends, but it is inappropriate, even disastrous in politics. "Love," she writes, "can only become false and perverted when it is used for political purposes."[62] The political realm, Arendt argues, is precisely the place where people who are not necessarily kin, who are strangers to each other, and who do not especially like each other can nevertheless meet and freely deliberate. Love is exclusive, not diverse and plural. "Love by its very nature is unworldly [. . .] it is not only apolitical but antipoliti-cal," Arendt writes.[63] "Love," therefore "is incapable of founding a public realm of its own."[64] Love and goodness, Arendt insists, simply are not and should not be political categories. "Goodness [. . .] is not only impossible within the confines of the public realm," she argues, "it is even destructive of it."[65] To insist that love, family, kin, and bloodlines must, even meta-phorically, shape politics is to exclude the stranger, the rival, the other. In politics, Arendt thinks, love is dangerous.

Martha Nussbaum, to the contrary, makes a strong argument for the centrality of love, specifically, love as compassion, to democracy. Every polity has its characteristic political culture; political cultures mobilize emotions through symbol and ritual. A political culture driven by fear, envy, and disgust is incompatible with democracy. Democracy requires a political culture in which citizens are genuinely concerned for each other and are willing to bear each other's burdens. "In the type of liberal society that aspires to justice and equal opportunity," Nussbaum writes, there are two tasks for the political cultivation of emotion. One is to engender and sustain strong commitment to worthy projects that require effort and sacrifice—such as social redistribution, the full inclusion of previously excluded or marginalized groups, the protection of the environment, foreign aid, and the national defense.

The other task, Nussbaum continues, "is to keep at bay forces that lurk in all societies [. . .] tendencies to protect the fragile self by denigrating and subordinating others [. . .] disgust and envy, the desire to inflict shame upon others [. . .] are present in all societies [. . .] Unchecked, they can inflict great damage."[66] Therefore, Nussbaum argues, that both citizens and political leaders express and enact compassion is essential. Only when love as compassion is widespread will democracy function; "love," Nussbaum insists, "matters for justice."[67] Compassion, ultimately, is what fuels a polity's commitment to equal justice under law.

Paul Kavieff writes that the Manhattan gangster Lepke Buchalter, even as a teenager, began to divide the world into

wolves and lambs, predators and victims, winners and losers, deceivers and deceived, the elite and the rabble. It is the elite few who grasp this truth and possess the courage and energy to act upon it.[68]

Buchalter thought that he and the gangsters were the elite few. In La Guardia, the lambs, victims, losers, deceived, and rabble had found their champion. The gangster film had met its match in the cinema of redemption.

5
Gangbuster
Thomas Dewey and Imperfect Justice

> As you retire to your room, gentlemen, I ask
> you to bear in mind that the people of this
> country look to you twelve men as to the
> course of justice in this country. Are we to have
> justice in the courts? Is justice to be effective in
> this country in the courts, or is it not?
>
> —*Prosecutor Thomas Dewey, final comments at
> the trial of Waxey Gordon, 1933*[1]

In the mid-1930s, on the heels of the Seabury hearings and inspired by Mayor La Guardia, New York launched a second judicial attack on gangland. The attack's leader was Special Prosecutor, and later District Attorney, Thomas E. Dewey, who would earn the *nom de guerre* "Gang-buster." Dewey's most dramatic moment was his prosecution of one of the underworld's key figures, Charlie "Lucky" Luciano, in 1936. The Dewey investigations put enormous pressure on the gangs and that pressure produced Murder, Inc. Dewey insisted that his raids, indictments, and prosecutions—often messy, controversial, and deeply ambiguous—were, ultimately, about justice. But what did Dewey mean, exactly, by "justice"?

This chapter explores New York's Dewey investigations of the mid-1930s and, especially, the Lucky Luciano trial of 1936. It will follow the stunning twists and disconcerting turns the search for justice took and conclude by sketching the ways in which ways in which this search for justice, ironically, gave birth to Murder, Inc.

In February 1935, Irving Ben Cooper, special counsel to the City of New York, reported that seventy-seven bail bondsmen in New York City had perjured themselves 1,584 times.[2] Cooper had been an investigator in the Seabury hearings, which, only three years before, had toppled New York's mayor, Jimmy Walker. Cooper had stayed on with the city, handling, among other things, an ongoing investigation of the city's court system. In his report, Cooper alleged that the police regularly arrested scores of numbers runners but that bail bondsmen almost immediately put up the money to spring the runners from jail. The bail bondsmen regularly listed fake names when asked who had provided the bail money; according to Cooper, the real person bailing out the numbers runners was the former bootlegger and current king of the numbers racket, Dutch Schulz. Schulz's numbers operation generated something like $100 million per year, and Schulz needed his numbers runners out of jail.[3]

Pressured by angry civic groups, Manhattan District Attorney William Copeland Dodge agreed to impanel a grand jury to investigate Cooper's charges. Meanwhile, Martin Mooney, a journalist with the New York American, reported that the fix was in, that Schulz, through Tammy Hall leader Jimmy Hines, had made sure that Dodge's grand jury would go nowhere. In fact, the grand jury went nowhere. And then, a very strange thing happened— the grand jury ran away. The grand jury foreman, Lee Thompson Smith, angrily complained that District Attorney Dodge was dragging his heals and that "every conceivable obstacle" had been put in the grand jury's path.[4] Relations between the grand jury and District Attorney Dodge quickly soured; the grand jury, led by foreman Smith, demanded that Dodge appoint an investigator of their choice; newspapers began reporting on a "runaway grand jury." Finally, the grand jury demanded that Governor Herbert Lehman appoint a special prosecutor.[5] Governor Lehman selected four prominent New York attorneys and ordered District Attorney Dodge to pick one of them as his special prosecutor. Meanwhile, the four attorneys named— Charles E. Hughes, Jr., George Z. Medalie, Charles H. Tuttle, and Thomas D. Thacher—announced that they had a better idea. They urged Lehman to appoint thirty-three-year-old Thomas E. Dewey as special prosecutor.[6]

Born in 1902 and raised in Owosso, Michigan, Thomas Dewey was Owosso's brightest boy. He graduated from the University of Michigan in 1923 and Columbia University's Law School in 1925. Intense, prim, sober, industrious, young Dewey made a fine corporate lawyer. He had thought of settling in Chicago, but, as he explained later, "I never liked Chicago. Chicago was [...] a gangster town with the lowest set of moral standards I ever saw in my life."[7] New York was not much better; Dewey's Owosso family had always held a dim view of New York and, especially, New York's crooked politics. Dewey would write that in New York, in the 1920s, during elections "fraud was a way of life [...] in many districts, too, gangsters were present to create chaos [...] Tammany Hall was all

Thomas E. Dewey campaigning for Governor, 1938. (*Brooklyn Eagle*, Brooklyn Public Library)

that my grandfather Dewey and the rest of the family always thought it was, only worse."[8]

Back in Owosso, the Deweys had always been civic-minded; Dewey's father was editor of the local newspaper, the *Owosso Times*. In New York, Dewey joined the Young Republicans, "mostly," he wrote, "young Wall Street lawyers," who "kept fighting in the good cause" of electoral reform. Outnumbered Republicans in New York quickly identified Tom Dewey as a rising star; in 1928, Republican leaders saw to it that the twenty-six-year-old Dewey was named a special assistant state attorney general to help supervise elections in New York City. It was a hair-raising experience. As soon as the polls opened—Dewey was a poll watcher in Harlem—tough guys began to show up. "Some had guns in evidence in their pockets. Some had guns bulging from holsters under their coats," Dewey remembered.[9] He continued: "Every policeman that day appeared to know this was politics, that Tammany Hall was in charge, and that if they attempted to enforce the law they would be sent to pound a beat in the far recesses of Staten Island."[10] Dewey learned, the hard way, that making any headway against Tammany Hall was next to impossible. In the mayoral election of 1929, Dewey and his Republican reformers supported Fiorello La Guardia against Tammany's Jimmy Walker. Walker won.

New York City's government was, Dewey later wrote, "foul." He understood that "the masses of the poor and the immigrants" saw in Tammany Hall their only friend,[11] but in his opinion, they had been duped. The Republican Party Dewey admired was the party of Lincoln, the friend of African Americans, and the opponent of slavery. The Republican Party was also the party of trust-buster Theodore Roosevelt, who, as New York City's police commissioner and later as New York State's governor, tried to replace government by payoff with government by impartial justice. Back in Owosso, Dewey's father and grandfather had been militant Lincoln–Roosevelt Republicans, and that Republicanism was what young Tom Dewey advocated in New York in the late 1920s.

In 1929, when the Depression began, Tom Dewey was a corporate lawyer with the firm of McNamara and Seymour. From his first days at the firm, Dewey impressed people; one of the people he impressed was attorney George Z. Medalie, who occasionally worked with McNamara and Seymour. In 1930, President Hoover named Medalie US Attorney for the Southern District of New York, that is, New York City—Medalie was the first Jewish American ever to be named US Attorney for the Southern District—and Medalie asked Dewey if he wanted to try his hand at criminal law. Medalie and Dewey were sworn in as US Attorneys in

1931. At twenty-eight, Tom Dewey became chief assistant US Attorney to Medalie, and thereby leader of Medalie's staff of sixty lawyers.

In 1931, the Seabury hearings rocked New York City. Seabury had launched a full-scale war against political corruption, and George Medalie and his young deputy, Tom Dewey, were eager to participate. Medalie was a NewYorker, a graduate of City College and Columbia, with a fondness for ancient Greek; he and his wife, Carrie Kaplan, sent notes to each other in Greek.[12] Once an assistant to District Attorney Charles S. Whitman, Medalie was a Progressive Republican respected by both Republicans and Democrats.

Medalie would be Dewey's guide in the harsh world of criminal law. Medalie taught Dewey to be aggressive, although Dewey needed little instruction in that department. He taught Dewey to be obsessive about facts, to amass witnesses, to interrogate witnesses relentlessly, and to scour telephone, bank, and any other records for the tiniest detail. Most important, he taught Dewey that a criminal trial was a drama and that it was essential not only to muster facts and master the law but to highlight the most compelling and emotion-laden stories, to "put a ruby nose" on the case, as Medalie liked to say. A prosecution had to be transformed into a narrative, with characters and plots, conflicts and resolutions, just like a movie; "you've got to give [the jury] a sort of motion picture of the evidence," Medalie said.[13]

Medalie and Dewey recruited the best New York lawyers they could find. Eventually, Dewey wrote, "[T]here were so many Phi Beta Kappa keys dangling from the watch chains of our staff that one of the General Sessions judges remarked that defense lawyers thought they should be classed as 'dangerous weapons.'"[14]

One of Dewey's first cases involved prosecuting vice cop Jimmie Quinlivan, whose career was uncovered during the Seabury hearings. Somehow, between 1927 and 1929, officer Quinlivan, despite his modest police officer's salary, had accumulated some $80,000 in, Dewey claimed, "graft taken from speakeasies and brothels."[15]

Dewey and his Phi Betta Kappa colleagues proved to be tireless prosecutors. They quickly moved up the food chain from crooked cops to the people who bought the crooked cops. In 1931, Medalie and Dewey indicted Legs Diamond for, among other things, tax evasion; Dewey handled the prosecution because several years before, when in private practice, Medalie had actually defended Diamond. Diamond was convicted, fined, and sentenced to four years in prison. Dewey promised to help NewYork State conduct its own prosecution of Diamond.[16] Medalie and Dewey went after numbers runners and Tammany politicians; they tried to catch Dutch Schulz, but he got away. They did arrest and interrogate Schulz's chief lieutenant, Abe "Bo" Weinberg, but Weinberg would not talk and was released. A few months later, he couldn't talk; Dewey's sources told him that Weinberg "was taken out in a boat on the Harlem River and was made to watch while concrete dried out around his feet and ankles. Then, in his concrete shoes, he was dumped overboard."[17] (E. L. Doctorow would re-create this gruesome scene in his Dutch Schulz novel, *Billy Bathgate*, and it would reappear in the 1991 film adaptation of Doctorow's novel.)

In 1932, after months of meticulous research, Medalie and Dewey caught a very big fish indeed—Waxey Gordon.

Born in 1888, Waxey Gordon—his real name was Irving Wechsler—began his criminal career as a pickpocket. In his thirties, during Prohibition, Waxey Gordon turned from picking pockets to driving beer trucks and then from driving beer trucks to organizing convoys of beer trucks, and with Dutch Schulz, he quickly became one of New York City's most prosperous bootleggers. "Heavy set and laconic," Dewey wrote, Gordon was "an old hand at gang wars, of course, and knew the rough underworld logic: what you take at the point of a gun you can lose at the point of another."[18] Gordon, in the 1920s, made millions of dollars, strutted through New York's speakeasies like a celebrity—Dewey called him a "showoff"[19]—and dared the authorities to come after him.

Medalie and Dewey came after him. They alleged that Gordon had failed to pay federal income taxes on a yearly income of at least $500,000. Gordon's trial began on November 20, 1933. Dewey was the lead prosecutor. He was meticulous and indefatigable. Over nine days, Dewey called some 150 witnesses and offered 939 exhibits.[20] The clash between prosecutor Dewey and defendant Gordon had all the drama of a Hollywood movie; stories ran through the court that witnesses' lives might be in danger. Testimony about Gordon's role in the brutal beer wars chilled the courtroom; the *New York Times* reported that "a ghostly parade of the names of dead North Jersey beer runners added a macabre touch in Federal Court yesterday, at the trial of Waxey Gordon for tax evasion."[21] In the middle of the Gordon trial, US Attorney Medalie retired, and Thomas Dewey, at thirty-one, was sworn in as Medalie's temporary replacement. Judge Frank Coleman, presiding over the Gordon trial, swore Dewey in as the new US Attorney for the Southern District of New York. Although reporters clustered around Dewey, he waved them away. "With the Gordon trial under way," Dewey said, "I am too busy at this time to be interviewed. There are 150 witnesses outside and today's work is carved out for me."[22] In his final remarks to the jury in the Gordon trial, Dewey insisted that the case was not simply about beer and bootlegging; it was not even about paying taxes. It was also about justice. Dewey concluded,

> As you retire to your room, gentlemen, I ask you to bear in mind that the people of this country look to you twelve men as to the course of justice in this country. Are we to have justice in the courts? Is justice to be effective in this country in the courts, or is it not?[23]

The jury convicted Gordon, fined him $20,000, and sentenced him to ten years in prison.

In November 1932, New York's Democratic governor, Franklin Delano Roosevelt, had been elected president. One by one, Democratic US Attorneys replaced Republican US Attorneys, and Dewey served as US Attorney only for a few weeks. Shortly after his conviction of Waxey Gordon, Dewey was replaced as by a Democrat and he went back to corporate law. Dewey later wrote, "I despised the kind of government most of our big cities had been getting, and the exploitation of people by their political leaders. I guess I was a full-fledged reformer at heart, but with no desire or impulse to hold public office as an occupation."[24] Yet even back in private practice, Dewey never forgot what he described as "our struggle against lawlessness of all kinds."[25] The *New York Times* would later note that as US Attorney young Dewey had received "wide publicity" as a "racket buster"; his record of seventy-two convictions from seventy-three indictments was, the *Times* thought, very impressive.[26]

A "reformer at heart," Tom Dewey, like Fiorello La Guardia, was a complicated man. Like La Guardia, Dewey was bursting with ambition, not just to make money as a corporate lawyer but also to become a public figure and not just as a politician but also as a champion of justice.

Tom Dewey had inherited his reformer's heart. Two generations before, Dewey's grandfather, George Dewey, had moved from tame Lowell, Massachusetts—the Deweys had been among Massachusetts' Puritan settlers—to the wilds of Michigan. He settled in the little village of Owosso, some twenty-seven miles outside Lansing, the state capital, and there, in the 1850s, the elder Dewey launched a ferocious campaign to purify America. George Dewey was a typical, if unusually intense, example of America's antebellum reformer, propelled by a passion for social justice. Fueled by hot revivalism, American reformers, determined to live up to the legacy of their Revolutionary War ancestors, enthusiastically set to work to mold a more perfect union. They attacked dueling and drunkenness; they called for public education and public investment in canals and highways; overnight, they built brand-new cities in the middle of nowhere. Mid-nineteenth-century reformers were convinced that securing Jefferson's "unalienable rights" was the task of their generation. Committed to individual civil liberties, the reformers were just as passionate about creating a righteous social order. Radical reformers asserted that even women and working class people had rights—to form unions, to agitate in public, and to vote. The most radical of the radicals claimed that America's two-hundred-year-old institution, human slavery, was a detestable moral evil utterly incompatible with a just social order, and therefore, slavery had to be destroyed.

In the 1850s, in Owosso, George Dewey was a fervent reformer. He was an argumentative man, who found, in journalism, a perfect outlet for his belligerence. He edited and published a series of small town papers, including the *Owosso Times*, all dedicated to the great war for social justice. When the Republican Party was formed, George Dewey became an intense Republican. To old George Dewey, the Democratic Party was the party of aristocrats, slavery, and secession. Republicans were the defenders of the common man's (and maybe even common woman's) republic and the liberators of the enslaved.

George Dewey was, one of Tom Dewey's biographers writes, "prickly and prone to attack" and utterly "convinced of his own rectitude."[27] He was also a man who believed that there is what Republican William Henry Seward called a "higher law"; that this "higher law," God's law, manifested itself both in a respect for unalienable rights and impartial justice, that rights and justice were best found in democracy, and that each person had a profound duty to defend democracy, rights, and justice from their many enemies—in his day, the ghastly "slaveocracy" that threatened to destroy the republic.

George Dewey fought the Civil War with "words instead of bullets," but the Deweys were proud that some two hundred assorted Deweys served in the Union Army.[28] When George Dewey died, his eulogist, Rev. George Wilson, explained:

> To such a man, the world of thought is a battlefield [. . .] He does not speak to please; he does not tarry to adorn with rhetoric; he does not look for stories to enliven, far less to amuse; he does not seek to provoke laughter but slaughter. Life is too serious in its great efforts to stop and laugh. The very voice of the man will gather to itself a quality [. . .] alive with the agony of intensity.[29]

That was Tom Dewey's grandfather.

Tom Dewey's father, George Martin Dewey, Jr., was not quite as belligerent as the elder Dewey, but he was every bit as dedicated to the principles of the Grand Old Party. Annie Louise Thompson, who married George Dewey, Jr. in 1899, added unflagging industry and her own hot temper to Dewey Republicanism. On March 24, 1902, when Annie gave birth to her son, Thomas Edmund Dewey, the local paper reported that "[a] ten-pound Republican voter was born last evening to Mr. and Mrs. George M. Dewey. George says the young man arrived in time for registration in the April elections."[30]

George Dewey, Jr. no longer had, like his father, the southern slaveocracy to fight, but he had plenty of causes of his own. Dewey, Jr. was a passionate Progressive and an admirer of Theodore Roosevelt. His little boy's initials, T. E. D., spelled, of course, T. R.'s nickname, and for a while, young Tom Dewey was called "Ted." When Tom was a little boy, the Republican Party had sprouted two poorly coordinated wings—a "standpatter" wing, increasingly dominated by plutocrats dedicated to preserving their privileges, and a "Bull Moose" wing, led by Theodore Roosevelt, which called for a host of progressive reforms, ranging from trust busting to government by civil servants not lobbyists to advancing the rights of workers and women to creating national parks. George Dewey, Jr. and his little son, Ted, were staunch Bull Moosers.

One central focus of Progressive reform was the new, immense, sprawling, immigrant-filled cities like Chicago and New York. These new industrial cities, as muckraker Lincoln Steffens reported in *The Shame of the Cities* (1904), were plagued by poverty, disease, broken families, broken sidewalks, crime, alcoholism, poor schools, terrible sanitation, filthy slums, and the outrageous exploitation of immigrant workers. Worse, all this was exacerbated by corrupt politicians, who, in league with criminals, stole the people's money. Among Progressive Republicans from Theodore Roosevelt to George Dewey, Jr., the name for the very archetype of the corrupt urban political machine was "Tammany." Old George Dewey; his son, George, Jr.; and his grandson, Tom, were sure that, as Tom Dewey later said, "Tammany Hall represents all that is evil in government."[31]

At the University of Michigan and later at Columbia, Tom Dewey was the smartest and certainly the most industrious student in every class. Blessed with a beautiful baritone voice, young Tom thought of becoming an opera singer, but practicality trumped artistry, and Dewey switched from music to law and planned for a career as a corporate lawyer. But for Tom Dewey, public life beckoned too. How could he be an Owosso Dewey if he abandoned the Republican Party's noble causes?

From his earliest days in New York City, Dewey, inspired by those passionate Owosso Republicans, became a Republican activist. Although Dewey, with his regimental mustache and perfect grooming, looked like the little groom on every wedding cake (as Clare Boothe Luce would meanly remark),[32] he had, like his grandfather, a powerful hunger for combat. What he seemed to have wanted was not just celebrity exactly but, rather, glory as well, that is, recognition for wise decisions and bold deeds done for the public good. And however ancient the idea sounded, Dewey was motivated by what his ancestors would have called "duty" and "patriotism." He had a duty to defend and advance democracy and justice; patriotism called him to be concerned not only with his own career and his own neighborhood but with the whole city and the country too. His patriotic duty demanded that he confront democracy's enemies—the "interests," the corrupt politicians, and the gangsters.

And so, in 1935, when the runaway grand jury demanded a special prosecutor, New York's top lawyers recommended Tom Dewey, and Governor Herbert Lehman asked Dewey to lead a special investigation into Manhattan corruption. Officially, Dewey worked for the hard-pressed Manhattan District Attorney William Copeland Dodge; in fact, Dewey reported to Governor Lehman.

Dewey went to work in July 1935. What he had in mind, he later wrote, was not simply chasing small-time politicians. The crooked politicians, he was sure, especially after his prosecution of Waxey Gordon, were in the pay of criminals. What was needed, Dewey argued, was "a frontal, and expert, attack on extortionists and gangsters." His "avowed purpose" was "to destroy organized crime and racketeering of all kinds."[33]

Dewey set up headquarters in the sixty-story Woolworth Building on lower Broadway, a block away from City Hall, near the US Attorney's office. He and his staff occupied some thirty-five offices, totaling around 10,500 feet of office space on the fourteenth floor. Working for Special Prosecutor Dewey were some twenty deputy assistant district attorneys, ten police investigators, ten accountants, four process servers, a chief clerk with three assistants, two grand jury reporters, twenty stenographers, and four messengers. The police department agreed to devote some seventy-five officers to Dewey's investigation, all "young policemen," Dewey wrote, "with no bad habits to correct."[34] Dewey thought of himself as one of the team of twenty assistant district attorneys; they were all between twenty-five and forty years old; "seven were members of Phi Beta Kappa. Practically all had won honors in the best law schools in the country. Columbia and Harvard Law Schools led with six apiece."[35] The twenty included Eunice Carter, the only woman, and African American, on the team. They were on, Dewey insisted, a moral crusade; one of Dewey's staff later recalled, "[W]e were the forces of decent living."[36] Dewey's lawyers thought of themselves as "Twenty against the Underworld." Dewey wrote, "[W]e were twenty lawyers against the world, and we now knew something of the monstrous nature of our job."[37] Tom Dewey had a cause worthy of the Deweys of Owosso.

In that summer of 1935, Dewey's police squad began making raids, and his young lawyers won indictments. In their first swoop, Dewey's raiders snagged twenty-two loan sharks, charged them, in 126 "meticulously prepared indictments," with 252 different crimes.[38] Dewey, however, had no intention of simply scooping up street-level criminals. He wanted to decapitate crime by prosecuting gang leaders. He was especially hostile to what he called the "Mafia." He wrote that "the Mafia was worse than the rest of the underworld. There was no honor among this breed of thieves, gunmen, robbers, narcotic peddlers, pimps, murders, and racketeers. The whole lot of them were not merely anti-social. They were slimy, cheating savages."[39]

As Dewey's raiders swept through gangland, a kind of "great fear" struck New York's gangsters. Sometime during that summer of 1935, Lucky Luciano, Frank Costello, Meyer Lansky, Bugsy Siegel, Lepke Buchalter, Albert Anastasia, Dutch Schulz, and others met to decide what to do. Schulz, outraged by Dewey's assault, insisted that the obvious response was to murder Dewey. Albert Anastasia added that he had personally scouted Dewey's office building and watched Dewey enter a corner store to make some telephone calls. Killing Dewey would be easy, Anastasia argued. Dewey's guards usually waited outside while Dewey went into the store; all someone had to do was take care of the guards, go into the store, and shoot Dewey. The others, however, were not so sure. Lepke allegedly said, "[W]e will all burn if Dewey is knocked off."[40] Luciano agreed with Lepke; the heat was bad enough as it was. Killing Dewey would only bring on an even bigger heat. Anastasia finally agreed with Luciano and Lepke; Schulz, furious, insisted that "Dewey's gotta go!" and announced that if no one else had the courage to go after Dewey, he'd do it personally.[41]

However, Lucky Luciano and the others decided that Schulz, not Dewey, had to go. If Dutch went wild and took a shot at Dewey, everyone would be in serious trouble. Anyway, Dutch had been acting crazy lately; he threatened everybody's business. And there was another consideration. Since the end of Prohibition, everyone had been scrambling to find other sources of income. The numbers racket was especially attractive. Schulz had expanded rapidly into numbers, especially in Harlem, threatening games run by Meyer Lansky and Bugsy Siegel. Schulz was making a fortune, but of course, he wouldn't share. So, if something were to happen to Schulz, his Harlem numbers business would be free for the taking.

On October 25, 1935,[42] around 6:00 p.m., Dutch Schulz walked into the Palace Chop House in Newark. He was staying out of New York City, where he was in deep legal trouble. With Schulz were Bernard "Lulu" Rosenkrantz and Abe Landau. Others drifted in and out that evening—Michael "Micky the Mock" Marks; Schulz's young wife, Frances Geis Flegenheimer; Schulz's bail bondsman, Max Silverman. Otto Berman arrived late. Berman, short and plump, was, like Arnold Rothstein and Meyer Lansky, a mathematical genius. Rothstein had nicknamed Berman "Avisack," after a winning racehorse. Damon Runyon would write a story that Hollywood turned into a hit film, *Little Miss Marker* (1934), starring five-year-old Shirley Temple. A minor character in the film is a racetrack gambler Runyon called "Regret" (after a winning horse). "Regret," played by Lynne Overmann, was modeled after Berman. Berman preferred the nickname, "Abbadabba"; he thought it sounded mysterious.

Berman had good news to report. Over the past six weeks, Schulz's numbers racket had taken in a total of $827,253.43 and had paid out $313,711.99, leaving, for Schulz and his associates, a profit amounting to an astonishing $513,541.44.

By 10:15 or so, there were only four customers left in the Palace Chop House, Schulz, Rosenkrantz, Landau, and Berman. Then, the bartender said later, "[T]he front door opened suddenly."

Two men burst in. The first barked, "Don't move, lay down." The men rushed the table where Rosenkrantz, Landau, and Berman were sitting and immediately opened fire. Schulz wasn't at the table. One gunman burst into the men's room, found Schulz, and shot him repeatedly. Schulz staggered out to the table and collapsed; the gunmen ran out; amazingly, Rosenkrantz and Landau, mortally wounded, managed to stagger to their feet and pursue the gunmen. Rosenkrantz collapsed after a few paces; Landau made it outside and fell dead on the sidewalk. The terrified bartender popped up from his hiding place behind the bar and called the police.

Mortally wounded, Dutch Schulz would somehow survive for another day, semiconscious, delirious, and mumbling a bizarre litany peppered with obscure names and places and favorite foods, all transcribed by a series of police stenographers. Stanley Walker would publish a parody of it in *The New Yorker*. A local professor, Walker joked, had identified Schulz's dying comment, "a boy has never wept nor dashed a thousand kim," as an expression of folk art. Walker wrote a doggerel commentary on it.[43] The beat writer William S. Burroughs would turn Schulz's last words into a screenplay, *The Last Words of Dutch Schulz* (1970). At one point, Schulz, who always considered himself "Hebrew" but was, in fact, nonreligious, asked to see a priest. He was thirty-three at the time of his death.

Everyone in New York knew that the most influential gangster in the city was Charlie "Lucky" Luciano. By 1935, Charlie Lucky had achieved a bizarre sort of celebrity status; Dewey cites a popular crime magazine that described Charlie Lucky this way:

> He was wily, rapacious. He was savagely cruel. For years, like some deadly King Cobra, this droopy-eyed thug coiled himself about the Eastern underworld and squeezed it implacably of its tainted gold. Nights were spent touring the Broadway hot-spots with gorgeous Gay Orlova, or another of the showshop beauties he was partial to. Then, if Broadway palled, his powerful private Lockheed plane would roar him away to Miami, Chicago, or Hot Springs, to be hailed there with open arms. He was the bookmaker's joy, the torch singer's delight, a Dracula masquerading as Good-time Charlie.[44]

Why Dewey included this bizarre citation in his memoir is unclear; maybe at some level, Special Prosecutor Dewey really thought he was battling a "deadly King Cobra," a "Dracula."

Everyone knew that Luciano was a rackets king, but how to convict him of a crime was the problem. He had been arrested repeatedly, but he managed to avoid prison because invariably evidence, or witnesses, disappeared. By 1935, layers of cutoff men separated Luciano from street crime. He was a bootlegger, but potential jurors actually liked the bootleggers who supplied them their liquor, and besides, by 1935, Prohibition was over, and selling alcohol was legal again. Luciano distributed narcotics; he was involved in murders, but proving anything would be next to impossible.

Then Eunice Carter, one of Dewey's "Twenty against the Underworld," had an idea. Carter was a graduate of Smith College and Fordham Law School. She had been involved in a number of cases involving prostitution. She argued that a serious racketeer like Luciano was almost certainly involved with prostitution, that prostitution was a nasty business, and that a jury might well convict Luciano on some sort of prostitution charge.[45]

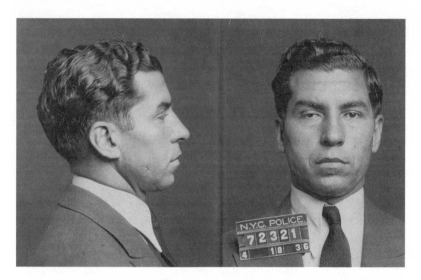

Charlie "Lucky" Luciano in 1936. (New York City Municipal Archives)

At midnight, January 31, 1936, Dewey's police squad swept through New York and raided a score of brothels; the next night, the Dewey raiders attacked some eighty more, and the raids would continue for the next several weeks. Police Commissioner Lewis Valentine vowed his support.[46] The raids, Dewey wrote, "were sensational in the extreme."[47] Newspaper headlines screamed about Dewey's "vice raids." Included in the dragnet were prostitutes and bookers, madams and gamblers, horrified citizens caught in embarrassing situations, and cynical hoodlums. Dewey's lawyers methodically interviewed each one. Most swore they knew nothing about anything. Dewey's prospectors, nevertheless, began discovering nuggets of information. Dewey rushed indictments to the Grand Jury.[48] Among those indicted was Charlie "Lucky" Luciano. The newspapers would invariably get his name wrong; they called him "Lucania" or "Luciana."[49]

Luciano fled New York and headed for Hot Springs, Arkansas, a gangster-friendly resort run by former bootlegger and Harlem Cotton Club owner, Owen "Owney" Madden. On April 1, 1936, Dewey obtained a warrant for Luciano's arrest. A small army of Arkansas lawyers challenged the warrant, but finally, Luciano was arrested and shipped back to New York. Dewey's original indictment charged Luciano and fifteen co-conspirators with multiple crimes (the number of defendants and the specific charges would vary as the investigation wore on).

The trial of Lucky Luciano and others began on May 11, 1936, and it was a tabloid sensation. Dewey claimed that New York's sex industry grossed something like $12 million each year. Dewey had indicted ten defendants (one would plead guilty amid the trial), but, as the *Brooklyn Eagle* pointed out, "the squint-eyed Lucania is the chief of the ten defendants."[50] Dewey's basic claim was that Luciano, with the help of his nine co-defendants, had taken over the sex industry, regularly used threats and violence against the sex workers, and, of course, paid not a penny in taxes on his enormous profits. After reorganizing the case several times, Dewey finally charged Luciano and his co-defendants with sixty separate counts. All ten were tried at once, making the trial gargantuan; each defendant had his own attorney, and some witnesses testified for or against one or another defendant; Judge Philip McCook had to struggle to keep the proceedings on track. One of New York's most prominent criminal defense lawyers, George Morton Levy, defended Luciano.[51]

Prosecutor Dewey proved to be an extraordinary courtroom actor. In 1940, Wolcott Gibbs and John Bainbridge published a profile of Dewey in *The New Yorker*, titled "St. George and the Dragnet." A Dewey prosecution, Gibbs and Bainbridge wrote, was just like a movie, with Dewey as the star; if New Yorkers "were already inclined to believe that they were taking part in a moving picture, [Dewey] did little to disillusion them."[52] Dewey, the profilers reported,

> is five feet eight and a half inches tall and he weighs a hundred and fifty-seven pounds stripped. His teeth, with centre gaps in both the upper and lower sets, are his most unfortunate feature; his eyes, next to the mustache, and the voice, his most arresting. These are brown, with small irises surrounded by a relatively immense area of white and Dewey has a habit of rotating them furiously to punctuate and emphasize his speech, expressing horror and surprise, by shooting them upward, cunning by sliding them from side to side behind narrowed lids. At climactic moments he can pop them, almost audibly.[53]

An obsessive planner and dogged examiner, Dewey had lots of other courtroom tricks. "If a ruling is unfavorable to the People," Gibbs and Bainbridge wrote, "Dewey will rise from his chair, slow and aghast, the blood mottling his neck, and cry, 'Do you mean to say that the court will not allow [. . .] etc.' Should the defense score a point, Dewey turns to the jury and beats his breast, to let them know the People are being crucified." He was skilled at throwing opposing lawyers off pace; if they seemed to be making progress, Dewey would ostentatiously stand up, stroll over to a water cooler—Gibbs and Bainbridge wrote that his "most annoying mannerism [. . .] is drinking water"—tug down a paper cup, sip and stare at his rival until his rival became befuddled. Once, a defense lawyer who knew Dewey's tricks scurried over to the water cooler and dramatically got Dewey his drink of water.[54] Remembering the Luciano trial, Gibbs and Bainbridge wrote that theatrically, thanks to Dewey, the trial was "a tremendous artistic success."[55]

One after another, bookers, madams, and prostitutes paraded into the courtroom, and the media was fascinated. Rose Cohen, twenty-five years old, was "a pert, dark-haired girl who graduated from the streets to evening gown disorderly houses."[56] Mildred Harris, a madam, "handsomely dressed in a black and white print gown, black coat, draped with silver fox, smart black hat trimmed with a white bow and wearing white gloves," explained that she had been a prostitute—"I had always been somewhat adventuresome all my life," she explained—and then a madam. Hoodlums demanded a share of her profits and threated to kill her and her girls if she did not pay up.[57] Bookers described how the sex industry worked. "The brisk business of booking women—like shipping cattle or carrots or cucumbers—was detailed [. . .] by Al Weiner, 27, who was schooled in the trade from knee-pants days by Cock-eyed Louis, his father," the *Daily News* reported.[58] Madams explained how they ran their brothels and whom they had to pay off. "A strident tongued madam of the old school," according to the *Daily News*, testified. Her name was Joan Marten; she was, the paper said, "a swart Rumanian." The *Brooklyn Eagle* described Marten as "a colorless figure compared with her demi-monde predecessors on the stand. She wore horn-rimmed glasses and dark clothing."[59] According to the *Daily News*, Marten was

> a rugged individualist of vice who fought tooth and nail against her elimination as an independent by the gunmen of Gotham's vice syndicate [. . .] when she entered the courtroom she brought with her the atmosphere of the dark, tenement-house rookeries where she retailed counterfeit love for $1.50. A jaunty spring straw-hat, fit for a maid of 18, surmounted her thinning black hair and struck a jarring note against her old winter coat.

Marten explained that she ran an independent bordello, but that hoodlums appeared and demanded a cut of her profits; if she didn't pay up, they threatened, they'd beat up her and her girls—or worse. Defense lawyer Sam Seigel tried to mock Marten by pointing out that she ran an unusually cheap and tawdry "$1.00 house." Marten heatedly responded that she actually ran a "$3.00 house" but that she'd had to cut prices down to $2.00 because of the Depression. The courtroom spectators laughed. Inspired, Marten went after attorney Seigel: "I think you talk funny," she said; "I'm laughing at you!"[60] According to the *New York Times,* Marten, "the dark-haired and bespectacled woman on the stand relished the opportunity to obtain revenge." Once, she claimed, when she refused to pay off the local hoodlums, "they smashed the furniture, pulled the couch apart and cut the upholstery with big knives."[61]

The seemingly endless parade of prostitutes provoked, among the mostly male reporters, detailed commentary. Betty Anderson was "blond and buxom"; Catherine O'Connor was a "vivacious 24-year-old redhead."[62] Shirley Mason, twenty-three years old, was "a scrawny prostitute."[63] Elinore Jackson, twenty-eight, was "slim, pretty, henna-haired and dressed in a becoming modest brown suit."[64] Margaret Martino was "a statuesque, composed, reddish blonde,"[65] while Mollie Leonard, thirty-seven, was "a rotund, solidly-built woman [who] wore a jaunty little hat cocked at a precarious angle over her right eye."[66]

They all had terrible tales to tell. They were all prostitutes, and some were madams. Hoodlums demanded a cut of their profits and threatened to beat or kill them if they did not pay up. If they resisted, the hoodlums would wreck their bordellos and threaten, as Thelma Jordan, also known as Buddy Stephens, "a plump brunette," testified, to slit the prostitutes' tongues.[67] One booker, Pete Harris, a "surly underworld character who lived in luxury by booking girls to disorderly houses," testified that he collected money from the prostitutes and madams and passed it along to the defendants, including Luciano.[68] Another booker, Danny Brooks, explained that a cut of the sex-industry money regularly went to cops and politicians.[69] One prostitute, Helen Kelly, who wore a "summery orchid flowered dress with matching pert straw hat," testified that when she tried to get out of the sex business, she was held prisoner until she agreed to go back to prostitution.[70]

Dewey methodically recreated for the jury New York's huge sex industry; he demonstrated that the industry was dominated by hoodlums who became rich from the prostitutes' sordid work; step by step he linked each defendant to the sex business. He showed the jury a huge chart, listing some 154 women arrested for prostitution. All had been quickly released because the fix was in; some cop or some judge had been paid off. "In a sing-song manner, Mr. Dewey chanted the records with the most constant theme of 'discharged,'" the *Brooklyn Eagle* reported.[71] Throughout the trial, Dewey insisted that the person behind this vast corrupt enterprise was the "Vice Czar," Charlie "Lucky" Luciano.

Dewey's key witnesses were at best shady characters, but they certainly were flamboyant. Joe Bendix, for example, was a hotel burglar and general-practice thief, who testified that Luciano had worked from his suite in the Waldorf-Astoria and had personally hired him to collect payments from bookers and madams.[72] Finally came Dewey's star witnesses, Nancy Pressler and Flo Brown.

Nancy Pressler, twenty-four years old, was, according to the *Daily News*, "a ravishing blonde" and "the Delilah of Lucky's love life." She was, she testified, Luciano's intimate companion. She was present, she said, on innumerable occasions when Luciano and others talked business, especially sex industry business. She vividly recalled an underling reporting to Luciano that one bordello was behind in its payments and Luciano responding, "[G]o ahead and crack the joint."[73] Her cross-examination, Dewey later wrote, "lasted eight and half hours, and once again every type of nauseating, insulting question was thrown at her."[74]

The prosecution's other key witness was Florence Brown. Brown, like Pressler, was both a prostitute and a drug addict. She was also known as "Cockeyed Florence" and "Cokey Flo." Cokey Flo was "a small, pale woman, with scarlet lips." Her "nerves twitched" as she testified.[75] Like Nancy Pressler, Cokey Flo swore that she had been present on a number of occasions when Luciano and the other defendants had discussed the sex industry. Once, she remembered, Luciano had said, "[W]e could syndicate the places on a large scale, the same as the chain stores. We could even get the madams on a salary or commission basis." She said that Luciano had boasted that the sex industry was "the same as the A & P stores are, a large syndicate."[76] Cokey Flo's testimony became national news.[77] According to the *Times,* Cokey Flo seemed to "enjoy herself." Twenty-eight years old and "shabbily dressed in blue," she was, in the *Times*'s opinion, "the most dramatic of the many witnesses." During her testimony, Luciano scribbled notes on a legal pad. When Cokey Flo was asked to identify Luciano, she pointed to "that man with the yellow pencil." Luciano "threw down the pencil in a gesture of disgust."[78]

Whispered threats rattled the courtroom. Dewey, at one point, hid several of his key witnesses in secret locations.[79] "Working with G-man secrecy," the *Daily News* excitedly reported, Dewey ordered the arrest of two women and a lawyer who were allegedly conspiring to commit perjury.[80] Courtroom bailiffs were heavily armed.

The defense heatedly pointed out that virtually all of the prosecution witnesses were criminals themselves; many had been in jail; many of the prostitutes were drug addicts, including both Nancy Pressler and Cokey

Flo Brown. The defense insisted that the witnesses gave such detailed and compelling testimony because Dewey had told them what to say. Luciano would later claim that Cokey Flo had been coached as if, Luciano said, she were the star of the popular 1906 play *Bertha the Sewin' Machine Girl*.[81]

Whatever the merits of the case, the media quickly decided that Luciano was guilty. He was "droopy-eyed," sullen," and "swarthy." The *Daily News* especially liked to point out that Lucky had run out of luck! One front-page photo showed Luciano, in handcuffs, stepping out of a police van; the caption read: "Change of habits for Lucky—not exactly like stepping out of a limousine into the Waldorf-Astoria, eh Lucky?"[82]

The prosecution rested on May 29, 1936, after calling sixty-eight witnesses.

The defense called, as its witnesses, a number of respectable business people, who testified to the defendants' good characters. "Unlike the pallid, shifty-eyed creatures Special Prosecutor Thomas E. Dewey had to drag from under the stones of Gotham's underworld," the *Daily News* reported, "defense witnesses are business people and even an assistant to D.A. Dodge!" (Assistant District Attorney Morris Panger was called to testify that prosecution witness Joe Bendix, the hotel thief, was, in fact, a career criminal).[83]

On June 3, the defense called on Lucky Luciano to testify. The defense led Luciano through a series of answers in which Luciano explained that he had quit school after the sixth grade and had worked as a laborer; yes, he had gotten into trouble with the law, but no, he had never been involved in the illegal sex industry.

Then came the showdown everyone had eagerly awaited. Special Prosecutor Tom Dewey cross-examined Lucky Luciano. "Droopy-eyed" Luciano, the *Brooklyn Eagle* reported, "spoke in a low voice." He was thirty-eight; he had been in trouble with the law since age eighteen.[84] The fight was uneven from the beginning. Dewey conducted what the *Times* called a "battering four-hour cross examination." Dewey was relentless; Luciano, evasive and monosyllabic. Luciano, whom the *Times* called "a beetle-browed defendant" and "a swarthy-faced witness," grudgingly answered Dewey's questions, and "one damaging admission after another was drawn from his sullen lips." Dewey forced Luciano to admit that he had been arrested repeatedly, that he had been a bootlegger, that several of his arrests were for possession and distribution of narcotics, and that he had regularly cheated on his taxes and lied under oath.[85] The *Daily News* reported that Dewey was amazing and that Luciano was stumbling. A photograph on the front page of the *Daily News* showed Luciano looking "glum" as he entered the courtroom. According to the *Daily News,* Luciano "cringed" on the stand as Dewey led him back through all his criminal convictions. "Halting and stammering," the *Daily News* reported, "his unusually warm, broad grin replaced by a sickly twist of his lips [. . .] [Luciano] proved to be his own worst witness."[86] Dewey pointed out that once Luciano had been arrested for having a car full of pistols and shotguns and 250 rounds of ammunition—what was all that for? Dewey demanded. For hunting "peasants," Luciano replied (he meant to say *pheasants*), and after a double take, everyone laughed. Luciano joked that when it came to prostitutes, "I gave to 'em, I never took." But under Dewey's merciless questioning, "sweat beaded his swarthy brow," and Luciano seemed to wilt on the witness stand.[87]

The defense rested. In their summary, the defense attorneys pointed out again just how unreliable the prosecution witnesses were. In their three-hour summation, the defense attorneys insisted that Dewey had actually "glorified" the world of madams and prostitutes and that he had staged not a legal prosecution but a kind of "thrilling courtroom drama." Dewey's drama, they insisted, was "a bordello extravaganza with beautiful vice madams for leading ladies, and a ballet of prostitutes."[88]

Dewey, in his dramatic summation, addressed the character of his witnesses directly. "We cannot get bishops, we cannot get clergymen, we cannot get bankers or businessmen to testify about gangsters, pimps, and prostitution," he said. He continued: "we must use the testimony of bad men. Otherwise, there would be no rule of law, there would only be the despotic, terroristic rule of the underworld [. . .] and your Lucianos [. . .] and all the others would run unchecked."[89]

The jury deliberated for six-and-a-half hours. There were now, including Luciano, nine defendants. At 5:25 a.m., on Sunday morning, June 7, 1936, the jury informed Judge Philip McCook that it had reached its decision. The jury found all nine defendants[90] guilty on all sixty-two charges.[91]

Judge McCook sentenced the defendants to varying punishments; he sentenced "a sullen but calm" Luciano to an incredible thirty to fifty years in prison.[92] A grim Tom Dewey applauded the convictions and described Luciano as "Public Enemy No. 1" and "the greatest gangster in America."[93]

Police Commissioner Valentine hailed Luciano's conviction.[94] Luciano biographer Tim Newark writes that Luciano's conviction "was a landmark in U.S. legal history as it was the first against a major organized crime figure for anything other than tax evasion. It was the pinnacle of Dewey's crusade against the underworld." Newark notes that Fiorello La

Guardia was jubilant. La Guardia told the press that Luciano "could never have run his rackets without the knowledge if not the connivance of some of the very people entrusted with law enforcement. I recommend that at least six public officials commit hara-kiri."[95]

Tom Dewey insisted that his was a single-minded pursuit of "justice," but what did he understand by "justice"? By justice, Dewey understood something very close to the ideas of philosopher, economist, and 1998 Nobel laureate Amartya Sen.

There are, of course, many different ways to understand "justice." John Rawls was certainly the most influential philosopher of justice in the twentieth century; he argued that one should think of justice as "fairness." Amartya Sen's thought is fundamentally shaped by that of Rawls, although ultimately Sen's thinking is quite different from that of Rawls.[96]

Where Sen agrees with Rawls, and, for that matter, with Achilles, is in the sense that justice is somehow fundamentally about "fairness." Fairness is the elementary notion that we are social creatures engaged in multiple relationships with each other and that because of these relationships, we "owe" each other certain things; as a minimum, we owe each other a kind of basic acknowledgment that each of us is there in the relationship and that each of us exists. Fairness is much more modest than some abstract notion of absolute justice; fairness is practical whereas justice is theoretical. Sen agrees with Rawls that "justice is partly a relation in which ideas of obligation to each other are important"; these obligations are what Kant called "imperfect obligations" in that they are often tacit, fluid, undefined, but nevertheless real.[97] Justice tends toward utopia; fairness toward practical wisdom.

Our sense of fairness, of justice-as-fairness, is triggered not so much by utopian visions of a perfectly just order as by the experience of unfairness in our limited, flawed, and very fallible world. "What moves us," Sen writes, "is not the realization that the world falls short of being completely just [. . .] but that there are clearly remediable injustices around us that we want to eliminate [. . .] manifest injustices that could be overcome." Our aim is not "to achieve a perfectly just world" but, rather, to "remove clear injustices,"[98] and "the identification of redressable injustice is not only what animates us to think about justice and injustice, it is also central," Sen writes, "to the theory of justice."[99] This modest vision is actually empowering. If our goal were perfect justice, we would be paralyzed; this side of the Heavenly Kingdom, no one could achieve that. If our goal is to repair a particular injustice, we are able to act.

Justice, Sen writes, does not call on us simply to compare actions to ideals. Justice instead calls on us to compare actions to other actions, alternatives to alternatives, choices to other choices, all informed by ideals but all imperfect, contradictory, contingent, and fallible. This understanding of justice obviates the need to achieve some sort of "consensus on what a perfectly just society would look like," which is, in any case, a political fool's errand.[100]

Dewey was no utopian. He was not attracted to what Sen calls "transcendental institutionalism," that is, "perfect justice" embodied in "perfect institutions."[101] His war on the gangs was pragmatic and nonideological. His aim was to restore a measure of fundamental fairness, not to construct the city of God. Here Dewey reflects not only the thought of Amartya Sen but also the older Progressive tradition. Richard Rorty, writing about John Dewey (no relation to Tom Dewey), argued precisely for this modest approach to justice. "The political discourse of the democracies," Rorty writes, "at its best, is the exchange of what Wittgenstein called 'reminders for a particular purpose'—anecdotes about the past effects of various practices and predictions of what will happen if, or unless, some of these are altered."[102] Prosecutor Dewey was never known for his personal modesty, but his understanding of justice reflects this cautious approach of Sen, Rorty, and John Dewey.

Justice-as-fairness, according to Sen, demands that we step beyond our own narcissism and acknowledge the presence of the other and the rights of the other, which, in turn, demand that we develop a certain impartiality, an ability to judge both our own actions and those of the other against some third standard. To be fair, then, justice must be blind.[103] Rawls argued that this external, third standard is some sort of "social contract"; Sen prefers Adam Smith's simpler notion of the "impartial spectator" (something akin to a disinterested umpire or informed conscience).[104]

Dewey thought of the law and its officers precisely as this kind of disinterested, impartial spectator who could fairly adjudicate disputes, save the innocent, and rebuke outlaws. However, Judge Seabury's investigation had shown that this disinterested entity had all but disappeared in New York, that at the grassroots level, with the cops on the beat and with the magistrates on their benches, disinterest had been bought out. Disinterest had been replaced not by ideology—always a danger, of course—but by something much more primitive—greed. If justice is, as Sen argues, based on fairness and is shaped by impartiality, justice had failed in New York. Therefore, Dewey's task was to resurrect the impartial spectator, an entity, a power that would be independent of the underworld and its ethos of the total market.

The impartial spectator, however, is no robot. Objectivity is not mechanical. To the contrary, the impartial spectator and the moral agent are inevitably shaped by what Adam Smith called "sentiments," that is, intuitions, emotions, and aesthetic responses.[105] Our sentiments, Smith thought, are educated quite early in life and then function as powerful guides in our understanding of justice. Hence, incidentally, the crucial importance of educating not only the reason but also the sentiments.[106] Dewey's courtroom histrionics, his tense radio broadcasts, the whole theatrical persona he adopted were, of course, manipulative and calculated, but they also were rooted in the understanding that Dewey shared with Sen and with Adam Smith, that justice is in part a matter of sentiment and that mobilizing sentiment for the sake of justice is precisely what a statesman must do.

Dewey and Sen also agree that discussion, "civic discourse," is central to justice. I do not possess justice alone. Justice refers to my relationships with others, and if these relationships are to be fair and respectful, they must include the ancient rhetorical skills of persuasion, of speaking and listening. What else did Dewey try to do but persuade the "gentlemen of the jury" to achieve justice? Justice is more forensic than it is metaphysical; that is, justice is concerned fundamentally with public debates about the right thing to do on earth, not speculation on what is perfectly right in the heavens. What Sen calls "public reasoning"[107] is the way we decide on what's fair. We transcend our egoistical "positional confinement," Sen writes, by asking others what they see; Sen notes that "changing places has been one way to 'see' hidden things in the world."[108] We find out whether Waxey Gordon and Lucky Luciano are guilty by asking twelve very different jurors to ask themselves, "[I]s justice to be effective in this country in the courts, or is it not?"[109]

Justice, Sen continues, is not simply about institutions and their processes, but about people and their choices. Rawls, according to Sen, tended to focus on institutions and processes, what Indian philosophers might refer to as *niti*. *Niti* means "justice," but suggests a kind of procedural, process-focused justice. *Niti,* Sen writes, while of course necessary, is really is too narrow. Justice, he writes, ought to be closer to what Indian thinkers called *nyaya,* another term for "justice," which means something like "social justice."

Like Seabury, called to defend the integrity of New York City's courts, Dewey was a champion, then, of *niti*, due process, and fair procedure. Dewey's campaign against the gangs, however, focused not simply on process and institutions but also on society and social fairness. Dewey charged Luciano with organizing prostitution because the charge was lurid and, therefore, certain to attract the media and because Dewey was pretty sure, he could get a conviction. Of course, Dewey's thinking was instrumental. Yet, a kind of *nyaya* was at work in Dewey as well. By focusing on the exploitation of women, on the manifest unfairness of the commercial sex industry, and on the outrageousness of hoodlum violence directed against the powerless, something like social justice was a subtext of the Dewey investigations. The ghost of Owosso abolitionism, speaking the language of *nyaya*, echoed in Dewey's Manhattan courtrooms.

Thomas Dewey's conviction of Lucky Luciano rocketed Dewey to fame. Luciano's trial occurred at the very peak of the public's fascination with gangsters; *Little Caesar, The Public Enemy,* and *Scarface,* had only been out for a few years and everyone was still eagerly talking about them. After the Luciano conviction, Dewey became a New York celebrity. New York Republicans promised him a dazzling future. His public image was transformed by popular culture. In 1935, the same year the Dewey investigations began, a radio drama called *G-Men* premiered on NBC radio; in January 1936, NBC renamed it *Gang Busters.* If gangsters could be hits in the movies, could gangbusters not be hits on the radio too? *Gang Busters* with its shrill sound effects—police whistles, screeching tires, and machine-gun *ratta-tat-tats*—and its allegedly true stories, was a huge hit. In popular jargon, "to come on like Gangbusters" meant to begin something with a bang! *Gang Busters* would stay on the radio until the 1950s. When he retired as New York's police commissioner, Lewis Valentine would be hired as a consultant by the radio show. In 1937, Hollywood rushed out *Marked Woman*, a gangster film about a brave gangbuster district attorney (played by Humphrey Bogart) who fought the mob and the courageous (if tainted) woman (played by Bette Davis) who boldly testified against the mob boss. Broadway presented *Behind Red Light,* a melodrama that depicted life in New York's sex industry. *Gang Busters* also appeared in comic-book form and later as an early television show; the TV show would be reorganized into two feature films, *Gang Busters* (1955) and *Guns Don't Argue* (1957).

During the Luciano trial, New York's media began to refer to Thomas Dewey as the "Gangbuster." Inspired by Luciano's conviction, Dewey and his investigators accelerated their "frontal attack" against New York's gangsters. Meanwhile, letters began to pour into New York addressed simply to "The Racketbuster." The real-life Dewey merged with the *Gang Busters* radio show and Humphrey Bogart in *Marked Woman.* Newspapers around the country began carrying New York stories about gangsters and the gangbuster. "If you don't think Dewey is Public Hero No. 1," the *Philadelphia Inquirer* wrote, "listen to the applause he gets every time he is shown in a newsreel."[110]

The media transformed Tom Dewey into a kind of fantasy hero. Meanwhile, Dewey masterfully used the media to create a heroic narrative around his investigations. In 1937, Dewey began a series of Sunday night talks on New York City radio; according to Dewey's biographer, Richard Norton Smith, Dewey's radio talks "electrified the city as no one else had since Franklin Roosevelt invented the Fire Side Chat."[111] Dewey's radio talks echoed *Gang Busters* in style and in content. He spoke in an earnest, police-report, no-nonsense, steely monotone. "Dewey's speeches, the result of an exhaustive group effort," Norton explains, "were staccato processions of facts and figures, crafted in short, powerful sentences that fell like hammer blows."[112] Reporter Walter Winchell said that Dewey sounded like some hard-boiled movie cop when he mocked New York's gangsters; Dewey, for instance, described the mid-level hoodlum, Tootsie Herbert, as "a slim, slick-haired fellow who cowed the nosey with cold eye or a crippling, unexpected blow." When he reported on the attempted murder of Max Rubin, an associate of gangster Lepke Buchalter and potential Dewey witness, Dewey told his radio audience, "Tonight, I am going to talk about murder—murder in the bakery racket." The attempted assassination of Max Rubin, Dewey explained, was "the frightened act of a desperate underworld. The racketeers have flung down their challenge. Tonight I accept that challenge."[113] Dewey's staccato tone set the standard for movie and television gangbusters, reaching its climax in Sergeant Joe Friday's (played by Jack Webb) "just the facts, Ma'am" machine-like delivery in the television series, *Dragnet*. In 1960, Walter Winchell, the radio journalist who liked to boast of his mob connections, narrated the story of Murder, Inc., for Dot Records. His narration included original music by T. F. Ogal and George Greeley. An FBI report noted that Winchell spoke in a "dramatic, staccato" style,"[114] much like Dewey's. According to a 1937 "Talk of the Town" report in *The New Yorker*,

> [t]he radio makes sissies of most public men [. . .] But not Mr. Dewey. No breakfast food company has found anything to approach the suave menace of that voice [. . .] We could wish, perhaps, that Mr. Dewey's face were as menacing as his voice. The mustache helps, of course. A fierce black beard, now—but that's asking too much.[115]

By 1937, it was hard to tell where the fictional *Gangbuster* ended and the real Tom Dewey began.

The Luciano conviction and the wave of other indictments transformed
Tom Dewey, corporate lawyer from Owosso, Michigan, into a kind of
public persona: half fantasy, half real. In 1937, gangbuster Dewey easily
won election as Manhattan's district attorney, where he continued his
prosecution of underworld figures and crooked politicians. In 1938, he
won another spectacular courtroom victory; he indicted, and convicted,
Tammany leader Jimmy Hines on thirteen counts of bribery and corruption. Jimmy Hines was Tammany's go-to guy with the underground; he
was especially close to Dutch Schulz. Saved by a mistrial in his first battle
with the law, Hines was finally put in prison by gangbuster Dewey. In
1938, Dewey lost a close race for New York governor; in 1940, he lost to
Wendell Wilkie in the race for the Republican presidential nomination. In
1942, however, Dewey was elected New York's governor and was reelected
in 1946 and, for a third term, in 1950. While governor, he was twice the
Republican Party's candidate for president. In 1944, Dewey ran against
Franklin Roosevelt, and in 1948, he ran against Harry Truman. Dewey
was defeated both times, but despite his defeats, Dewey, "the Gangbuster,"
remained a hero to millions of Republicans and a major force in American
politics from the 1940s into the 1960s; Tom Dewey died in 1971.

Dewey's victories against the underworld came at a high price, however. As special prosecutor and then as district attorney, Dewey was forced
to live as a kind of mirror image of a gang boss. He worked in a fortified
office; he traveled surrounded by scowling armed guards; he made important telephone calls from corner candy stores because he feared that
his office telephone might be tapped. Dutch Schulz really wanted to kill
him, and Schulz was not the only one. During the Luciano trial, everyone
was sure that somebody, maybe even Dewey, was going to be killed. His
days were spent with killers, prostitutes, madams, and bookers. Dewey
had always been a fussy person; he disliked shaking hands and washed his
hands after touching doorknobs; his war against the mob did nothing to
reduce his nervous tics. During the investigations, for example, he got in
the habit of insisting, when dining in a restaurant, that he have a seat with
his back to a wall so no assassin could shoot him from behind.[116]

Worse, his entanglement with the mob left a bitter taste. His spectacular conviction of Luciano, for example, and Luciano's extraordinary sentence—thirty to fifty years in prison for organizing prostitution—seemed
to some critics excessive, a put-up job. Gangsters scoffed at the idea that
Luciano's chief occupation was prostitution; Meyer Lansky would always
insist that Luciano had been railroaded; "the whole thing was a frame-up,"
Lansky claimed.[117] Months after Luciano's conviction, Dewey's case be-

gan to unravel. Several of his star witnesses, including Nancy Presser and "Cokey Flo," recanted their testimony. They claimed Dewey had coached them, told them what to say, and promised them rewards if they helped convict Luciano. Dewey and his staff, shocked, insisted that the mob had gotten to "Cokey Flo" and the others and frightened them into recanting. Dewey responded to Luciano's defense team's demand for a new trial with a tidal wave of affidavits from other witnesses; the courts sided with Dewey and Luciano's conviction stood. Still, the whole thing proved an exhausting and thoroughly sordid business.[118]

Then, a decade after the conviction, in 1946, Governor Tom Dewey stunned New Yorkers by ordering that Charlie Lucky be released from prison. Luciano had not been pardoned (his conviction stayed on his record), but Dewey had commuted his sentence. Dewey agreed to let Luciano go, and Luciano agreed to depart immediately for Italy. The whole bizarre case was shrouded in mystery.[119]

During World War II, New York City became America's strategic link to wartime Europe. Thousands of ships sailed from the United States to Europe carrying tens of thousands of troops and millions of dollars of equipment. For the Axis, crippling New York's harbor would cripple the whole Allied war effort. No wonder that people like Navy Captain Roscoe McFall, of naval intelligence in New York, fretted. Ships in New York's harbor were serviced by armies of stevedores; many of the stevedores were immigrants, and many of them came from Italy. Captain McFall and the navy worried that some Italian stevedores might be sympathetic to Mussolini, or that Mussolini could infiltrate saboteurs into the stevedores' ranks. When the passenger ship *Normandie* burst into flames in New York Harbor on February 9, 1942, the navy was sure that enemy saboteurs had torched the ship.

Who controlled New York's docks? Not the navy and not the New York police. Brooklyn's docks, for example, were controlled by Albert Anastasia's hoodlums. McFall and the navy decided that they had no choice; the US Navy, with the help of New York City and New York State, would have to reach an understanding with the underworld.

Naval intelligence officer Charles R. Heffernden met with Socks Lanza, who ran the Fulton Fish Market for the mob. Socks Lanza talked to Albert Anastasia, Meyer Lansky, Frank Costello, and others. Luciano's attorney, Moses Polakoff, became involved. They all agreed to help the war effort, they said; their price was Luciano's release from prison. After the war, the navy said that the gangsters had actually been cooperative; they had policed the docks and passed information along to navy spies. After the *Normandie* fire, which in fact may have been just an accident, there was no sabotage on the New York waterfront. Just what sort of agreement had been reached remained a point of controversy; it appears that Heffernden, on behalf of Naval intelligence, agreed that, when the war was over, if the gangsters had cooperated, then the navy would endorse a request that Luciano's sentence be commuted. This was a deal between the US Navy and the hoodlums; the state of New York, it appears, and Governor Dewey were not involved.

When the war ended, Luciano's attorney, Polakoff, filed a request for a commutation of Luciano's sentence. The navy endorsed the request, so, too, did the state's parole board. Commuting Luciano's sentence would be, for Dewey, personally infuriating and politically damaging. However, refusing to honor the deal could damage naval intelligence, which might well require underworld assistance again someday. Governor Dewey stoically decided that he had no choice. He commuted Luciano's sentence. He explained that

> upon the entry of the United States into the war, Luciano's aid was sought by the armed services in inducing others to provide information concerning possible enemy attack. It appears that he cooperated in such effort, though the actual value of the information is not clear. His record in prison is reported as wholly satisfactory.[120]

In 1946, after a decade in prison, Lucky Luciano sailed from New York, tearful friends waving good-bye, and returned to Italy. Dewey did his best to avoid the issue, insisting that the Luciano case was a matter of national security. When reporters asked Charles Heffernden, Luciano's former navy intelligence handler, his opinion, Heffernden said that Luciano was just an ordinary informant, nothing special. Both Democrats and Dewey's Republican rivals would regularly criticize Dewey for the commutation.[121]

Everyone speculated about Dewey's motives. According to an FBI memo, "considerable opinion exists to the effect that Luciano was not guilty of the charges for which he was convicted and that Governor Dewey's parole of Luciano was motivated partly as an easing of Dewey's conscience."[122] Dewey himself would say little about it other than to repeat his 1946 claim that Luciano's release was in recognition of Luciano's aid to US intelligence.[123] In 1954, New York State's chief legal investigator, William Herlands, produced an exhaustive, 2,600-page report for Governor Dewey, which confirmed that Luciano had, indeed, aided US intelligence and that the commutation of his sentence was appropriate.

Because the report dealt with intelligence and national security, however, it was not released until 1977.[124]

Luciano headed back to Italy, but quickly surfaced in Havana. Harassed by US authorities, Luciano returned Italy and to a mysterious life. Some said that he was simply a retired businessman; some said that he played a major role in drug smuggling from the Middle East, through Sicily and Marseille, to the United States, in what eventually would be called "The French Connection" (itself the focus of a famous film of the same name).[125] No one ever knew for sure.

In 1936, after his spectacular conviction of Lucky Luciano, gangbuster Dewey decided to go after the next leading hoodlum in New York, Louis "Lepke" Buchalter. Lepke dominated the needle trades in Manhattan; he controlled the major trucking lines that linked New York to the rest of the country. Lepke's people had infiltrated both businesses and unions. Lepke was tied to Luciano, Albert Anastasia, Frank Costello, Meyer Lansky, Bugsy Siegel, and all of New York's other criminals. Having convicted Luciano, Dewey would now go after him.

Like everyone else, Lepke had followed Luciano's trial with great interest. The key to Luciano's conviction was the array of witnesses Dewey called against him. Had there been no witnesses, there would have been no conviction. The calculus was simple—if Lepke were to elude Dewey, Lepke would have to eliminate any possible witnesses. He could eliminate the witnesses himself, of course; he could have his lieutenant, Mendy Weiss, see to that. Lepke and Weiss, though, knew that it'd be dangerous for them to act directly; they'd need someone else, someone not directly linked to them, to do their work for them. Sometime in the mid-1930s, Lepke spoke with his friend, Albert Anastasia. Would Anastasia help? Yes, he would. Anastasia knew people in Brooklyn who could do what Lepke needed to have done. Out of this agreement, Murder, Inc., would be born.

6
Murder, Inc.
"I Got Used to It"

[Assistant District Attorney Burton Turkus to Abe Reles]: "Did your conscience ever bother you? [...] Didn't you feel anything?"
[Reles to Turkus]: "How did you feel when you tried your first law case?"
"I was rather nervous," I admitted.
"And how about your second case?"
"It wasn't so bad, but I was still a little nervous."
"And after that?"
"Oh [...] after that, I was all right; I was used to it."
"You answered your own question [...] It's the same with murder. I got used to it."[1]

Violent death, Thomas Hobbes argued, is the greatest of evils.[2] Murder, Inc., was in the business of violent death. The leaders of Murder, Inc., would themselves suffer violent death; as a result of the 1940–41 Murder, Inc., trials, seven men connected with Murder, Inc., would be sentenced to death and be electrocuted at Sing Sing prison. Violent death infected the very air around The Corner in Brownsville inhabited by Murder, Inc. To understand Murder, Inc., means to enter into the Brownsville gang's sinister world of mayhem and murder; that is the task of the first part of this chapter. The second part of this chapter then focuses on the three Brooklyn murders that would send the members of Murder, Inc., to their own deaths—the killings of Joe Rosen, Whitey Rudnick, and Puggy Feinstein. Finally, the chapter concludes by trying to think through the moral meanings of all these murders. If, as Hobbes says, violent death is the greatest of evils, how should we think about all this great evil? What can we say?

Abe Reles had been in trouble since he was a teenager.[3] Reles stood about five feet five inches tall; by the time he became famous, in 1940 and 1941, he weighed about 160 pounds. He had brown eyes. He accumulated a variety of tattoos over the years—on his right forearm, he had a tattoo of a bird, and above it were the words "True Love" and below it "Mother" and "A.R. 1921." Below this, he had a tattoo of a "grotesque character," a "dwarf-like female." On his right wrist, he had a kind of chain tattoo. On his left forearm he had a heart with two female heads and "A.R. 1931." His fingers were stubby and "clubbed."[4]

As a teenager, Reles hung out with the guys on street corners in Browns-ville, especially on the corner of Livonia and Saratoga Avenues, in front of Midnight Rose's candy store. Sometimes he'd go a few blocks away to Louis Capone's coffee shop, on Pacific Street off Eastern Parkway. Louis Capone was into a lot of things and knew a lot of people. Sometimes even Albert Anastasia, Brooklyn's most powerful gangster, would drop by Ca-pone's coffee shop. Reles first met Capone around 1928, or maybe it was 1929. Twelve years older than Abe Reles, Capone was one of the "older guys," when Reles was "a wild kid." Like the other wild kids, Reles did things for Capone. Reles would later remark,

> Louis [Capone] asks me to do the first job for him. Happy [Maione] and him drive me to one of them little streets near Pleasant Place over in Ocean Hill. Louis points to the house, and tells me what room this bum lives in. I go in and shoot the guy five times. One of the slugs goes in the back of his head and takes one of his eyes out. After that, I do a lot of jobs for Louis when he tells me [. . .] Louis was always very nice to me.[5]

When Abe Reles was a twenty-something hoodlum, the boss of Browns-ville was Meyer Shapiro. He and his two brothers, Irv and Willie, and their circle of allies ran the neighborhood. The Shapiros collected extortion pay-ments from all the convenience stories and small businesses and brothels in Brownsville; they took a cut from all pots in all the poker and craps games; they were bootleggers, narcotics peddlers, and thieves. Brownsville, like many New York neighborhoods, had a vibrant illegal economy, and in that illegal economy, the Shapiros had just about a complete monopoly.

In the 1920s, Abe Reles was a "worshipful punk"[6] who hung around the Shapiros; there were lots of young guys just like Reles. Martin "Buggsy"

Goldstein was one, and Harry "Pittsburgh Phil" Strauss was another. They ran errands, collected money, threatened the recalcitrant, and waited for the Shapiros to accept them as real gangsters. People called Reles "Kid" or sometimes "Kid Twist." The gangster life meant violence, which equaled masculinity, which meant power, which meant the ability to have the sorts of things the working stiffs in the neighborhood could only dream of, which meant status and respect. Teenager Abe Reles desperately wanted to be part of that world.

After several years as a criminal gofer, Reles began getting itchy. He wanted a bigger piece of the action—maybe a brothel to manage (there were at least fifteen in Brownsville, all owned by the Shapiros),[7] maybe a small crew of criminals of his own to boss around. When slot machines became all the rage—pushed by Frank Costello and his people—Reles, Goldstein, Strauss, and others went from restaurant to restaurant and bar to bar in Brownsville, demanding that the owners install the slots. Anyone who refused got his head broken. The slots were gold mines; weekly collections brought in sacks of nickels. However, all the money went up to the Shapiros and, beyond them, to the mysterious gangsters in the center of the underworld. Not much was left for guys like Abe Reles.

Willie Shapiro was a minor player, a sort of court jester; he did not matter. Irv was the second in command; his chief duty was enforcing his older brother's decisions. Meyer Shapiro was the real boss, and he was grasping, suspicious, and violent. He had no intention of sharing anything with Kid Twist Reles, Buggsy Goldstein, Pittsburgh Phil, or any of Shapiro's other young henchmen. "I'm the boss of Brownsville," Meyer Shapiro boasted.[8] But by 1930, some of Meyer Shapiro's subordinates were unhappy. "Why do we got to take the left-overs?" Reles angrily said to Buggsy Goldstein; "We should cut a piece. The hell with them guys," the Shapiros.[9]

Buggsy Goldstein was an early ally. Buggsy was short and bulldog looking, like *Little Caesar*'s star Edward G. Robinson. His friends called him "Buggsy" because he was always goofing around. Once, in a police lineup, Buggsy Goldstein joked that he was only number six on the police department's list of wanted Brooklyn criminals; Buggsy said, "I should get a better spot [. . .] I'm working on it."[10]

Harry Strauss—"Big Harry," or "Pep," or "Pittsburgh Phil"—was, Assistant District Attorney Turkus would write, "the dandy of the outfit. Pittsburgh Phil would fairly purr when you referred to him as the Beau Brummel of the Brooklyn underworld. To others, homicide was purely business; to Pep, it was practically ecstasy. He reveled in manslaughter;

delighted in death [. . .] He was as vicious as a Gestapo agent, as casually cold-blooded as a meat-grinding machine in a butcher shop." According to Turkus's count, Pittsburgh Phil would eventually kill more than thirty men.[11] Reles later told Turkus, "[T]he way Pep went, it was like we put on a whole new troop."[12] Pittsburgh Phil could be hard to work with; he saw himself as Reles's ally, not his subordinate. Seymour "Blue Jaw" Magoon, one of the "kids" who ran errands and stole cars for the gang later testified that Pep was very prickly about his status within the gang. "When he was with his superiors in the mob," Magoon testified, "he wined and dined them, and made a show at splurging, while with his equals or subordinates, he would argue when it came his time to pay." Strauss, Magoon said, liked to boast about the murders he had committed: "on occasion, Harry would tell me, more or less in a spirit of braggadocio, about the murders in which he participated or of which he knew. I would then cut him short with a 'you told me that before.'"[13]

Reles found other critical allies in the nearby neighborhoods of Ocean Hill and East New York. Harry "Happy" Maione—"he wore such a surly look that when he walked along the street, the neighbors would actually pull down the shades,"[14] Burton Turkus joked—had his own gang. Maione brought with him that speedy runner, Frank "the Dasher" Abbandando,[15] and Vito "Socko" or "Chickenhead" Gurino. Gurino, prosecutor Turkus would say, "was probably as savage as any of that band who would commit any crime. He was five feet eight and 265 pounds" and, although only in his twenties, looked much older. He had, Turkus wrote, "the manners of a wallowing animal and the habits of an oaf." Gurino was a baker by trade, and in Ocean Hill he owned five little bakeries that also acted as fronts for his other activities. He was also a member of a Bakers' Union local, from which he stole union dues.[16]

Reles almost certainly received a go-ahead from the most important people in Brooklyn, especially Albert Anastasia, although there is no clear evidence that Anastasia was part of Reles's conspiracy. Historian Albert Fried thinks that Louis "Lepke" Buchalter also approved Reles's rebellion, although again, there is no clear evidence of Buchalter's involvement.[17]

Reles launched his rebellion in the summer of 1930; it raged for a whole year, and it was a strange and brutal thing.[18] On June 4, 1930, Meyer Shapiro and some of his gang members were standing around outside the Globe Cafeteria on Sutter Avenue, in Brownsville. Two cars slowly drove by and the men inside opened fire. Meyer Shapiro and his people immediately returned fire, and the car sped off. Shapiro was wounded in the stomach but recovered quickly.[19]

Meyer Shapiro, and his brothers Irv and Willie, could not leave Brownsville; if they did, Reles would immediately seize all their businesses. Yet
everywhere they went in Brownsville—and Brownsville, at no more than
three miles square, was a small place—Reles and his people were lurking.
The Shapiros changed their routines; they slept here and then there. Reles
followed. At one point, one of the Shapiro's guys, Joey Silvers, contacted
Reles and whispered that he could tell Reles were the Shapiros were.
Based on Silvers's tip, Reles and others hurried to a parking lot and found
the Shapiros' cars. Reles used an ice pick to puncture the cars' tires so
there would be no getaway. Alas, for Reles, it was an ambush. The Shapiros
opened fire. One of Reles's people, George DeFeo, was killed; Buggsy
Goldstein was hit in the face; Reles was wounded in the stomach. The
Shapiros ran away. Goldstein and Reles recovered. (Some months later,
Joey Silvers would be shot to death by persons unknown.)[20]

During that long year, from the summer of 1930 until the summer of
1931, the Shapiro and Reles gangs battled at least eighteen times.[21] At
one point, Meyer Shapiro spotted Reles's girlfriend walking along the
sidewalk; Shapiro grabbed her, pulled her into his car, drove off with her,
attacked her, and dumped her on the side of the street.[22]

Finally, in July 1931, the tide turned. One dark night, Irv Shapiro
stepped into the darkened foyer of his apartment building on Blake
Avenue. He snapped on the light. A hidden gunman shot him to death.
On August 31, 1931, Reles stood in front of a poolroom on Sutter
Avenue; a car roared by, and men in the car blazed away at Reles; they
missed. The gunmen did shoot the windows out of an adjacent store and
just missed killing terrified shoppers. "The lives of hundreds of pedestrians and shoppers were endangered by this fusillade," the New York Times
reported.[23] Days later, another gun battle erupted on New Lots Avenue;
scores of shocked pedestrians watched as gunmen fired at each other then
sped away in their cars.[24] Two months later, armed men finally caught
up with Meyer Shapiro; they pulled him into a car and sped off. Meyer
Shapiro's body was found later in an abandoned building on Manhattan's
Lower East Side.[25] Poor Willie Shapiro, the last of the brothers, would suffer a terrible end. In 1934, he simply stopped hiding, and Reles's people
easily caught him. His body was later found stuffed in a laundry bag buried in the sand along Canarsie Flats. He had been brutally beaten. An autopsy found sand in his lungs, so he must have been buried alive.[26]

Finally, in the fall of 1931, Abe Reles, twenty-five, was the new boss of
Brownsville. Reles and his allies lost no time in taking over all of the Shapiros' businesses. They collected extortion money from all Brownsville's

businesses and brothels; they took over the gambling, loan-sharking, theft, and fencing in the neighborhood; they pedaled illegal beer, whiskey, and narcotics. They took over an incredibly popular craps game that usually was held in a building on the corner of State and Court Streets in Brooklyn. Everyone, workers and businesspeople and boys playing hooky from high school, went to shoot craps there. Louis Benson ran the games for Reles. Benson was an enormous man; he weighed well over four hundred pounds, so naturally everyone called him "Tiny." He'd been a cab driver, but when he became too huge to fit behind the wheel, he quite driving and did odd jobs for Abe Reles. Tiny collected payments for loan sharks; he ruled the craps games with an iron fist and scrupulously passed along to Reles a cut of every pot.[27]

Reles's headquarters was Midnight Rose's, and most days, Reles and the others could be found on The Corner at Livonia and Saratoga Avenues. Rose Gold, a "white-haired grandmother," who ran the store, seemed to those who saw her to be nothing more than a little old lady. Once, when she was arrested in 1939, the *New York Daily News* described her this way:

> She was a drab figure, little more than five feet tall, wearing an old-fashioned black turban. She peered nearsightedly through silver-rimmed nose spectacles. Wisps of grey hair fell over her forehead.

No one, the *Daily News* added, would ever believe that this "wizened old woman's" little candy store was "the clearing house for Brooklyn's prostitution, policy, and bail bond rackets."[28] When in trouble with the law, Gold hired the best criminal defense lawyer in Brooklyn—Burton Turkus.[29]

Reles called his gang "the Combination."[30] The Combination never numbered more than a score of people, more or less. Reles, Goldstein, and Strauss formed one faction; Happy Maione, Frank "the Dasher" Abbandando, and Vito "Socko" Gurino formed another. A small number of "bat boys" orbited this inner core. The "bat boys" were neighborhood teenagers eager to join the gangster life. Sholem Bernstein was an exceptionally skillful car thief; he would later admit, "I stole maybe seventy-five, a hundred cars [. . .] whenever I got orders."[31] Anthony "Dukey" Maffetore, Julie Catalano, Abraham "Pretty" Levine, and Seymour "Blue Jaw" Magoon did things for the combination's leaders. As the *New York Times* remarked, "the younger hangers-on of the street gangs seek to win the notice and the approval of the gangsters they look up to by doing a 'strong-arm' job for them."[32]

Dukey Maffetore's story was typical. In 1931, when Reles took over Brownsville, Dukey was sixteen. He had had trouble in school and dropped out; his parents could not control him. He worked briefly in a lightbulb factory and then worked as an iceman and a plumber's helper. After he got fired from a job when he was seventeen, he, as he later testified, started "hanging around corners and craps games." He ran errands for Reles, Goldstein, and Maione. "Big Harry" (Strauss) "[gave] me the o.k. to shylock," Dukey later testified, so Dukey started making loans and collecting interest. Abe "Pretty" Levine was his partner in the loan shark business. Dukey and Pretty got to be very good at stealing cars, especially cars needed for murders.[33]

The Combination's crimes were secret, but the members were very public. By 1931, everyone in Brownsville knew Abe Reles. The police, of course, knew Reles and the others and regularly arrested them on suspicion of one crime or another. Reles would strut into the precinct station, pull out a huge wad of money, peel off a few hundreds, toss them to the desk sergeant for his bail, and strut back out.[34] By referring to Reles in 1937, as "Brooklyn's Public Enemy No. 1,"[35] the New York Times would link this relatively minor local hoodlum both to celebrity criminals like Al Capone and John Dillinger and to the still-popular gangster movie starring James Cagney, The Public Enemy. Abe Reles had certainly come up in the world.

In February 1934, Reles and most likely Strauss assaulted gas station attendant Charles Battle and murdered Alvin Snyder. Reles was convicted of third-degree assault and sent to prison for three years.[36] With Reles away, the Combination quickly bifurcated into two allied gangs, one led by Strauss and Goldstein and the other led by Maione and Abbandando. The two factions regularly cooperated, but keeping order in Brownsville, and fending off rivals, proved to be very hard.

For example, Jimmy "Blue Eyes" Silvio had a brother, "Bot." In 1935, Bot Silvio went missing. Abe Meer and Irving Amron had snatched him; they demanded that Blue Eyes pay a ransom of $8,000 to get his brother back. Blue Eyes paid the ransom, and Bot was freed. Blue Eyes then went to Pittsburgh Phil and demanded that he kill Meer and Amron.

On September 15, 1935, Dukey Maffetore was hanging out with Walter Sage on The Corner when Buggsy Goldstein, Harry Strauss, and Sholom Bernstein hurried over. Strauss told Maffetore and Sage to go snatch a car and then to go find Meer and Amron. They were to tell Meer and Amron that they needed to go to some sort of meeting with Phil and Buggsy. Maffetore and Sage found Meer and Amron and drove them to Thatchford Avenue. When Meer and Amron got out of the car, Strauss ran over and shouted, "[T]his is a stick-up!" He and Goldstein pushed Meer and Amron against a wall, stepped back, and began shooting. For some reason Goldstein's weapon did not go off. Meer was killed, but Amron only fainted. Strauss and Goldstein bundled Amron into the car with Maffetore and Sage; then Strauss, Maffetore, and Sage drove off with the unconscious Amron. They took Amron, now coming around, to Mutt Goldstein's home (Mutt was Buggsy's brother). They beat Amron up and then loaded him back in the car. Buggsy Goldstein followed in a back-up car. Driving down the street, Sage shot and killed Amron; Maffetore stopped the car; everyone leaped out and jumped in the backup car Goldstein was driving, leaving only Amron's lonely corpse in the first car. Strauss would later mock Goldstein for his sorry performance that day. Even at point-blank range, Strauss said, Goldstein couldn't hit his target; Goldstein insisted that it wasn't his fault, his weapon had misfired.[37]

Meanwhile, at the very same time, in 1935, the Ambergs emerged as an even greater threat.

Hyman, Louis, and Joey Amberg were mirror images of Abe Reles, Harry Strauss, Buggsy Goldstein, and the others. Teenage street-corner hoodlums, the Ambergs were bootleggers, thieves, and assassins. In November 1926, armed with smuggled-in guns, Hyman Amberg staged a daring attempt to escape from New York's notorious prison, the Tombs. Amberg almost escaped; when he was finally cornered by guards, Hyman Amberg killed himself.

Although in and out of jail, Joey and Louis (known as "Pretty") Amberg were back on the street by the mid-1930s, and when Joey Amberg heard that Abe Reles was in jail, Amberg decided that the time was ripe for him to take over Reles's businesses in Brownsville. However, Joey Amberg faced at least two major problems. In the summer of 1935, Joey Amberg had murdered a gangster by the name of Hy Kasner. Amberg and others stuffed Kasner's corpse in a sack and shoved it down a sewer, assuming that the sewer would carry the corpse off into the ocean. The sewer did not; Kasner's corpse popped back up from the sewer, and word circulated that Joey Amberg was Kasner's killer. That was a problem for Amberg because Kasner was a friend of both Albert Anastasia and Louis Capone. Amberg's second problem was that Reles's associates, especially Strauss and Goldstein, and no intention of being taken over by Joey Amberg. Louis Capone and Albert Anastasia met with Lucky Luciano at the Saratoga Race Track and complained about Joey Amberg; Luciano gave them "the O.K." for Amberg's killing.[38]

On September 30, 1935, Joey Amberg and his driver, Manny Kessler, pulled into a garage on the corner of Blake and Christopher Avenues. They were apparently headed for some sort of meeting with Pittsburgh Phil Strauss; he owned the garage. When Kessler and Amberg stepped out of their car, two men rushed up, announced that they were police officers, and ordered Amberg and Kessler to face the garage wall. When Amberg and Kessler did, the two men immediately opened fire and killed them both.

No one ever knew just who the killers were. One might have been Happy Maione; another might have been Strauss or Buggsy Goldstein; an early police report speculated that the killers were Goldstein, Strauss, and maybe Louis Capone.[39] Other reports claimed that Philip Mangano and Julius "Red" Pulvino, two of Albert Anastasia's men, had been the killers.[40] According to one witness, after shooting Amberg and Kessler, the two killers got confused and ran off in opposite directions, then turned around and leaped into a getaway car just when a local cop shouted at them to stop and opened fire.[41] As for the last Amberg, Louis "Pretty" Amberg, he was killed several weeks later. His body was left in a car, which was set on fire; one of the women associated with the Reles gangsters tossed the match.[42]

When Abe Reles was released from prison in 1937, he reconstituted the Combination. Reles was very much a hands-on gangster. For instance, once a grocery store and garage owner in Brownsville, Joe Litvin, asked to borrow money from Reles. He asked for $5,000. Reles agreed to the loan; Litvin would have to pay back the $5,000, of course, as well as an additional $1,000 per week for every week that the loan was outstanding. Litvin, however, could not pay the interest and went, without telling Reles, to Pittsburgh Phil to borrow more money. When Reles learned what was going on, he was furious.

On the night of October 17, 1939, Reles; Pittsburgh Phil's brother, Alex; and Max Golob, whom the gang members called "the Jerk," went off to talk to Joe Litvin at his garage. They did not find Litvin, so they began slashing all the tires they could find in and around the garage. Litvin's son, Rube Smith, ran out and attacked Reles. "I was having a helluva time with him," Reles told Burton Turkus, but the Jerk ran over and stabbed Smith to death. "The Jerk is a good man," Reles assured Turkus.[43]

By then, the Combination had become active in much bigger things. By the mid-1930s, Mayor La Guardia and his police commissioner, Lewis Valentine, had declared war on the mobs. Special Prosecutor Thomas Dewey vowed to put Lucky Luciano in prison and then go after Lepke Buchalter. Panic gripped the underworld. Everyone knew that witnesses were the key to the war. If La Guardia, Valentine, and Dewey could find enough witnesses, they could cripple the underworld; if the gangsters could intimidate or murder enough witnesses, they would win. Lepke Buchalter, Albert Anastasia, and gangland's other leaders, whom Abe Reles vaguely called the "Syndicate," demanded that witnesses be liquidated. Lepke and Albert A. ordered Abe Reles and the Brownsville boys to hunt down dangerous witnesses. And "that," Reles later told District Attorney Turkus, "is how we got to be a big outfit [. . .] handling the contracts for the Syndicate."[44] They became, as a police report explained, "men engaged in the business of murder."[45]

In the end, three murders would seal the fate of Murder, Inc. The killings of Joe Rosen, Whitey Rudnick, and Puggy Feinstein would eventually send the Murder, Inc., killers to the electric chair.

Joe Rosen was a trucker. He drove for Garfield Trucking out of Passaic, New Jersey, and later the New York and New Jersey Trucking Company.[46] He and his fellow drivers hauled freight back and forth from eastern Pennsylvania and New York City. By 1932, Lepke Buchalter and his lieutenants Mendy Weiss and Gurrah Shapiro had begun to shake down the truckers. They demanded a cut from all the trucking contracts, and if not paid off, they slashed truck tires, set fires to truck loads, and threw acid in drivers' faces.

Joe Rosen would not be intimidated. In 1934, Lepke got him fired; Rosen was accused of petty larceny; he denied the charge, but his company fired him anyway. He found a new trucking job, but the company also was under Lepke's control.[47] Rosen quit and threatened to "go to Dewey." To make a living, he opened a little convenience store at 725 Sutter Avenue, in Brooklyn. In the spring of 1936, ominous-looking men began dropping by the store, asking to speak to Joe. According to Joe's wife, Ester, Gurrah Shapiro and Lepke Buchalter came by; they wanted some cigars, she remembered, so she gave them some Robert Burns cigars. Later, Max Rubin, another Lepke lieutenant, came by with a couple of other guys. Ester Rosen told police that they said to Joe,

> "Be a good fellow. We know we done you dirty, but be a good fellow. First of all you have to get out of the place [. . .]." My husband says: "I can't get out. You have to have money to get out." They said: "you don't have to worry about that; we will take care of it." They told him: "if you know what's good for you, you have got to get out of here."[48]

Ester told police that others came by the store and said, "Listen, Joe, you got to get out of town, they are hot on the trail [. . .] the upper-ups ordered that you must go away."[49]

Joe Rosen, murdered by Murder, Inc., on Lepke Buchalter's orders. (*Brooklyn Eagle*, Brooklyn Public Library)

Rosen again threatened to go to Dewey. Lepke told Rosen to stay away from Dewey. Lepke tried to bribe Rosen, and frighten him, but nothing worked.[50] In June 1936, Dewey shocked the underworld by convicting Lucky Luciano, and Dewey vowed to go after Lepke next. Lepke now decided that he had no choice. "I stood enough of this crap," Lepke exploded. "That son of a bitch Rosen, that bastard, he's going around shooting off his mouth about seeing Dewey. He and nobody else is going any place and doing any talking. I'll take care of him."[51] Lepke ordered one of his gunmen, Paul Berger, to drive to Brownsville and identify Rosen for Mendy Weiss. Berger drove slowly past Rosen's store and pointed Rosen out to Weiss. Weiss now took over. Weiss reconnoitered the area around Rosen's store; he strolled into the store, looked around, and strolled out again. He talked to Louis Capone; Capone talked to Pittsburgh Phil Strauss.

Capone ordered Sholem Bernstein to "clip" a car. Bernstein did—a two-door coup. Bernstein also had an inspiration. He had an acquaintance named "Muggsy," who was a car thief, pull the radio out of the car so that if the car were later found, the police would think it was just any old car stolen for its radio. Bernstein showed the stolen car to Capone. Capone was furious; how could the whole crew climb in and out of a two-door? But it would have to do. Capone drove with Bernstein along Sutter Avenue and pointed out Rosen's store. "That is where somebody is going to get killed," Capone said to Bernstein.[52]

Early on Sunday morning, September 13, 1936, Bernstein drove up to Rosen's store on Sutter Avenue. In the two-door coup with him were Mendy Weiss, Harry Strauss, and another of Louis Capone's associates, Jimmy Feraco. Joe Rosen stepped out of his store—he and his family lived in the back—picked up a bundle of newspapers, and walked back into the store. Weiss, Strauss, and Feraco clambered out of the car. Feraco stood watch. Weiss and Strauss stepped into the store, pulled out their pistols, and shot Rosen to death. They ran back outside and the three of them, Feraco, Weiss, and Strauss, shoved themselves through Bernstein's two doors. Bernstein drove off to a prearranged rendezvous. Bernstein later testified, saying, "[T]hey were all telling me this way and that way [. . .] I was very nervous myself."[53] Louis Capone waited at the rendezvous in one car; Philip "Little Farvel" Cohen, in another. Bernstein and the others abandoned the two-door murder coup, split up, and drove off with Capone and Little Farvel Cohen.

That Sunday morning, Officer Guglielmo Cappadora was cruising along Sutter Avenue on a tediously routine patrol, checking out the traffic lights. Suddenly, he spotted someone in front of Rosen's store, waving hysterically. Officer Cappadora pulled over and ran into the store. Sprawled on the floor, amid a bloodied clutter of Sunday papers, lay Joe Rosen riddled with bullets.[54]

When they escaped, Sholem Bernstein had second thoughts about that car radio. Muggsy had it. The radio had a serial number; the serial number could connect Muggsy to the murder car and to Sholem. Bernstein hurried over to Muggsy's house grabbed the radio, broke it into pieces, drove to Canarsie, and threw the radio parts into the ocean. Later that day, Bernstein saw the report of Rosen's murder in the newspaper. "I seen a picture of the killing, and the name," he would later testify. "I didn't know the man."[55]

When Mendy Weiss reported to Lepke Buchalter, Weiss was livid. Allie "Tick Tock" Tannenbaum, who was with Lepke, remembered Weiss's angry account of the killings. Lepke asked, "[Is] everything all right?" Weiss replied, "Everything is okay. Only [. . .] that son of a bitch Pep" (meaning Pittsburgh Phil Strauss). Weiss continued: "I give him strict orders not to do any shooting, but after I shoot Rosen, and he is laying there on the floor, Pep starts shooting him." Lepke replied, "[A]ll right, what's the difference [. . .] as long as everybody is clean and you got away all right."[56]

Joe Rosen's son, Harold, had no doubt about the reasons behind his father's death. The police asked Harold Rosen, "Is it your impression and your conclusion that the motive for the killing of your father was to prevent him from telling Dewey about the practices of Lepke, Gurrah, or any other men?" Harold Rosen answered, "That is it."[57]

Joe Rosen's 1936 murder would remain unsolved for the next four years.

On May 25, 1937, around 7:40 a.m., police officers Francis Schneider and Jim Reilly, patrolling in Brooklyn in their police cruiser, got a call to investigate an abandoned car, a black Buick sedan, on Jefferson Avenue, between Evergreen and Central. They hurried to the site and peered into the car. Jammed in the back seat was a corpse. Whoever it was had been hit in the forehead with some sort of weapon, strangled with a rope, and stabbed repeatedly.

On the body, the officers discovered a poorly typed note:

> Freind George: Will you please meet me in N.Y. some day—same place and time—in reference to what you told me last week. Also, I will have that certain powder that I promised you the last time I seen you. PS. I hope you find this in your letterbox still sealed. I remain your freind, you know, from DEWEY'S office.[58]

The note was addressed to George Rudnick.

The battered corpse was taken to the morgue. The police quickly tracked down Rudnick's mother, Dora, who identified him. The coroner reported that Rudnick was about six feet in height, and skinny, no more than 140 pounds. He had been stabbed with an ice pick some sixty-three times. He had a gaping wound on his forehead. He had also been strangled; the rope was still around his neck. The "certain powder" referred

George "Whitey" Rudnick's body. (City University of New York, John Jay College, Lloyd Sealy Library, Special Collections)

to in the odd note no doubt referred to narcotics. Detectives knew that George Rudnick—everyone called him "Whitey"—was a drug addict, or as Turkus described him, "a skinny hophead."[59] The reference to "DEWEY'S office" was a warning. For some reason, Rudnick had been identified as a potential Dewey witness; his gruesome fate was a warning to future witnesses.

His murder remained unsolved—until the Murder, Inc., investigation began in 1940. The investigators learned that sometime in the spring of 1937, Pittsburgh Phil and Abe Reles had been talking on The Corner. Phil said: "I got info George Rudnick is talking to the law [. . .] we got to take him. Let's go up and see Happy and the Dasher." The Dasher, Phil added, "is pally with Rudnick. He would come with Dasher faster than any of us."[60] Abe Reles had known Rudnick for a long time; Reles would tell Turkus, "Whitey was my friend for fifteen years."[61]

On or about May 20, 1937, in the evening, Anthony "Dukey" Maffetore was hanging around The Corner with Pittsburgh Phil. Phil told Dukey and Dukey's partner, Abraham "Pretty" Levine," to steal a car and bring it to Strauss's home; the next night, Dukey and Pretty took the car to a garage on Atlantic Avenue near Eastern Parkway.

Meantime, Pittsburgh Phil and Abe Reles invented what they considered a clever ruse. They tracked down an old typewriter. The typewriter had no ribbon spool, so Reles had to hold a piece of ribbon in the typewriter, while Phil typed. Phil typed "Freind George." Reles objected that *friend* was spelled wrong. They tore the note out of the typewriter and tried again. Phil again typed "f r e i n d." Reles again objected. They got into what Reles later described as "quite a rhubarb" about the proper way to spell "friend"; Phil's misspelling prevailed.[62] "This will do a lot of good for Lep, when they find a dead man with a note," Phil pointed out, meaning Lepke Buchalter. When the note appeared in the newspapers, Phil was sure that it would frighten anyone from going to Dewey. Alas, the note was for naught. It never appeared in the news. "The god-damned cops," Phil complained; "the letter didn't get in the papers."[63]

Now, everyone waited for Rudnick. Rudnick hung around the neighborhood and did odd jobs to earn money for his drugs. Around 4:30 a.m. on the morning of May 24, 1937, Reles spotted Rudnick wandering down the street; Reles alerted the Dasher Abbandando. Abbandando hurried over to Rudnick; Abbandando got into his car, and Rudnick got in with him. Abbandando drove off to the garage on Atlantic Avenue.

Abbandando and Rudnick got out of Abbandando's car and stepped into the garage. Suddenly Abbandando grabbed Rudnick; Harry Strauss jumped out of the shadows, looped a rope around Rudnick's neck and began strangling him; as Rudnick kicked and struggled, Strauss began stabbing him furiously with an ice pick. When Rudnick finally collapsed, Abbandando and Strauss tried to shove his corpse into the sedan Dukey and Pretty had stolen. Happy Maione, in the garage too, helped. Rudnick was awfully tall, however, too tall to fit easily into the sedan's backseat. Abbandando, Strauss, and Maione had to push and pull him to squeeze him in. "The bum don't fit," somebody grunted.[64] Abe Reles appeared and watched as the others shoved the corpse into the car; when Rudnick's corpse let out a loud sigh, Phil, startled, started stabbing him again. Happy Maione grabbed a meat clever, shouted, "[L]et me hit this bastard for luck!" and whacked Rudnick's corpse on the head.[65] Rudnick's corpse quieted. Julie Catalano drove the stolen car, with Rudnick's corpse in it, over to Jefferson Avenue and abandoned it; another car picked Catalano up, and they drove off. Curious neighbors spotted the car a few minutes later and called the police.

Sometime in the fall of 1939, Pittsburgh Phil told Abe Reles that Albert Anastasia had a job for them. Reles liked to think of himself as the boss of the Brownsville Combination, and that Strauss would communicate directly with Anastasia irritated him.[66] Strauss had had dinner with Anastasia; Albert wanted to protect Vince Mangano from a stool pigeon. Strauss said, "Albert gave me a contract to take some guy, 'Puggy,' from 14th Avenue, Borough Park. He wants him knocked off." The stool pigeon's name was Irving "Puggy" Feinstein.[67]

Puggy Feinstein had always wanted to be a boxer. He had had several bouts and about the only thing he accomplished was getting his nose flattened and earning the nickname "Puggy." Puggy Feinstein was a minor character in Brooklyn; he gambled, lost, and borrowed from the loan sharks. He worked for a while for Vince Mangano.

In 1939, Puggy decided to go straight. Whether he really intended to testify against Vince Mangano is unclear, but under the circumstances, with La Guardia, Dewey, and Police Commissioner Valentine putting the big heat on everyone, Mangano was not taking any chances. Mangano asked Anastasia for help. Anastasia told Pittsburgh Phil to take Puggy for a ride.

On the night before Labor Day, Puggy Feinstein and friends were cruising around Brooklyn in Feinstein's new car, when Feinstein said that he wanted to drive over toward Brownsville. He wanted to pay off that fat loan shark named Tiny Benson. He parked near The Corner. He said he would be right back.

Puggy walked up to The Corner. Strauss, Reles, and Buggsy Goldstein were hanging out there. They did not know Puggy. Puggy asked whether they had seen Tiny. No, they hadn't. Who was asking? Feinstein told them his name. They were astonished! The very guy they had been hunting for had just walked up to them! Pittsburgh Phil said to Reles, "That's the 'Puggy'! You can see by his kisser!"[68]

While Feinstein uncertainly waited, Reles, Strauss, and Goldstein went into a whispered consultation. Phil said to Reles, "Now that we've got him, what are we going to do?" Reles replied, "What are you going to do, burn up the corner?" Phil replied, "You are moving anyhow, we'll bring him over to your house." Reles said, "What? My house?" And Phil replied, "What's the difference? I won't make no noise. Once I mug him, you know, he stays mugged."[69] So that was the plan: Goldstein and Dukey Maffetore would drive Feinstein around Brooklyn on a phony hunt for Tiny. Reles and Strauss would rush over to Reles's house. Goldstein and Maffetore would then drive Feinstein over to Reles.

While Goldstein, Maffetore, and Feinstein drove around in circles, Reles and Strauss rushed to Reles's home. When they got there, Reles wife, Rose, and Goldstein's wife, Beatrice, were getting ready to go the movies. Reles and Strauss hurried them out. Reles's mother-in-law stayed behind and went to bed.

Reles started looking for an ice pick and length of rope. He could not find them. He tiptoed into his mother-in-law's bedroom and asked her where they were. The rope was down in the basement, she said; the ice pick was in the pantry.

Harry Strauss helped himself to a glass of milk.

Buggsy Goldstein, Dukey Maffetore, and Puggy Feinstein drove up. They got out of the car. Puggy stepped through Reles's front door and into the house. Harry Strauss leaped behind Feinstein and tried to get a rope around Feinstein's neck, but Feinstein shrieked and kicked, and the two of them tumbled onto Reles's couch. Goldstein started punching Feinstein. Reles turned the radio up to drown out Feinstein's cries. Feinstein shouted, "Don't hit me, don't hit me, I got the money," but no one was listening. Everyone was wrestling around on the floor; Pittsburgh Phil shouted, "[T]he bastard bit me!" Reles started jumping on Feinstein's stomach; Strauss finally got the rope around Feinstein's neck and then proceeded to tie him "into a little ball," Reles later testified. Then Strauss began "punching" him with the ice pick.

It had been quite a battle. Dukey spotted Reles's ring on the floor; Pittsburgh Phil shouted, "[M]y watch is missing!" They found the watch (it was broken), and then Phil cried, "The bastard bit me in the hand! [. . .] [M]aybe I am getting lockjaw!" Looking at his hand, Strauss, distressed, asked Reles, "Have you got mercurochrome in the house?"[70]

The problem now was what to do with Feinstein's corpse. There might be some sort of physical evidence in Puggy's teeth, left there when he bit Pittsburgh Phil. Strauss insisted that Puggy's corpse be burned. Maffetore and Goldstein ran off and got a can of gasoline; they returned and all of them trundled Feinstein's corpse into the car. Strauss told Maffetore and Goldstein to take the corpse over to the "dumps," off Flatlands Avenue, a city dump where refuse was constantly smoldering, and burn it. No one would find Feinstein's burned body there. However, Maffetore and Goldstein got lost and finally picked a random lot in southeast Brooklyn. They dragged Feinstein's corpse out of the car and dumped it into the empty lot. Goldstein doused the corpse with gasoline and tossed a match on it. With a *whoosh*, the corpse burst into flames; Goldstein jumped backward with a scream; the flames had singed his eyebrows. Maffetore and Goldstein jumped back into the car and raced back to Reles's. Meantime, Seymour "Blue Jaw" Magoon showed up at Reles's house. Magoon drove the shaken Goldstein—"I nearly got burned," Goldstein cried, pointing to his eyebrows—back to the gas station so Goldstein could return the gas can; on the way, Goldstein told Magoon what had happened.[71]

That Labor Day night, Mrs. Louise Mauer, who lived next door to the lot, looked out her window and saw "an unmerciful big blaze." She ran outside with a pail of water. Two neighbor boys ran over too. To their shock, they saw a charred human form in the middle of the blaze. The boys ran off and found a policeman.

The top of Feinstein's body was badly burned but not the bottom. Goldstein had splashed gasoline over Feinstein from the waist up, but not the waist down. Feinstein's brown and white saddleback shoes and white socks were as good as new, and they, together with a ring and a scrap of paper in his pocket, helped police identify him.

The next day, Puggy's friends from the night before were still looking for him. They drove by The Corner again and spotted Buggsy Goldstein. They asked Goldstein if he had seen Puggy. "Puggy who?" Goldstein replied.[72]

In 1940, gang member Seymour "Blue Jaw" Magoon testified against his old pals Buggsy Goldstein and Pittsburgh Phil Strauss. He explained how they and Abe Reles had murdered Puggy Feinstein; how they had shoved Puggy's body into a car, driven off to that vacant lot, dumped the body, and then set it on fire; and how Buggsy had leaped back with a shriek when his eyebrows ignited.

Then, after the killing and the burning of the corpse, what did the killers do, the prosecutor asked.

Well, Blue Jaw said, they all decided to go out for a lobster dinner.

What happened at the dinner?

They ordered their meals, Blue Jaw explained. Then Pittsburgh Phil began teasing Buggsy in the mean sort of way Phil had. "We sent you out for a can [of gasoline,] and you take an hour," Phil complained. Blue Jaw said that Buggsy's feelings were hurt, and that Buggsy replied, "You're always picking on me." Reles boasted that he, and not Phil or Buggsy, had really taken care of Puggy. "You didn't know how to strangle the guy," Reles said to the others. "I knocked him out when I jumped on his belly."

"Then what?" the prosecutor asked.

"Then the lobsters came," said Magoon.[73]

Puggy Feinstein would receive a touching obituary. When he learned of Feinstein's fate, attorney Sydney V. Levy wrote this brief letter to journalist Eddie Zeltner, who wrote a column about Brooklyn life for the *New York Daily Mirror*:

> Dear Ed:
>
> I desire to write a few words concerning Puggy Feinstein. Puggy and I played punchball together in the neighborhood. He was a small fellow, and wanted to be a big shot. So, we took different paths. But both paths are so closely entwined that we should understand those who take a path we just miss. He, too, had a fine background.
>
> Last year, Puggy enthusiastically told me how he was going straight [...] The cause of his return to his proper environment was that he was in love with a respectable Flatbush girl.
>
> But after he had bought the furniture and planned the wedding, a neighborhood boy went up to the girl's folks and told them of Puggy's past. This broke up the match and broke his heart.
>
> He reverted to type. And now I read that Puggy was a torch-murder victim.
>
> He was a swell punchball player.[74]

Gangsters killed people for a variety of reasons. Often the killings were purely instrumental; in a lawless world, informers, rivals, and competitors had to be intimidated or killed. In this sense, hoodlums were not much different from, say, the Tudors or the Medicis. As the fictional Michael Corleone (Al Pacino) says, in *The Godfather—Part I*, his father is just another "powerful man."

Sometimes people were murdered as favors by one set of gangsters to another. For example, John Bagdonowitz, in the 1920s, was a minor gangland figure in New Jersey. People called him "the Polack." For some reason, Bagdonowitz decided that he had had enough. He told everyone that he had quit the rackets, and he disappeared into the wilds of Long Island. Then, in 1933, Walter Sage, one of the Brownsville boys, happened to be in Albertson Square, a little town on Long Island's southern shore, and who does he spot but John Bagdonowitz. Sage hurried back to Brownsville. "Remember John the Polack?" he asked the boys. "Well, I bump into him out on the Island. He looks like he's doing all right, but I don't know how he can take it out there. Nothing is doing. I'm glad to be back in civilization."[75] The Brownsville boys helpfully passed the news along to friends in Newark that they'd found John the Polack.

The friends in Newark, as expected, replied that they wanted Bagdonowitz dead. The Brownsville boys said they would take care of it. A gunman named Joe Mercaldo and Vito Gurino, that enormous "oxlike" man, got the job. Julie Catalano drove the car. Abe Reles went along "for the ride." They drove off into Long Island. Walter Sage had given them what he guessed was Bagdonowitz's home address. The car from Brownsville pulled up in front of Bagdonowitz's home. Gurino and Mercaldo walked up to the front door and knocked. Bagdonowitz's wife answered the door. Gurino and Mercaldo said that they were detectives looking for John Bagdonowitz. Bagdonowitz's wife called for John. When John Bagdonowitz came to the door, Gurino and Mercaldo shot him to death and ran back to the car. The car roared off before anyone in the neighborhood knew what had happened.[76] The killers felt no particular hostility toward Bagdonowitz; they were simply doing a favor for their Newark colleagues.

People were killed too because they broke the rules. Walter Sage, the man who had spotted John Bagdonowitz, had been one of the Brownsville boys for years. He was one of the gang's top earners. When Frank Costello began pushing slot machines, the Brownsville boys eagerly helped out, going from bar to bar and store to store, encouraging people to install the slots, threatening to beat them up or kill them if they refused. Walter Sage also ran slot machines way up in the Catskills, and they were a gold mine. Everyone from the city tried to escape New York's brutal summer heat by running up to the Catskill Mountains. Up there were resorts for the rich and cabins for the poor. When people went up to the Catskills, they wanted to have fun, and for many, having fun meant gambling. The slot machines produced mountains of money, and Walter Sage and his longtime friend and ally, Irving "Big Gangy" Cohen, got rich.

Walter and Big Gangy, of course, were supposed to share their wealth with their friends back in Brownsville. However, by the summer of 1937, Abe Reles, Harry Strauss, and the others were suspicious. They had heard that Walter was skimming the profits, pocketing money that he should have sent back to them. Reles and Strauss were furious. Sage would have to go. They decided that Sage's friend, Big Gangy Cohen, would have to kill Sage. Strauss went up to the mountains to supervise.

Up in the Catskills, Strauss tracked down Pretty Levine who happened to be vacationing there. He ordered Levine to get his car. Levine got his car and, in the middle of the night, in front of the Evans Hotel, he waited. Strauss walked over and got in. Another car went past; Levine pulled out and followed it. "A scream [. . .] came from the other car," Burton Turkus would later report. Walter Sage, Gangy Cohen, and an associate named Jack Drucker were in the first car. Sage sat in the front passenger seat. Drucker suddenly leaned forward, jerked his arm across Sage's neck and put him in a headlock—something the gangsters called "mugging"—and then started stabbing Sage with an ice pick. Drucker stabbed Sage some thirty-two times. The first car pulled over onto the shoulder of the road. In the darkness, Sage's body was pulled out of the car and was tumbled into the trunk of Levine's car. Levine and Strauss drove off to a nearby lake. Sage's corpse was lashed to a pinball machine; machine and body were dumped in the lake. Pretty Levine later told the court about his role in Sage's killing. Turkus asked him, "Did you drive a man by the name of Walter Sage up to that town [Lock Sheldrake]?"

A. No, sir. I didn't drive him.
Q. Were you in the car that was being driven with Walter Sage.
A. Alive?
Q. Alive or dead [. . .]
A. Yes.
Q. Was he alive or dead?
A. Dead [. . .]
Q. Was this man Sage killed with an ice pick?
A. I don't know [. . .] a couple of fellows took him out and that's all.[77]

The killers had assumed that a body as punctured as Sage's would sink, especially when lashed to a pinball machine. They were wrong; ten days after the murder, Sage's corpse somehow had wiggled loose from the pinball machine and bobbed to the surface. When Pittsburgh Phil heard about it, he was disgusted. "With this bum, you got be a doctor, or he floats," Phil remarked.[78] Sage's murder, much like Bagdonowitz's, was a practical matter. Sage was skimming from the profits, thereby breaking a fundamental rule of the gangster's "social code," so he had to be punished.

(Gangy Cohen would, after Sage's murder, embark on a remarkable adventure. He caught a train out of the Catskills and headed west. He made it all the way to Los Angeles. Cohen knew people who knew people in Hollywood; he began hanging around film sets and eventually was cast as a minor player. He performed in several films—as a hoodlum and as a police officer! In 1940, a real police officer back in the Catskills was in a theater watching a movie when who should he suddenly see in the film but Gangy Cohen! A warrant was quickly sent to the Los Angeles police; Cohen was arrested and shipped back to New York. In 1944, Cohen and Drucker were tried for Walter Sage's murder. Cohen insisted that Drucker had actually killed Sage and that Drucker and Levine had then tried to kill Cohen—that was why he fled. On May 5, 1944, Cohen was acquitted; Drucker was convicted of second-degree murder and sentenced to twenty-five years to life in Attica.)[79]

If some killings were strictly business, others had a strange, crazy quality to them. Plenty of psychopaths were loose in the underworld, and sometimes violence was the product of some psychological explosion. On August 23, 1939, for example, three members of the Brownsville gang, Happy Maione, Vito Gurino, Frank Abbandando and others decided to hang out at the Parkway Casino, in Ozone Park. When the club closed, a seventeen-year-old dancer climbed into their car, and they all drove off, the girl thought, to party until dawn. Instead, they drove to a nearby parking lot where the men attacked her. They acted wildly like a pack of animals. They took her home and told her to keep quiet or they would "bury her alive." They gave her mother $500 to keep her quiet. Neither the girl nor her mother kept quiet. They went to the police. However, other than the girl herself, the only other witnesses to the crime were the perpetrators, so no arrests were made.[80] The next day, according to later police reports, there was a heated argument on The Corner about just what had happened the night before. Happy Maione called Abbandando "an animal." But, Maione added, it did not really matter because the girl was "a bum." Julie Catalano said to Vito "Socko"/"Chickenhead" Gurino, "[W]hat's the matter with you? Aren't you married?" Gurino replied, "Don't you know how it is when Happy is in the party? It's why I like to go any place where he is at."[81] In the neighborhood, Gurino himself was rumored to be a rapist.[82]

Violence equaled power equaled masculinity, and performing "masculinity" played a key role in all the violence too, something Hollywood eagerly incorporated into the gangster film. In the gangster movies, as

David Ruth points out, "destructive impulses in need of repression had become defining badges of virility."[83] Fred Gardaphé argues that issues of masculinity were central to the lives of young Italian American men both on the street and in the gangster films, and violence and power were crucial to definitions of masculinity. In Italy, Gardaphé writes,

> the world outside the home was considered a manly domain, while the domestic front was controlled by women. In American cities during the early part of the twentieth century, different ethnic groups controlled different neighborhoods. Movement could be dangerous when crossing the street meant entering a neighborhood patrolled by a hostile group. Consequently, Little Italies across the country became stages for the public display of manhood as Italian-American men protected their home turf from invasion, and these neighborhoods were breeding grounds for street gangs.[84]

Something very like this also operated in largely Jewish, immigrant, struggling, working-class neighborhoods like Brownsville. Manhood, power, violence, and dominance were all fatally linked.

For example, in 1933 a nineteen-year-old thief named Alex "Red" Alpert offered to sell Harry Strauss some stolen jewelry. "I've got some nice stuff here," Alpert said. "[G]imme three G's for it. It's worth a lot more."

Pittsburgh Phil responded, "I'll give you seven hundred." Phil was one of the leaders of the gang; Alpert was just a petty thief. Alpert angrily replied: "You know what you can do for seven hundred [...] you can go to hell."

Phil was outraged, insulted, and furious at Alpert's public display of disrespect. He demanded that Alpert be killed.

Killing Alpert would be a trick. Alpert was aggressive and cunning; he would be on the lookout for Phil. So Phil told Pretty Levine to kill Alpert, but Levine bungled the job. Furious, Phil demanded that Abe Reles and Buggsy Goldstein take care of Alpert. Reles and Goldstein tried to talk to Alpert, but Alpert was a hardhead. So they killed him.[85]

Killings could be strictly business, or crazy, or some sort of affirmation of manhood and dominance. Sometimes killers killed because they were frightened of being killed. Reles's ally Sholom Bernstein, for example, drove the car in Joe Rosen's murder. Later, during a trial, Bernstein was asked,

Q. Did you ever have any reason [...] to kill Rosen?
A. Never knew his name until I saw the papers the next day.
Q. Your [...] reason for participating?
A. Fear of being killed.

Bernstein continued: "[Once] they [the Reles gang] killed a friend of mine,"
and I happened to go and look for him and they all got around
me and they just said they just killed my friend and you better go
home and keep your mouth shut. In other words, meaning that I
would be killed.

Did he go home and keep his mouth shut? he was asked. Was he really
that afraid? Bernstein replied, "[T]hat's right, all the time. One day, I took
home another friend of mine and the next day he was killed. Always in
fear of them."[86]

Killers killed for instrumental reasons, because they were crazy, because
they linked power with masculinity with violence with respect to posses-
sions. Whatever their reason, how are people to think about this great evil?

We could, of course, ignore the killers' choices, agency, and responsibility, in other words, their moral "wickedness," and focus instead on the
impersonal push and pull of psychology and sociology. However, as Mary
Midgley points out, when we reduce evil to some sort of psychological
and sociological mechanics and ignore matters of agency and responsibility, "public wickedness vanishes into a social problem." When we refuse
to name and examine actors and their public wickedness, that is, when
we fail to discuss wickedness in terms of agency and responsibility, we risk
losing the power of "self-direction" and "moral judgment."[87] So, according to Midgley, we must consider agency and responsibility when we reflect on evil. Judith Butler agrees: "those who commit acts of violence are
surely responsible for them; they are not dupes or mechanisms or an impersonal social force, but agents with responsibility." Yet, Butler continues,
"on the other hand, these individuals are formed," that is, conditioned by
their world, and "to take the self-generated acts of the individual as our
point of departure in moral reasoning is precisely to foreclose the possibility of questioning what kind of world gives rise to such individuals."[88]
There is, after all, a "situational theory of evil," according to which "ordinary people," placed in extreme conditions, can engage in utterly dreadful
actions and then, when returned to normal circumstances, can return to
something like normal life.[89] So, following Midgley and Butler, we ought
to think about both agency and the agents' moral worlds.

In doing so, we might consider radical evil, stupid evil, and grotesque evil.

Writing about Nazi evil in World War II, Hannah Arendt, in *Totalitarianism*, evoked Immanuel Kant's concept of "radical evil." Morality, Kant
insisted, is tied to reason. Rationality means clarity and morality. When
we are irrational, we become immoral. Some forms of immorality are

not totally devoid of rationality, and therefore, we can comprehend them. However, some forms of immorality are so divorced from rationality that they become literally unspeakable. This sort of unspeakable evil is what Kant thought of as "radical evil." Slavoj Žižek has this in mind when he writes about the "inherently mystifying" confrontation with violence; a mark of authentic testimony about the encounter with violence and evil is its inarticulate quality. A concentration camp witness, for example, "able to offer a clear narrative of his camp experience would," Žižek continues, "disqualify himself by virtue of that clarity."[90] Arendt's notion of radical evil, however, goes beyond Kant. Radical evil, Arendt argues, is not just nonhuman, it is profoundly antihuman; its aim is ultimately the destruction of humanity as such. Radical evil is an antiworld, an underworld, pure negation.[91]

Unspeakable evil is committed by actors who are utterly outside the human realm of reason and discourse. The agents of radical evil are irrational, monstrous, subhuman; they are moral monsters who inhabit a nonhuman "underworld." Tony Camonte in *Scarface* approaches this sort of monster; as the film progresses, he becomes increasingly uncanny, unhinged, simian, violent, and crazy. His brutal "gutter ending" seems well deserved.[92]

Throughout the 1930s and 1940s, journalists, politicians, and law officers experienced Murder, Inc., in particular and gangsters in general as radically evil.

In the mid-1930s, as the antigangster crusade began, President Herbert Hoover, FBI Director J. Edgar Hoover, Mayor La Guardia, Police Commissioner Valentine, Prosecutor Dewey, all vowed to destroy the mobsters. US Attorney General Homer Cummings warned the Daughters of the American Revolution that "we are now engaged in a war that threatens the safety of our country, a war with the organized forces of crime."[93] Criminals were "types,"[94] not persons; they were feral, antisocial, beyond redemption, bad from birth, and profoundly evil, and they had to be mercilessly destroyed. Dewey's citation from the hysterical crime magazine that described Luciano as a "deadly King Cobra" and "a Dracula" is not untypical.[95] Burton Turkus's memoir unfailingly describes the gangsters he knew as "moral imbeciles," "gorillas," and "brutes."[96] According to Turkus, "about the best you could say for Reles was that he was an animal in human guise."[97] Mendy Weiss, Lepke Buchalter's lieutenant, was, Turkus recalled, "a hulking monster."[98] The others were just as bad. Sending these subhumans off to be electrocuted was, for Prosecutor Turkus, a public duty he happily fulfilled; writing of the defendants, he calls them "the seven killers I had the pleasure of putting in the electric chair."[99] In his 1947 memoir, Police Commissioner Valentine wrote, "I can only lift my voice in praise of men like Mayor O'Dwyer, Governor Dewey, Mayor La Guardia, and our policemen, for blasting out of existence the Lepkes, Gurrahs, and Releses."[100]

Not only were individual gangsters inherently evil, they represented, collectively, a shockingly evil force in American life. Tom Dewey heightens the drama of his prosecutorial task by describing how his small staff of twenty lawyers battled a vast, evil, criminal conspiracy. Remembering the first days of his 1935 investigation, Dewey writes,

> We were twenty lawyers and we now knew something of the monstrous nature of our job. We were coming to realize that nobody really believed in us. The press said it did. Public figures said they did. The citizens said they believed in us [...] The hard fact, was, however, that our principal enemies, cynicism and fear, seemed overpowering. The victims of organized crime did not believe that anything could be done.

Democracy itself was at stake. Crime undermined the very foundations of democracy, but many thought, Dewey wrote, that "nothing would break the hold of the underworld except a dictatorship." The only force defending democracy from crime and dictatorship was Dewey's lonely band of lawyers.[101]

Maybe there were times when even the killers recognized the shocking quality of their actions. In 1935, Happy Maione learned that a bookmaker was having trouble with a hoodlum named John "Spider" Murtha. Maione did not like Murtha anyway and, according to Turkus's notes, "wished to do the [bookmaker] an unsolicited favor."[102] Maione, Frank Abbandando, and Max "the Jerk" Golub followed Murtha to the Palace Hotel in Brooklyn where Murtha was staying with Marie "Flo" Nestfield. On March 3, 1935, around 10:45 a.m., Murtha and Nestfield stepped out of the hotel and began walking along Atlantic Avenue.[103] Two men hurried up behind them, told Nestfield to step aside, shot Murtha eight times, and then fled.[104] The investigation of Murtha's shooting went nowhere. One material witness, Joseph Ciancemino, who ran the Parkside Restaurant on Rockaway Boulevard in Ozone Park, which was described in a police report as "a rendezvous of such men as Frank Abbandando, Harry Maione and others of the same ilk [...] men engaged in the business of murder," refused to talk. Ciancemino not only refused, he was "contumacious, obstructive, conceals facts, [and] furnishes false and perjured testimony."[105]

Marie Nestfield told the police that she saw nothing, recognized nobody, had no idea why Murtha had been killed.[106] One bystander, Minnie Jones, however, later told police that one of the gunmen, she identified him as Harry Maione, stood frozen for a second, "his whole body was shaking, but still holding the smoking gun, and his face had a look of complete terror on it, as if he was scared to death of what he had done."[107]

There is radical evil, but there is also stupid evil.

In the 1950s, Hannah Arendt wrote of the radicality of evil, but in 1961, Arendt began writing of the "banality of evil." In her controversial reporting on the 1961 Adolf Eichmann trial, Arendt was struck by just how banal, how stupid, and how totally mindless Eichmann seemed to be. Eichmann, to Arendt, did not appear to be Satan; to the contrary, Eichmann seemed to be a petty bureaucrat, who, obsessed with routine and his head filled with clichés, had not had an original thought in his life. Arendt may well have been wrong about Eichmann, as her many critics have argued— Eichmann was probably much more consciously malevolent and less stupid than Arendt thought[108]—but her analysis of what Lars Svendsen calls "stupid evil"[109] remains compelling.

Stupid evil is mindless, boring, thoughtless, tedious, and routine. In a brutal world, brutality becomes numbingly normal. When he thought about Brownsville in the 1920s and 1930s, when he compared Brownsville, say, to Manhattan's Lower East Side, what struck Sammy Aaronson, was that "Brownsville was tougher. More guys carried guns and instead of six beatings a day there were six an hour."[110] In Brownsville, murderous guys like Murder, Inc., were "normal." Reles had this sort of bored normality in mind in the following exchange with prosecutor Turkus:

> [Assistant District Attorney Burton Turkus to Abe Reles]: "Did your conscience ever bother you? [. . .] Didn't you feel anything?"
> [Reles to Turkus:] "How did you feel when you tried your first law case?"
> "I was rather nervous," I admitted.
> "And how about your second case?"
> "It wasn't so bad, but I was still a little nervous."
> "And after that?"
> "Oh [. . .] after that, I was all right; I was used to it."
> "You answered your own question [. . .] It's the same with murder. I got used to it."[111]

These murderous guys also seem, in retrospect, remarkably stupid. In 1939, for instance, Louis Capone and some of his hoodlum friends tried to shake down the local Hod Carriers and Builders Union. Capone wanted to increase the percentage of union dues he stole. However, he ran into some genuine trade unionists who were not afraid of him and who refused to pay him off. Capone wanted these union opponents dead. He demanded that two union members, Cesare Lattaro and Antonio Siciliano, kill Capone's opponents. Lattaro and Siciliano refused; Capone decided to have the two of them killed instead.

Capone spoke with Happy Maione; Maione organized the double murder. Around 1:30 a.m., on the dark morning of February 6, 1939, Julie Catalano was fast asleep with his wife in their apartment on East New York Avenue. A scratching and tapping on his window woke him up. The Dasher and Happy Maione waved Catalano to his front door. He opened the door; they told him to get up, get dressed, and go snatch a car. They had a "piece of work" to do. Catalano would later explain that "when he [Maione] says 'piece of work,' he means we go to kill somebody." Catalano complained: "Jesus," he said, "another one?" Maione angrily replied, "What the hell, must I always explain to you when I need you?"[112] Catalano hurriedly pulled his clothes on, ran out, found a car, and drove to meet Vito Gurino, Maione, and Abbandando. When he drove up to the meeting spot, he spotted Gurino and the Dasher—but at the Dasher's side was some woman. Gurino, Abbandando, and the woman got in Catalano's car. To his shock, Catalano discovered that the woman was Happy Maione, dressed in skirt and hat. He said to Maione, "[Y]ou look like a real broad! You got the face of one. Not bad."[113] Later, Catalano was asked, "Did [Maione] have a women's hat?" Yes, Catalano answered, "with a feather."[114]

Catalano drove Gurino, Abbandando and Maione to the basement apartment Lattaro and Siciliano shared. It was dark, well past midnight. Gurino got out of the car to stand watch. According to Catalano: "Abbie [Abbandando] had Happy under the arm like you hold a girl and he tapped at the door and the guy opened the door. He said 'who is it?' He said, 'Frank.' He knew Frank."[115] Lattaro and Siciliano opened their door and looked at the man and woman. Abbandando and Maione immediately opened fire. They fired six or seven shots. Abbandando and Gurino jumped back into the car. Meanwhile, Maione was attacked by Lattaro and Siciliano's dog; he shot the dog and ran out to the car and jumped in. The killers roared off into the chilly Brooklyn night, Maione, in drag, clutching his smoking gun and feathered hat.[116]

The members of Murder, Inc., were not Napoleons of crime.

Radical evil, of course, applies to the killers of Murder, Inc., and so, too, does stupid evil. Perhaps the odd mix of the two triggered both the gasps and the guffaws in the courtroom when Abe Reles and the others told their stories.

There is radical evil; there is stupid evil; there is also grotesque evil.

The notion that evil can, in some way, be grotesque and even, in an odd way, comic is very old. During the European Middle Ages, for instance, theatrical villains were presented as distortions and caricatures. Villains had humped backs, warty noses, and clawlike fingernails. Scary though they might be, they were also, as caricatures, comic; medieval audiences could cope with evil by mocking it. Shakespeare critic Charles Norton Coe writes that "Elizabethan audiences sometimes regarded villains as stock comic characters,"[117] and Charlotte Spivack is struck by the "union between comedy and iniquity" in Shakespeare.[118] Spivack explains that the metaphysical roots of Shakespeare's understanding of evil go back to antiquity. If, as the Greeks liked to do, we try to think about "reality," or, say, "being," we might eventually agree with Parmenides that "being" "is." Talking about "nothing" as if "nothing" were actually "something" is nonsensical. Therefore, there is only "being" in multiple shades and gradations. If we call the fullness of being "good," then what we call "evil" is not so much another, alien, other reality, but rather, it is a distortion, a diminution, a limitation of being. As diminished and distorted being, evil hovers on the brink of the "unreal." Spivack notes that Shakespeare certainly thought in terms of what Arthur Lovejoy famously called the "Great Chain of Being." From God, that is, the Supreme Being who is the very fullness of being, down through endless gradations of lesser beings, humans occupy an odd place. More fully being than other creatures, humans are less fully being than God. An individual person, for instance, does not "be" for millennia, then out of nowhere, suddenly "be's" for a few decades, and then, just as suddenly, ceases to be for the rest of eternity. According to Lovejoy, the human person is

> a strange hybrid monster; and if this gives him a certain pathetic sublimity, it also results in incongruities of feeling, inconsistencies of behavior, and disparities between his aspirations and his powers which render him ridiculous.[119]

C. S. Lewis, Spivack adds, endorses Lovejoy's argument that there is something inherently odd, even ridiculous about humanity.[120] Even good humans are odd; evil humans are even odder.

Evil, as Spivack writes, exists "existentially but not essentially."[121] Existentially, evil certainly has weight and power, even odor; we sense its doleful presence. Essentially, though, evil is not an alien reality but a diminished and distorted form of the one reality, the one being, which we all share. Evil is powerful and dangerous, but there is also something odd, weird, vaguely unreal, and grotesque about it too. Evil triggers fear, but evil can also trigger a kind of amazed and derisory laughter.

The movies very early on identified this caricature, grotesque quality in gangsters. They are recognizably human beings like us, but strange and twisted. In the movies, gangsters were instantly recognizable. They lounged on street corners and flipped coins, like the gangsters portrayed by George Raft. They talked funny; they mumbled; they distorted their faces and spoke out of one side of their mouths. They ended sentences with "see?" the way gangsters portrayed by Edward G. Robinson did or punctuated their sentences with clipped phrases like "What do you hear?" or "What do you say?" the way James Cagney's gangsters did.[122] They dressed garishly; they were parodies of proper businessmen. Gangsters wore black shirts and white ties and silk suits with shoulders much too big, like the loveable thugs in *Guys and Dolls*. During the New Deal, a subgenre of gangster films flourished, the "gangster comedy." In films like *Little Miss Marker, The Lemon Drop Kid,* and *Little Miss Glory*, gangsters were recognizably gangsters, but they acted like clowns and had hearts of gold.[123]

At times, the Murder, Inc., gangsters appeared almost comic. Their bigshot strutting on their frowsy Brooklyn street corner, their tawdry headquarters at Midnight Rose's, and their bizarrely clumsy crimes, all made them seem like denizens of Damon Runyon stories. The peripheral figures around the Brownsville gang were bizarre and grotesque, like "Tiny" Benson, the enormous bouncer and loan shark, and "Oscar the Poet." Oscar "the Poet" Friedman liked to wander around Brownsville reciting poetry; Wordsworth and Kipling were his favorites. Oscar had a special, secret talent. In a jiffy, he could dismantle hot cars and hide their parts. If a murder car was not left with its corpse on a street corner, it was driven to a garage where Oscar the Poet, chattering "Tinturn Abbey" or "Gunga Din" to himself, would take it apart.[124] In the courtroom, all the defendants spoke in heavy Brooklyn accents and with fractured grammar; their street jargon typically had to be translated; juries were amazed by their bizarre murders, for example, the case of John "Mummy" Friscia. Just why Friscia was killed is a bit obscure; he'd just murdered his former partner, Joe Kennedy, so maybe his killing was his punishment for killing Kennedy. In any case, Mummy Friscia was taken for a ride. He was holding the strap just above the car window when he was shot. When the killers—Maione, Reles, and Strauss—tried to dump the body, they could not get the strap out of the dead man's hand. In a panic, they hacked the strap loose from the car and pushed the body, still clinging to the strap, onto the street. According to Turkus's records, "[b]y a cadaver spasm, or 'dead man's clutch,' the side-strap remained in his hand when his body was dumped from the death car, at Williams Place and Herkimer Street, Brooklyn." The telltale strap helped the police trace the murder car.[125] There were other gruesomely comic moments, like Reles and Strauss arguing about how to spell *friend* or Strauss pleading for mercurochrome after murdering Puggy Feinstein because Puggy had bitten him; or like Buggsy Goldstein leaping backward in terror after singeing his eyebrows when he tried to incinerate Puggy; or like the gang arguing about the finer points of Puggy's murder over lobster dinner. As radically evil as Murder, Inc., was, it was also both remarkably stupid and utterly grotesque.

In January 1940, Harry Rudolph was doing a little time on Rikers Island. Harry was not a particularly bad guy. The police knew him as "Rudy" and laughed that "he's off his rocker"; they called him a "full mooner," a lunatic. That January, Harry Rudolph was angry. Years before, his old friend, Red Alpert, had been murdered because he had insulted Pittsburgh Phil Strauss. Rudolph had been an eyewitness to the murder. Out on the street, Rudolph had never made an issue of it, but now, in prison, Rudolph saw a way both to curry favor with the law and to get revenge on Alpert's killers.

On a piece of stationery from the City Workhouse on Rikers Island, Rudolph scribbled a note to the Brooklyn district attorney:

> Dear Sir:
>   I am doing a bit here. I would like to talk to the District Attorney. I know something about a murder in East New York.[126]

Brooklyn's district attorney, William O'Dwyer and his assistant for homicide, Burton Turkus, wondered what Rudolph had to say.

7

A Theater of Ethics
Mr. Arsenic and the Murder, Inc., Trials

> I know something about a murder in East
> New York.
>
> —*Harry Rudolph*[1]

The Murder, Inc., trials were a spectacle, a circus, a tragedy, and a soap opera; they were a tabloid aphrodisiac. They began in the spring of 1940 and ran until the late fall of 1941, and at times, the Murder, Inc., trials got bigger headlines than the war raging around the world. There were five major trials and any number of smaller legal actions. Seven defendants, including key figures in the Brownsville gang, were convicted, sentenced to death, and executed. And then, in November 1941, the Murder, Inc., investigations screeched to a sudden and shocking conclusion. The theatricality of the trials struck everyone, and this theatricality was not incidental to but actually central to the trials' moral meanings. If legally the trials were about the prosecution of crimes, morally the trials were about ritually purging the accused from New York City's moral space. The trials were a kind of deep play, a dramatic ritual, a theater of exorcism, culminating, after an elaborate ceremony, in the killing of the killers. This chapter considers each of the Murder, Inc., trials in turn and concludes with an investigation into the relationship between theatricality and morality and between drama and conscience.

In 1940, Bill O'Dwyer was Brooklyn's district attorney, and he was an ambitious man. Just a few months short of fifty, O'Dwyer had lived the New York immigrant's dream. Born in Ireland, he had studied for the priesthood but, at twenty, had left the seminary and headed for New York. Affable, smart, and ambitious, O'Dwyer began as a common laborer but then worked his way onto the police department. From the police department,

O'Dwyer had gone to Fordham University's law school; from law school he went into politics. Bill O'Dwyer was a Tammany Democrat, and as a reward for his loyal service, Tammany helped get him elected judge. In the 1930s, Brooklyn was as plagued by crime and corruption as Manhattan; eventually Governor Herbert Lehman appointed a special prosecutor for Brooklyn, just as he had appointed Tom Dewey to investigate Manhattan. John Harlan Amen, Brooklyn's special prosecutor, found in Brooklyn's judicial system what Dewey had found in Manhattan's—incompetence, corruption, and crime.[2] Brooklynites bitterly complained about the performance of their district attorney, William F. X. Geoghan, and in 1939, Judge O'Dwyer ran against Geoghan for Kings County district attorney and won. During the campaign, O'Dwyer vowed to purge the district attorney's office of political hacks and to crack down on the gangs.[3]

Many Brooklynites hated the gangs. In October 1935, "Dan S." wrote to the police, complaining about gangsters:

> Dear Sir, please take notice that you will stop a new gang war for revenge if you will pick up (Dopey) Red Levine and his partner Pretty Amberg. Red Levine if he is sweated will tell you who committed the last few murders in Brooklyn and New York. You can always find him any night in Ratner's Restaurant on Delancey Street. Dopey Levine is right now the king pin of the mob who are causing plenty of damage in this town and it is high time he was put away where he belongs so that people will be able to breathe easier. I understand he was instrumental in the disappearance of Bo Weinberg in a fight on the numbers racket.[4]

On February 9, 1940, an anonymous writer wrote this furious letter to the new Brooklyn district attorney about the guys who hung out on The Corner:

> these bums none of them work, they own beautiful homes and cars. They do all the plotting and the boys are got to steal then they go and gamble down to Mike "Gooty" R.'s basement [. . .] and if the boys lose anything they lend them money and they charge high interest if they can't pay they have places for them to steal so they can pay the loan [. . .] Mike R. knows who they are but collects $3 a day and don't care. The place is usually full of boys especially on Sunday. Policeman [sic] come and go but they don't care. Specially one tall cop that is dark, husky built, looks Italian and is Jewish [. . .] he tips them off when to break the gambling. The cops work with the

crooks because Sunday the place was packed. Harry Maione, Frankie Abbandando, and Angelo Catalano are responsible for robbing of the machines of the vocational school and all the robberies around the neighborhood [. . .] Frank Abbandando lives very comfortable and very nicely on no work. Vito Gurino never works, likewise with Maione and Catalano and Reles they plan everything [. . .] Frankie R. [. . .] helps sell tickets of lottery and stolen stuff is very friendly and member of them [. . .] Please honorable Mayor and Magistrate get rid of these leaders to bring piece [*sic*] to the stores and boys of East New York.[5]

Another anonymous letter denounced Frank Abbandando, called on the district attorney to take action against the Brownsville gang, and ended, "I desire to see justice meted out."[6]

Bill O'Dwyer wanted to be New York's mayor, and he had seen what being a gangbusting district attorney had done for Tom Dewey's career. From the moment he took office, on January 1, 1940, O'Dwyer was determined to go after Brooklyn's mobsters.

One of the first people O'Dwyer appointed to his staff was Burton Turkus. Burt Turkus was thirty-eight in 1940. He was a native Brooklynite, born in Prospect Park. He was the son of Jewish immigrants—his father was a watchmaker and his mother a seamstress—and he attended Brooklyn's Manual Training High School. After high school, Turkus worked nights as a Western Union operator and attended New York University (NYU) by day. After earning his law degree from NYU, Turkus began practicing law in Brooklyn in 1925. He was a criminal defense attorney in the office of Meier Steinbrink. Steinbrink took a liking to young Turkus. In 1925, he wrote a letter to a White House staffer he knew, Bascom Slemp, describing Turkus as "a young lawyer associated with my office," and explained that Turkus "is in Washington on his first visit [. . .] he would appreciate the opportunity of meeting the President."[7] Turkus quickly made quite a name for himself; years later, people would remember that the young Turkus "dazzled judges and juries alike."[8] A 1933 profile of Turkus, in *The Brooklyner,* noted that he was "one of the town's better attorneys," and "a pretty good boxer" too![9] Turkus was active in the Temple B'nai Sholaum Congregation and a wide variety of other civic and charitable groups.[10] Always perfectly groomed and, like Tom Dewey, sporting a neatly trimmed regimental mustache, Turkus looked like a young David Niven, the Hollywood actor.[11] Still single at the time of the Murder, Inc., investigations (he married at forty-five), Turkus

District Attorney William O'Dwyer (*left*) and Assistant District Attorney Burton
Turkus (*right*), in 1946. (*Brooklyn Eagle*, Brooklyn Public Library)

was, for years, one of Brooklyn's handsomest and most eligible bachelors.
When William O'Dwyer was elected Brooklyn (Kings County) district
attorney in November 1939, he asked Turkus to become an assistant district attorney. Politically independent, Turkus leaned toward the La Guardia Fusion liberal Republicans.[12] On January 1, 1940, Turkus became
assistant Brooklyn district attorney, in charge of the homicide division.[13]
Only days after taking office, O'Dwyer and Turkus received that odd letter from Harry Rudolph, the prisoner on Rikers Island.

O'Dwyer and Turkus interviewed Rudolph. Rudolph angrily told them
that "those rats" (meaning the Brownsville gang) "killed my friend Red
Alpert [. . .] and I saw them do it."[14] According to Turkus's records, Alex
"Red" Alpert was, at the time of his murder, nineteen years old and a
"small-time hood"; he was shot to death on November 25, 1933. His
murder was unsolved; there were no witnesses—no witnesses, that is, until
1940, when Harry Rudolph contacted the Brooklyn district attorney.

"I'll tell you who did it, too," Rudolph continued. "Those Brownsville guys—Reles and Buggsy and Dukey Maffetore [...] I saw Kid Twist and Buggsy and Dukey kill my pal."[15]

Turkus was immediately interested. New York State law was written to protect the defendant; the only way to convict an accused murderer was to get a confession or to get eyewitness testimony from someone who was not an accomplice. Testimony from accomplices was almost always ruled out of order as tainted; an accomplice who testified against a fellow defendant might simply be trying escape guilt by blaming someone else. So accomplice testimony was of little use. The only testimony that mattered, then, was that of eyewitnesses who were not accomplices. But finding such eyewitnesses was very hard. Killings happened quickly, often in the dark of night; eyewitnesses, if there were any, were often afraid to testify, and often they disappeared too. Getting homicide convictions was very difficult. No wonder that when Turkus became Brooklyn's assistant district attorney, something like two hundred unsolved murders were still on the books in Brooklyn.[16]

But here was an eyewitness, not an accomplice, who swore that he had seen Abe Reles, Buggsy Goldstein, and Dukey Maffetore murder Red Alpert.

On February 2, 1940, Turkus ordered the arrest of Maffetore.

When police lieutenant John "Big John" Osnato heard that Harry Rudolph had put the finger on Dukey Maffetore, he was immediately intrigued. As of 1940, Osnato had been a police officer for thirty years. As a *New York Times* profile of Big John later reported, Osnato, as a young cop

> went through the usual cop routine—settled tenement house rows, pacified truculent drunks, shot mad dogs, tried store doors at night, harried waterfront bootleggers and listened wearily to foreign sailors who were rolled by doxies.

In the 1920s, Osnato worked in Brooklyn, "when mobsters were dumping competitors' corpses in Brooklyn lots and detectives were weary with trying to keep bootlegging to a decent minimum." In 1925, Osnato and other officers broke up a brawl at "a shoddy night club on 20th Street, near the Gowanus Canal"; one of the brawlers arrested and later released was "a heavy-set young visitor from Chicago" named Al Capone.

As a detective, Osnato knew everyone in the Brooklyn underworld and cultivated a sprawling network of informers. One of his many informers was Harry Rudolph. Rudolph was "a stool pigeon and something of a Fagin." Once, Osnato angrily warned Rudolph that if he tried to sell Osnato any more phony information, he would find himself in a lot of trouble. To wiggle himself back into Osnato's good graces, Rudolph concocted a crackpot scheme. First, in the middle of a dark and freezing night, he broke into a store's loft and stole bundles of clothes. Then, he hired three teenage boys to load the stolen clothes into a truck and drive the truck to a garage on the corner of Broadway and Lorimer Street in Brooklyn. When the boys were on the way to the garage, Rudolph hurriedly called Osnato and told him he had a hot tip about some stolen goods! Osnato and his partners caught the boys; when they described the man who had put them up to the job, Osnato knew it was Harry Rudolph.

Osnato contacted District Attorney O'Dwyer and, with O'Dwyer's permission, went to see Dukey Maffetore in his jail cell. Maffetore grimly told Osnato that he was not talking to the cops. Osnato responded, "I know the mugg that turned you in. I know you had nothing to do with the Red Alpert job. I want to get you out of this mess." Osnato knew all Maffetore's friends in the Reles gang. Reles and the others, "they get all the gravy," Osnato said to Maffetore, while little guys like Maffetore take all the heat. Osnato left, and returned a few days later with Maffetore's favorite cigarettes, Pall Malls. A few days later, Osnato arranged for Maffetore's wife to visit him. All the while, Osnato reminded Maffetore that he, and he alone, would be charged with Red Alpert's murder, and if, and when, he were found guilty, he would go to the chair.[17]

Dukey Maffetore, Turkus would later write, was twenty-five, "a sleek young man who read comic books while the rest plotted murder."[18] He was a batboy, an errand runner who started hanging out on The Corner when he was twenty. Pittsburgh Phil gave him some money to set him up in loan-sharking. One of Maffetore's specialties was car theft; whenever anything serious was happening, Reles or Strauss would send him out to steal a car. He was the wheelman in a variety of crimes, but he had never been convicted of anything. But now, he was facing the electric chair for, ironically, a murder he had not committed. Osnato, O'Dwyer, and Turkus told Maffetore all about Harry Rudolph's continuing accusations. Rudolph said that he had been approached by a bail bondsman and that the bail bondsman had said that "it's worth five grand to me if I change my story and square Reles and Buggsy and put them on the street and let Maffetore take the rap."[19] The Brownsville gang was trying to set Maffetore up to take the fall. After talking to his wife, Detective Osnato, District Attorney O'Dwyer, and Assistant District Attorney Turkus, and after pacing in his cell and wringing his hands, Maffetore agreed to talk. He knew who really killed Red Alpert. It was Buggsy Goldstein and Abe Reles. O'Dwyer ordered the arrest of Goldstein and Reles.[20] Maffetore told O'Dwyer and Turkus that his partner, Abraham "Pretty" Levine knew all about the Alpert murder too. Levine was arrested and almost immediately agreed to talk.

Levine knew all about the 1933 murder of Red Alpert. He told Turkus about Alpert's argument with Harry Strauss over the stolen jewelry. He explained how furious Strauss had become, about how Strauss had told Levine to kill Alpert and how Levine had bungled the job. He explained how Strauss had then told Walter Sage, Alpert's friend, to kill Alpert. "I saw Walter Sage with Buggsy and Pep and Reles," Levine told Turkus. "Then Buggsy comes over to me and Dukey. He says, 'Youse two better go sleep together some place tonight. Something is gonna happen.' I had a room over on Williams Avenue then. Dukey and me stay there that night. The next day, I read in the paper where something happens. Red Alpert got hit."[21]

Once they started talking, Maffetore and Pretty Levine could not stop. Levine told Turkus about Walter Sage's 1937 murder. The two told Turkus all sorts of gangland gossip. But Rudolph remained the key. His eyewitness testimony might be just enough to send Abe Reles to the chair. "And then," Turkus writes, "Mrs. Kid Twist Reles walked into the district attorney's office. "'My husband,' she announced, 'wants an interview with the Law.'"[22]

New York police had arrested Abe Reles on January 19, 1940, on a vagrancy charge, the all-purpose charge police used to harass hoodlums. Reles had been arrested for vagrancy many times; this time, he quickly appeared before the magistrate and paid his $1,000 fine, "as if," Burton Turkus writes, "he were buying a pack of cigarettes." On January 25, 1940, after Harry Rudolph had spoken with Turkus and after Turkus had sent the police after Reles, Reles turned himself in. Reles was sent to the Tombs. Happy Maione, also picked up on a vagrancy charge, was already there. Reles said he wanted to speak to a detective he knew, John J. McDonough, whom the *Times* later called "a square shooting detective." Reles said, "[A]ll right. I'll talk. Get John McDonough at Miller Avenue Station. He is one of the few cops I ever knew to be honest."[23] On March 21, after meeting with his lawyers, Reles sent a note to his wife, Rose, "a medium blonde," the *Brooklyn Eagle* reported,[24] and asked her to contact District Attorney O'Dwyer.[25]

Turkus had Reles brought to the district attorney's office. Reles was, Turkus concluded, "a moral imbecile,"[26] "an animal in human guise";[27] "there was something in Reles' physical bearing, and a look in his eye, that actually made the hair on the back of your neck stand up."[28]

Frank Abbandando joined Harry Maione in jail. Neither had anything to say. Part of an interrogation of Maione went like this:

Q. Harry Maione [. . .] are you working?
A. I have a tailor business.
Q. How's business.
A. I make a living.[29]

Reles, however, wanted to talk. "He was definitely not a cornered criminal," Turkus remembered; "his whole attitude was the insolent assassin."[30] On March 22, 1940, Reles met with District Attorney O'Dwyer. Burton Turkus remembered that the day had a red box around it on the calendar; it was "Good Friday." Reles agreed to sing. O'Dwyer agreed to treat him as a prosecution witness in protective custody, not a criminal defendant. Everything, of course, was tentative; everything depended on just how cooperative Reles turned out to be and just what sort of evidence emerged about what sort of crime. But the March 22 deal was enough to get the investigation started.

By Turkus's reckoning, Reles, from June 11, 1930, when he was first charged with murder, until February 1940, when he turned himself in, had been arrested on average "once every seventy-eight days."[31] He had been in prison six times for short periods; although he was frequently arrested, he was rarely convicted. He had committed at least eleven murders; Turkus was sure that he was involved in at least fourteen others.[32]

For days and then weeks, Reles regaled O'Dwyer, Turkus, and their assistants with gangland gossip and eyewitness accounts of murders. He agreed to tell his stories under oath, in the courtroom, as a prosecution witness. The "major mystery,"[33] as Turkus put it, was why Reles agreed to turn state's evidence. He certainly hadn't changed his ways or his attitude. In the spring of 1940, he had a wife, a child, and another child on the way, but he did not seem particularly concerned with their fates.

His most obvious motivation was survival. If he had learned one lesson on the street, it was how to survive, even if his survival meant the betrayal of everyone else. He had worked for Meyer Shapiro and then killed Meyer Shapiro and Shapiro's two brothers. He had worked with Walter Sage and had Walter Sage killed. He had known Whitey Rudnick for years, the tall, skinny drug addict, and had watched while Rudnick was murdered. Now he was cornered; Harry Rudolph's testimony about his role in Red Alpert's killing could send Reles to the electric chair. Betrayal was the price of his survival, so, of course, he betrayed. "I am not a stoolpigeon," Reles angrily told Turkus. "Everyone one of those guys wanted to talk. Only I beat them to the bandwagon. They would be hanging me right now, if they had the chance."[34]

In talking to Turkus, District Attorney O'Dwyer, and their staff, and later, in testifying in trial after trial, Abe Reles found an even more compelling motive for his actions. By talking, Reles became the center of attention. "Reles' song was a full-length opera,"[35] Turkus wrote. Turkus was constantly amazed at the delight Reles seemed to take in talking. "He was an excellent raconteur, if you like your killings right from the feed bag,"[36] Turkus remarked, and again: Reles was "an extrovert with an outsized ego, he derived much pleasure from the horror he stirred up with tales of the terrible deeds of himself and his buddies."[37]

Word quickly leaked that Abe Reles, the "dapper little Brownsville gangster," had turned state's evidence. The *Brooklyn Eagle* announced that he would "blow the lid off" the murder case.[38] A wave of panic swept through the underworld as O'Dwyer said that he had other gangsters in his sights, including Joe Adonis, Albert Anastasia, and Lepke Buchalter.[39]

Turkus's investigation roared along like gangbusters, much like Thomas Dewey's had. Reles was his star witness. Reles's story was backed up by Dukey Maffetore, Pretty Levine, and later Allie "Tick Tock" Tannenbaum, Julie Catalano, Seymour "Blue Jaw" Magoon, Sholem Bernstein, and several others, all of whom had agreed to testify.[40] Turkus arrested Frank "Little Frankie" Galluccio, who boasted that years ago, he had been the one to scar Al Capone's face because Capone had made insulting comments about Galluccio's sister. Galluccio knew nothing about Murder, Inc., so Turkus threw him back.[41] The police rounded up scores of other people who had seen something or knew somebody. They rounded up the rest of the Brownsville gang, including "sportily garbed" Louis Capone, who, the *Brooklyn Eagle* thought, might have been the actual head of the "fantastic syndicate."[42] Police arrested unnamed "Mystery Women" including one "very beautiful girl" and briefly held them as potential witnesses.[43] Rumors swirled around the accelerating investigation, and people whispered that witnesses might be bribed—or killed.

O'Dwyer, Turkus, and their witnesses traveled with an escort of heavily armed detectives.[44] The *Brooklyn Eagle* urged O'Dwyer and Turkus to press on. In an editorial titled "A 'Murder for Money' Racket," the *Eagle* exclaimed that investigators had come across a "fantastic story." We Brooklynites, the editorial continued, "cannot stand for having our streets turned into shooting galleries." The editorial was shocked by the murderers' disdain for life; "to the killers in these cases," the editorial argued, "[human life] must be regarded as no different from that of the lowliest beast." In conclusion, the editors wrote, "we hope that District Attorney O'Dwyer and the police will be able to press these cases to such a conclusion that the 'murder for money' racket here will be effectively smashed."[45]

Housing Reles and the other gangsters who had turned state's evidence was a problem. They could not be kept safely in a regular jail, so Turkus built a kind of fortress to house them. "We had to set up a vault," he wrote,

> that was entrance-proof and invasion-proof. The result was an arrangement, short of a fortress, as human ingenuity could devise. Virtually one entire floor in one of the large downtown Brooklyn hotels was appropriated [. . .] no one could get off an elevator at that floor unless he had been checked in below. The informers were kept in one large suite, which could only be entered by a single door—and that was backed by strong shiny bolts. A system of mirrors was aligned [. . .] so that all approaches were under observation [. . .] Night and day a squad of detectives stood guard. They had pistols and rifles and pump guns [. . .] The ultra-security precautions even impressed the thugs. "Machine guns and shot guns and what all else they got," an awed Sholem [Bernstein] murmured. "When I go to sleep, two detectives sit in the room all night," he reported to his wife.[46]

For eight weeks, from March to May 1940, Burton Turkus and his assistants scrambled to construct their initial case. At first, they had planned to indict Frank "the Dasher" Abbandando and Max "the Jerk" Golob for the 1935 murder of John "Spider" Murtha,[47] but when Golob agreed to cooperate with the prosecution, Turkus decided to try Abbandando, Harry "Happy" Maione, and Harry Strauss for the murder of Whitey Rudnick. However, Strauss hinted that maybe he, too, would make a deal, so Turkus changed plans yet again.[48] Turkus finally decided to proceed against just Maione and Abbandando.[49]

On May 13, 1940, at 10:00 a.m. in Brooklyn's Criminal Courts Building, not far from the Brooklyn Bridge, in the first of the Murder, Inc., trials, "the Law and Murder, Inc., came face to face at last, with the chips down," as Turkus remembered.[50] The People, represented by Assistant District Attorney Turkus, charged Harry "Happy" Maione and Frank "the Dasher" Abbandando with the 1937 murder of George "Whitey" Rudnick.

Maione and Abbandando were represented by some of Brooklyn's finer defense lawyers; money seemed no object. Maione and Abbandando began their trial with the kind of arrogant, dismissive attitude, which was *de rigueur* for gangsters. Both had been in court multiple times; both had done time in prison; both had escaped multiple charges. Turkus began with the methodical examination of bystanders—people who knew Rudnick, who had seen Rudnick, and who could place Rudnick in Brownsville in the spring of 1937. And then, Turkus began to parade his star witnesses, beginning with Dukey Maffetore and Pretty Levine, friends of Maione and Abbandando, who knew all about Whitey Rudnick's death.[51] Maffetore, "a slender, swart youth," the *Herald Tribune* reported, nervously told "a tale of cheap racketeering"; he was "filled with such terror that he took only two quick glances at the defendants' faces." Maffetore explained how he'd stolen the car in which Rudnick's corpse was later found. Pretty Levine, somewhat more composed, confirmed Maffetore's testimony.[52]

And finally came the star of the show. Burton Turkus called on Abe Reles to testify. Reles was, the *Herald Tribune* wrote, a "squat, hard-faced, Brooklyn racketeer" who "showed scarcely a tremor" as he spoke, in a "thick, husky tone.[53] Reles was, said the *Brooklyn Eagle,* "a short, squat, tough guy." Reles took up his position in the witness chair, and with only occasional prompts by Turkus, regaled the court with the story of Rudnick's murder, complete with juicy bits of gangland gossip. Reles testified for more than six hours; he had an astonishingly precise recollection of days, times, and shards of conversation. He described the whole gruesome murder—Abbandando luring Rudnick to the garage, Strauss and Maione leaping from the shadows and grabbing Rudnick, Strauss stabbing Rudnick manically with an ice pick, the clumsy struggle to jam Rudnick's lanky body in the backseat of the car, Rudnick's corpse sighing, and Maione whirling around and whacking the corpse in the head with a meat cleaver.

Prosecutor Turkus asked Reles about his relationship with Rudnick.

Q. (Turkus). At one time had you been friendly with [Rudnick]?

A. (Reles). I was friendly with him all the time.

Turkus asked Reles to describe how the decision to kill Rudnick had been made. Reles explained that he and Harry Strauss were hanging around on The Corner. Strauss said to Reles, "You see I told you that bastard Whitey Rudnick is a stool pigeon. I seen him coming out of Harry Browser's car." Strauss continued: "[T]he bum has got to be taken." Reles said that he, Reles, had shrugged and said, "If he's got to be taken we will have to take him."[54] Strauss and Reles talked over the issue with Frank

Abbandando. The Dasher said, "[A]s soon as everything is all set, it will be easy to get him, one, two, three." Turkus asked whether the Dasher and Rudnick had been friendly. Reles replied, "Very friendly."[55] Turkus tried to paint an image for the jury of the fragile, skinny, Rudnick getting in the car with the burly Abbandando. Turkus asked Reles, "By the way [. . .] at that time, about how heavy was the Dasher, do you think?" Reles shrugged and replied, "I never weighed him."[56]

Reles's "fantastic tale," the *Eagle* reported, "was not without its humorous spots." Unlike the *Herald Tribune,* the *Brooklyn Eagle* thought Reles a little nervous when he began. Dressed nattily in a business suit, Reles twisted a handkerchief around his fingers and at first, stared at the ceiling. He spoke in the sort of "thick, husky voice, sometimes heard from a pugilist who has been subjected to blows on the throat." His Brooklyn accent was thick, and his grammar badly fractured, but once he got going, he held the courtroom in thrall. His story about the "rhubarb" he and Pittsburgh Phil had about the spelling of *friend* in the note inserted in Rudnick's pocket, provoked a burst of laughter from everyone in the courtroom.[57] His account of Rudnick's murder was graphic. Frank Abbandando had led Rudnick into the Sunrise garage; once in the garage, the others jumped him. But killing Rudnick was no cakewalk. When Reles stepped into the garage, "Happy says, 'It was not as easy as it looked.'" Getting Rudnick's corpse into the car was another headache. According to Reles,

[t]he Dasher got the body by the feet and Happy and Harry [Strauss] had the body by the head and shoulders and they start putting the body in the car. When they were about to put the top of the body in the car, to push it, it made a kind of noise, a cough or sneeze or something, and somebody remarked that the bum ain't dead yet, and they dropped him on the running board. With that, Harry [Strauss] jabbed him with the icepick a couple of times, and Hap Maione hit him with the cleaver over the head [. . .] The body would not fit in the car and the Dasher had to squeeze his knees to make him fit.[58]

The courtroom was fascinated. Reles wowed everyone. According to Turkus,

here he was, in front of the judge and jury no less—and blowing the roof off. He was reciting chapter and verse. And putting in the punctuation too. Reles had them gasping [. . .] He was the star of the show [. . .] and how he knew it! He was Kid Twist, the ham. He loved that spotlight."[59]

When, at long last, Reles finished and had stepped down from the witness stand, Happy Maione glared at him. Suddenly Maione lunged at Reles and screamed, "You stool pigeon son of a bitch [. . .] I'm gonna kill you [. . .] I'm gonna tear your throat out!"[60]

Turkus had other witnesses to follow Reles. Julie Catalano, the kid who stole cars with the gang and who had been a particular favorite of Maione's, testified about Rudnick's grim fate. Catalano, the *Eagle* reported, was "handsome and nervous, his palms alternatively beating against the arms of the witness chair and gesturing wildly." Catalano "spoke in the slang of the underworld"; his "picturesque speech and belligerent manner brought laughs to the faces of the two defendants." However, all in all, like Reles, Catalano "seemed to enjoy the spotlight."[61] The *Herald Tribune* described Catalano as "a swaggering, tough-talking gangman"; he was "jet-haired, slender, and [used] gestures to illustrate almost every answer."[62] The attendant at the garage where Rudnick was murdered, Joseph Liberito, also known as Joe Liberto, Kaiser Bill, and Joe the Baker, knew the killers and placed them all in the garage the night Rudnick was killed.

The defense did what it could. It argued that Maione was at his grandmother's funeral the night of Rudnick's murder, and four of Maione's aunts and two of his cousins confirmed this,[63] but the funeral director admitted that he had not actually seen Maione that night. Carmine Scaffo, whose testimony had originally supported Maione's innocent plea, dramatically changed his story under Turkus's questioning and admitted that he had committed perjury. Why? Because, Scaffo nervously explained, he had been threatened by Maione's brother.[64] Maione and Abbandando, of course, denied knowing anything about anything or doing anything to anybody.[65]

The trial lasted ten days. On May 23, after only about two hours of deliberation, the jury found Harry Maione and Frank Abbandando guilty of first-degree murder. According to the law, the conviction carried an automatic death sentence; Maione and Abbandando were to be sent to Sing Sing prison, where, at a date to be determined, they were to be strapped into a chair and electrocuted. Maione and Abbandando's lawyers vowed to appeal the convictions.

No sooner had the Maione and Abbandando trial ended, than Turkus and O'Dwyer prepared for their second trial. This time, Buggsy Goldstein and Pittsburgh Phil Strauss would be tried for the murder of Irving "Puggy"

Feinstein. Buggsy and Pittsburgh Phil's trial was scheduled to begin on September 4, 1940. All the same witnesses would be called; Abe Reles would again be the star.

But first, that summer of 1940, Burton Turkus and Abe Reles had an appointment in Los Angeles.

Los Angeles authorities were vigorously investigating the murder of Harry "Big Greenie" Greenberg, Los Angeles's first ever gangland-style slaying. The Los Angeles police were sure that Benjamin "Bugsy" Siegel was behind Big Greenie's murder. They contacted the New York police, who contacted Burt Turkus. Did Turkus's star witness, Abe Reles, know anything about Bugsy Siegel and Big Greenie Greenberg? Abe Reles knew everything.[66]

Bugsy had been the muscle in the Bugs and Meyer Gang. Sometime in the late 1930s, with the blessing of the New York gangsters, Bugsy Siegel went to California to seek his fortune. He certainly was not the only New Yorker headed to the Golden State. Hollywood was full of New York directors, writers, and actors. All sorts of New York entrepreneurs and artists had headed west. Barney Ruditsky, New York's most famous police detective, moved to Los Angeles after putting in his twenty years with the New York Police Department. Born in London, raised in South Africa, a young American soldier in World War I, Ruditsky had worked his way up from beat cop to detective. He helped break up a crime ring known as the "poison ivy gang," and he knew every gangster in New York. In 1934, he had arrested Abe Reles for attacking the garage attendants Charles Battle and Alvin Snyder. Ruditsky's memoir, *The Lawless Years*, was later turned into a television show. In Los Angeles, Ruditsky opened a restaurant, *Sherry's*, which became a home away from home for expatriate New Yorkers, including Bugsy Siegel. In 1949, Siegel's Los Angeles ally, Mickey Cohen, was wounded in a gun battle outside *Sherry's*.[67]

Siegel was a natural in Los Angeles. Movie-star handsome, a meticulous dresser, and charming when he wanted to be, "a raconteur extraordinary, the hood from the East," Turkus wrote, "became the darling of the very screen society he was muscling—while he was muscling it."[68] Siegel moved into a Beverley Hills mansion and began a flamboyant relationship with Virginia Hill, a young woman with a passion for hoodlums. Siegel had learned from Lepke Buchalter how to shake down unions and management and with gunmen from Chicago and New York, Siegel began labor racketeering in Los Angeles. He formed an alliance with local criminals like Jack Dragna and Mickey Cohen and energetically launched, or took over, New York–style businesses—gambling, drug smuggling, bookmaking, prostitution, and so on. Where such things already existed, Siegel and his allies demanded payoffs; where they did not exist, Siegel started them.

Abe Reles knew lots of stories about Bugsy Siegel. One story he told would send Burton Turkus, and then, under guard, Reles and several other informers, out to L.A. to testify against their old friend Bugsy.

Reles' story went like this: when Dewey began putting pressure on Lepke, one of Lepke's gunmen, Harry "Big Greenie" Greenberg, began to waver. Maybe, to save himself, Big Greenie would cooperate with Dewey. Lepke became suspicious. Fearful that Dewey could not protect him from Lepke's ferocious retribution, Big Greenie disappeared. Lepke ordered that Big Greenie be killed. Word came to New York that Big Greenie was in Montreal; Lepke rushed Albert "Tick Tock" Tannenbaum to Montreal with orders to kill Big Greenie. Big Greenie hurried to Detroit, hoping for help from Detroit's Purple Gang; Tick Tock came after him. Finally, Big Greenie fled to Los Angeles. Lepke sent word to his old friend, Bugsy Siegel, that he, Lepke, would appreciate it if Bugsy would eliminate Big Greenie.

Meanwhile, Reles continued, Sholem Bernstein, who worked with both Reles and Lepke, hurried out to Los Angeles to help Siegel. Sholem's specialty was car theft. Bugsy wanted Sholem to clip a car to be used in Big Greenie's murder. Bugsy insisted that the stolen car be left in a parking lot. Sholem replied that that was crazy; in New York, when you stole a car, you switched license plates and then hid the car in a garage somewhere. Stealing a car and just leaving it in a parking lot would never work. Bernstein was right. He stole a car and left it in a parking lot, just like Bugsy had ordered. The car's owner called the police, just like Bernstein said they would, and recovered the car. After arguing angrily with Siegel, Bernstein, disgusted, walked off the job and headed back to New York.

Back in Los Angeles, Siegel; Tick Tock Tannenbaum; Siegel's brother-in-law, Walter Krackow; and another gunman named Frank Carbo plotted Big Greenie's murder.

On the night before Thanksgiving, 1939, Harry Greenberg stepped out of his modest Los Angeles home and drove off to buy a newspaper. When he drove back home, a car on his street flashed its lights as he went by, a signal to a second car that Greenberg was on the way. Greenberg slowed his car, pulled into his driveway, and stopped. A man ran up to the driver's side window. Greenberg rolled the car window down and looked up. The man shot Greenberg in the face, ran off, and jumped into a waiting car. The car roared away. No one knew who the gunman was; maybe it was Bugsy Siegel himself, maybe not. Harry "Big Greenie" Greenberg had the unhappy honor of being, as Turkus put it, "Southern California's first important gangland cadaver."[69]

The Los Angeles police arrested Bugsy Siegel, and the district attorney charged him with Big Greenie's murder. Turkus hurried Reles to Los Angeles to testify. All Reles could testify to, of course, were underworld rumors. In fact, there was very little evidence against Siegel. The jury found him not guilty.

There was a curious coda to the story. After his acquittal, according to Reles, Bugsy Siegel rushed back to New York to complain bitterly about Sholem Bernstein. All the top New York gangsters, according to Reles, gathered to hear Siegel's complaint. Reles, who claimed to have attended this curious trial, spoke in Bernstein's defense. "Sholem got word from New York that his mama is going to cash in," Reles said that he told the gangster court. "Sholem is a good boy [. . .] you all know how a mama is. It makes it easier to go, if her boy is sitting there by the bed, saying nice things—he loves her and she is getting better and like that." That was why Bernstein abandoned Siegel. Siegel wasn't impressed, but the gangsters apparently were moved; they decided to leave Sholem Bernstein alone.[70] Bernstein, like Reles, would later turn state's evidence and be one of Burton Turkus's key informers.

In September 1940, the murder trial of Harry "Pittsburgh Phil" Strauss and Martin "Buggsy" Goldstein, the second of the Murder, Inc., trials, finally began in the same Brooklyn Courthouse in which Turkus had just convicted Harry Maione and Frank Abbandando. Strauss and Goldstein were charged with the September 4, 1939 murder of Irving "Puggy" Feinstein.[71]

The trial of Strauss and Goldstein opened with a bang—some joker set off a firecracker in the courthouse. Worse, something very odd had happened to Harry Strauss. Pep had always been the snazzy dresser of the troop, but even before the trial began, Strauss had refused to bathe or shave, refused to get a haircut, and stalked around his cell murmuring and drooling. He was a sight at the defense table; he seemed to be a complete lunatic. According to the press, Buggsy Goldstein was sharply dressed in a "well-pressed blue serge suit [. . .] white shirt and maroon tie." Harry Strauss, on the other hand, had a "heavy stubble" and wore a "wrinkled light grey flannel suit over a blue V-necked sweater"; during the opening of the trial, Strauss "stared vacantly" toward the judge.[72]

Strauss's lawyers argued that their client had gone crazy and was not able to participate coherently in his own defense. Turkus and the prosecution team argued that Strauss was faking. The trial paused while a team of three psychiatrists examined Strauss. The psychiatrists asked Strauss, in his cell, whether he knew Abe Reles. Sure, Strauss said, "Reles comes under my bed every night [. . .] but my brother comes and chases him away!" and "Reles flies in here through the window; he tries to kill me."[73] But the psychiatrists were not impressed. Their conclusion: Strauss was faking. In any case, trial Judge John J. Fitzgerald ruled that the issue was whether Strauss was sane at the time of the murder, which no one denied. Whether the jury wanted to consider his current insanity, if he really were insane, when they deliberated, that was their choice.[74]

As for Martin Goldstein—he seemed to be his jovial, "buggsy" self. He had committed between ten and fifteen murders,[75] and he seemed to enjoy the attention he was getting. Short, stocky, and jowly, he reminded Turkus, and everyone else, of "Edward G. Robinson [. . .] the movie mobster." Buggsy smirked for photographs and shouted jokes to the reporters.[76]

Seating the jury was hard because just about everyone in New York had heard of the case by now, and, according to the defense, many potential jurors were already "tainted."[77] Finally, a jury was selected, and the trial began. Turkus had added yet another informer to his string. Vito "Socko/Chickenhead" Gurino, Happy Maione's old pal, had disappeared. However, suddenly, Gurino showed up screaming hysterically in a Manhattan church. His wife, Gertrude, said that Socko was terrified that he would be murdered. He agreed to testify for the prosecution. To keep Gurino focused, Turkus indicted him for three different murders.[78]

Turkus marched out informer after informer to testify against Strauss and Goldstein. Even Abe Reles's mother-in-law testified, putting Strauss and Goldstein at the murder scene, Reles's home. Had she not known that Reles was a murderer? His mother-in-law replied, "I didn't know Abe was a killer. He was a family man and was certainly good around the house."[79] The key witness was again Abe Reles, whom the *Brooklyn Eagle* now described as the "singing star" of the "murder-for-money mob."[80]

Just as in the Maione–Abbandando trial, Reles "reveled in the spot light."[81] He changed his story some; now he admitted to only eleven murders; he seemed entirely calm and matter of fact when he did so. Throughout his testimony, the *Herald Tribune* noted, "the swarthy witness showed no embarrassment."[82] For some five hours, he told the court all he knew about Puggy Feinstein's murder, which was everything. Reles admitted that yes, he, too, was a killer; "murder was his business, he made plain," reported the *Eagle*. The *Eagle* added that Reles was "kinky-haired, low of brow, and generally nondescript in appearance; he spoke with an impediment suggesting a mouthful of marbles."[83] Reles explained that Vince Mangano had complained about Puggy Feinstein to Albert Anastasia; that Anastasia had told Pittsburgh Phil to get rid of Puggy; that one night, out of the blue, Puggy had shown up on The Corner looking for the loan shark, Tiny "the Blimp" Benson;[84] and that Puggy was driven to Reles home where Strauss and Goldstein—and Reles—had killed him. Reles added that Puggy had bitten Phil and that Goldstein and Dukey Maffetore had taken Puggy's corpse away and burned it.

Then Turkus called Seymour Magoon. Magoon testified that he had gone to Reles's home that night. Goldstein and Maffetore drove up after setting Puggy's corpse on fire. Magoon agreed to drive Goldstein back to the gas station to return the gas can. According to Magoon, Goldstein said, "Dukie and I just burned somebody." When Magoon asked what had happened, Goldstein explained Feinstein's fate:

> Strauss, Abe, and I strangled him and after strangling him Duke and I went out and burned him. I'm coming back from there now. Take me to the gas station, I have to pay the guy and give the can back.[85]

Throughout Magoon's testimony, Strauss sat staring and mumbling. Buggsy got more and more agitated. Magoon had been his understudy, his protégé; now Magoon was sending Buggsy to the chair. As Magoon ended, Buggsy leaped to his feet and shrieked, "[H]e's burnin' me!" His lawyer pulled him back to his seat. Buggsy burst into tears.[86] Recovered, Goldstein focused his anger on Turkus. "That Turkus, that Turkus," Goldstein said to reporters, "they ought to call him Mr. Arsenic. He's poison."[87]

The defendants' lawyers, Leo Healy for Goldstein, Daniel Prior for Strauss, presented no serious defense. Strauss chattered to himself; asked what day it was, he replied, "[S]ame as any day." The bailiff tried to swear Strauss in; Strauss was so confused and incoherent that he was dismissed. Goldstein testified in his own defense; he swore he was innocent.[88] Turkus had nothing but contempt for him and called him "that sniveling, crawling creature."[89]

The trial of Harry Strauss and Martin Goldstein lasted two weeks. On September 19, 1940, both were found guilty of the murder of Irving "Puggy" Feinstein. "Strauss [. . .] drew patterns with the thumbs of his slightly extended hands on the linoleum-topped defense table while the jury foreman pronounced his doom," the *Eagle* reported. "Goldstein beat a nervous tattoo with unflexed fingers while he leaned forward, his entire face corrugated with an intense grimace of fearful concentration." When the foreman finished announcing the guilty verdict, Goldstein, "like a schoolboy," raised his hand. "Can I say something?" he asked the judge. "No," Judge Fitzgerald answered. "Can't I say a word [. . .] a little word?"

Buggsy pleaded. "No!" the judge responded. But Buggsy spoke anyway: "I want to thank the jury for what they have done."[90] Strauss and Goldstein were sentenced to death a few days later. At the sentencing, Strauss was still distracted and seemingly confused. Goldstein appeared, for the first time, "without an immaculate white shirt and tie." Asked if he had anything to say, Buggsy replied, "I want to thank the court for the charge he made sending us to our deaths [...] and I only hope that the same applies to you and your family [...] I am willing to die like a man."[91]

The *Brooklyn Eagle* congratulated Turkus and O'Dwyer on the conviction. The Reles gang was responsible for at least eighty-three murders, according to the *Eagle*'s tally. The paper continued:

It is doubtful a more important murder conviction has ever been found in Brooklyn [...] the revelations of the trial were shocking—indeed, incredible. For years, men have been "disposed of" here, on order, for fees, which were often cut rate. Life meant absolutely nothing to this mob.[92]

Then for Turkus and O'Dwyer came a surprising defeat. Happy Maione's and the Dasher Abbandando's lawyers had appealed their clients' convictions. The lawyers had accused Turkus and O'Dwyer of coaching some witnesses and intimidating others; they complained about the immunity given Reles and the other prosecution witnesses; they argued that the trial judge's final instructions to the jury were incorrect, and with that last technicality, the appeals court agreed. In December 1940, the appeals court ordered a new trial for Maione and Abbandando.[93]

So the third Murder, Inc., trial was a reprise of the first. In March 1941, the retrial of Happy Maione and the Dasher Abbandando began.[94] Judge Franklin Taylor ruled that women would not be eligible to serve as jurors because the case was too gruesome; besides, the court had no place to house women jurors.[95]

All the figures from the first trial reappeared in the retrial and defense lawyers scrupulously compared testimony from the first trial with testimony from the retrial, hoping to find discrepancies and confusion. Turkus, however, just as scrupulously held his witnesses to exactly the same testimony as they had given before. There were endless squabbles between defense and prosecution about who said what when, but in general, the prosecution's case held strong. Rumors again ran through the court about threats to witnesses.[96] Dukey Maffetore once again told about stealing the car used to carry Whitey Rudnick's corpse.[97]

The defense did its best to scramble the testimony of the prosecution witnesses. For example, the defense worked hard to prove that Maffetore was actually a murderer as well, and therefore, his testimony was tainted. In one exchange, the defense brought up the murder of Puggy Feinstein. The defense asked Maffetore, "You brought Puggy Feinstein to Reles' house?"

A. Yes, sir.
Q. You saw a rope and ice pick in that house too, didn't you?
A. No, sir.
Q. You did not see a rope?
A. I did see a rope but I didn't see no ice pick.
Q. You saw a rope being put around Feinstein's neck too, didn't you?
A. Yes, sir.
Q. You took the body out of the house after it became a corpse too, didn't you?
A. No, sir.

Dukey explained that he personally had not removed Feinstein's corpse from Reles's house. The defense resumed:

Q. Didn't you drive that corpse?
A. I had to drive the car [. . .]
Q. Now, that is not the only car that you drove, is it, with a dead body in it of a man that had been murdered?
A. I did not get that.
[Question repeated]
A. No, sir.
Q. How many more cars did you drive with dead bodies in them of men that had been murdered?
A. One more [. . .]
Q. In addition to that did you drive cars with men in them who on the same night that you drove it were killed?
A. Yes sir, but I did not know they were going to be killed [. . .]
Q. How many men were killed in machines you were operating when you were operating them?
A. What machines?[98]

Reles was just as cocky as he had been at the earlier trials. Yes, he admitted, he was a "big mogul" in the rackets. The defense pressed the point that Reles himself had committed multiple murders, maybe ten, maybe a dozen. "Would you hesitate to take a human life?" the defense asked. "Before I didn't," Reles responded, "but now I would not take a life." He had reformed, Reles claimed.[99] Reles insisted that Rudnick's murder had actually been plotted in Happy Maione's home. Maione, enraged, leaped to his feet, screamed at Reles, and hurled his water glass at him; everyone in the courtroom jumped, and Reles ducked.[100]

For the second time, the jury agreed with the prosecution. Maione and Abbandando were again convicted, and on April 14, 1941, they were again sentenced to die by electrocution.

In May 1941, O'Dwyer and Turkus prepared the fourth Murder, Inc., trial, the trial of Irving "Knadles" Nitzberg for the 1939 murder of Albert "Plug" Shuman. Assistant District Attorney Julius Helfand handled the case. Thirty-eight years old, he was a Brooklyn native. He had graduated from Boys High School in Brooklyn and had earned his law degree from New York University in 1923. He had been with the Brooklyn district attorney's office since 1935.[101] All the regular witnesses—Abe Reles, Tick Tock Tannenbaum, and Seymour Magoon, among others—lined up to testify for the prosecution.

Nitzberg was charged with the murder of Plug Shuman on January 9, 1939.[102] Shuman had worked for Lepke Buchalter, but when Dewey's Big Heat began, Lepke began to suspect that Shuman might run to Dewey. Lepke asked Albert Anastasia to get rid of Shuman; Anastasia told Reles to take care of it.

Killing Shuman was complicated; Shuman knew, and mistrusted, everyone in Brownsville. He did have an old friend from the Bronx, though, Irving "Knadles" Nitzberg. (*Knadles* is a Yiddish variation on the German word for dumpling, *Knödel*. Sometimes people just called Nitzberg "K."). Abe Reles contacted Knadles Nitzberg and told him Nitzberg's friend, Plug, had to go.

On January 9, 1939, Nitzberg and Tick Tock Tannenbaum offered to take Schuman off to play cards. Tannenbaum drove. Schuman sat next to him in the front seat. Nitzberg sat in the back, behind Schuman. Abe Reles followed in a second car. Tannenbaum testified: "I was to ask Knadles for a cigarette and that was the signal to start shooting." Tick Tock turned and asked Knadles for a cigarette, and Knadles shot Schuman twice in the head. Tannenbaum pulled the car to the curb; he and Nitzberg leaped out and jumped in the car Reles was driving. Reles sped off. Later, "while sipping a bottle of soda water," Tannenbaum asked Reles "[S]o, what's it all about? Who was this guy and why did we kill him?"[103]

Reles, again, was the star witness. He explained, as he had before, that his "business was murder in Brooklyn." He added: "Lepke was one of my bosses." He explained that he had been present when Lepke had ordered

Schuman's murder. "In December 1938," Reles explained, "Mendy Weiss and I visited Lepke at his hideout apartment where Mendy told Lepke that Plug Schuman was speaking to Inspector McDermott [...] Lepke said, 'If he is giving information against me, go out and take him.'"[104] Reles then confirmed Tannenbaum's account of the murder. Defense lawyer James Ryan got Reles to admit that yes, he'd killed eleven people. "Have you a conscience?" Ryan asked angrily. "I don't know what you mean," Reles replied. "Did you feel bad for killing others?" Ryan persisted. "Looking upward and pursing his lips," Reles replied, "Well, it was the way I was living."

Judge Peter Brancato interrupted and informed that jury that Reles "had no conscience" and was a "living tiger."

"Have you believed in God?" defense attorney Ryan asked Reles.

"Yes sir [...] I always believe in God," Reles answered.

Ryan continued: "When you were killing others for money did you believe that there was a God?"

"Yes I did," Reles replied, "but you must remember I had my manner of living."

Why had Reles agreed to testify? "It was love of my family," Reles said, "and the way I was living. I had one child and I was expecting another. And I was disgusted with the way I was living. The killing and all that."[105]

The Kings County jury took just eighteen minutes to convict Nitzberg of Plug Schuman's murder; sentenced to death, Nitzberg "smiled sardonically."[106]

However, there was a catch. The only eyewitness to the killing was Tick Tock Tannenbaum, and he was an accomplice to the crime. Although Tannebaum insisted that Nitzberg was the killer, Nitzberg claimed that Tannenbaum was the killer. Reles had followed with the second car, but Reles had not seen the actual killing. Nitzberg's lawyers appealed; the appeals court struck down the conviction and ordered a new trial. Freed after the second trial, Nitzberg would eventually go to jail but on a lesser charge.[107]

The next Murder, Inc., trial did not belong to O'Dwyer and Turkus; it belonged to their colleagues in New Jersey, but the key player in the case was again their star witness, Abe Reles. Reles had solved the murder of Dutch Schulz.

Dutch Schulz had been shot to death in October 1935. His murder remained unsolved for five years, until 1940, when Abe Reles agreed to talk. One of the first things Reles talked about was the murder of Dutch Schulz.

Reles recounted all the gangster lore he knew about the murder, about how Schulz had threatened to kill Dewey, about how the other big shots, especially Lucky Luciano, had decided to kill Schulz. Reles revealed that the man who killed Dutch Schulz and three of Schulz's men that October in 1935 was Charlie "the Bug" Workman. The trial of Charlie Workman for the murder of Dutch Schulz and others opened in Newark in June 1941. O'Dwyer and Turkus provided their New Jersey colleagues with Abe Reles and Tick Tock Tannenbaum. The Workman trial was messy; eyewitnesses to the shooting proved to be unreliable; Reles and Tannenbaum could only provide hearsay; Workman changed his plea back and forth. After a two-week trial, Workman was sentenced to life in prison.[108]

On June 12, 1941, the State of New York electrocuted Harry Strauss and Martin Goldstein. Both had appealed their sentences, but their appeals had been denied.[109]

Buggsy Goldstein continued to clown around almost to the very end. When he was sentenced, he said to Judge Fitzgerald, "I would like to 'pee' up your leg." The judge, who was hard of hearing, asked the clerk, "[W]hat did he say?" Goldstein repeated his comment, the clerk carefully translated it: "[H]e says he would like to urinate on your honor's trousers." Goldstein scoffed. "[Y]ou cannot go to your death in a nice way, you might as well go in a bad way." In his last shouted comments to reporters, Goldstein said, "I would die happy if I could knock off Turkus and take care of Judge [John J.] Fitzgerald [. . .] just tell that rat Reles I'll be waiting for him [. . .] maybe it'll be in hell; I don't know. But I'll be waiting. And I bet I got a pitchfork." Pushed in a police cruiser, Goldstein squirmed, hollered, and barked. "Too bad I can't hold Reles' hand when I sit in that chair," Goldstein shouted. "Reles in one hand and that dirty bastard [Seymour] Magoon in the other."[110]

The night before the execution, Goldstein's father, brother, and sister-in-law paid Goldstein a last visit, but he would not see them. At 11:03 p.m. on June 12, 1941, Goldstein stepped into the execution chamber. Burton Turkus later reminded his readers that Buggsy had not stepped through what "fiction writers" called a "little green door." Describing Goldstein's execution, Turkus was thinking, or assumed his readers would be thinking, of gangster movies. In *Angels with Dirty Faces* (1938), the tough gangster Rocky (James Cagney) prepares for the electric chair. His childhood friend, Jerry (Pat O'Brien), who had become a priest instead of a gangster, urges Rocky to pretend to be a coward. That way, Rocky would help dim the allure of the hoodlum life and discourage the neighborhood kids from leading a life of crime. Rocky agrees and feigns cowardice. One of the kids, Soapy (Billy Halop), says, "At the fatal stroke of eleven p.m., Rocky was led through the little green door of death." Turkus helpfully explained that the door to the death chamber in Sing Sing was neither little nor green.[111] Buggsy quietly sat in the electric chair while the executioners strapped him in. He was electrocuted a few minutes later.

Harry Strauss stayed disheveled and crazy almost to the very end. Just before his execution, though, he shaved, got a haircut, and cleaned himself up. His companion, Evelyn Mittelman, paid him a last visit. Pittsburgh Phil then, only minutes after Buggsy's death, followed him to the electric chair.

Buggsy's widow, Beatrice, would file a double-indemnity claim with Buggsy's insurance company, claiming a double payout because Buggsy had died unexpectedly and suddenly from unnatural causes. The insurance company rejected Beatrice's claim.[112]

The Murder, Inc., trials were extraordinary spectacles. They reminded people of the movies. Bill O'Dwyer, Brooklyn's district attorney, became a star. *Life* magazine, in April 1940, ran a glossy if grisly exposé of "Murder, Inc." and presented Bill O'Dwyer as the brave, gangbusting Humphrey Bogart–like district attorney.[113] *Look* magazine, in June 1940, ran a celebrity spread all about Bill O'Dwyer, with photos of O'Dwyer looking stern in his office and O'Dwyer relaxing in front of his radio at home. *Look* titled its piece "The Murder Trust Buster." The story explained that O'Dwyer's brother, John, a bystander in a gangland shootout, had been killed and that John's killing inspired O'Dwyer's vehement hatred of gangsters. "'Murder, Inc.'" is on the skids," *Look* told its readers, "and tough Bill O'Dwyer, 49, ex-hod carrier, bricklayer, dock-worker, cop, lawyer, and judge, is riding the headlines as 'Crime Buster No. 1.'" His wife, Kitty, thought he looked a little bit like the Hollywood actor Robert Taylor, who often played the good district attorney in gangster films; Kitty called Bill "District Attorney Robert Taylor."[114]

Burton Turkus, the assistant district attorney who actually prosecuted most of the cases, "does not conform to the general pattern of the prosecutor," Turkus's cowriter, journalist Sid Feder, explained. Turkus

> dotes on the theatrics of the courtroom and the criminal trial [. . .]
> He looks like the movie version of the D.A.—suave, dynamic in conversation, sharp. Meeting him, one can readily believe that, as prosecutor, he did put seven men accused of murder in the first degree into the chair. Before that, in private practice, on the other hand, he defended seventeen men accused of murder in the first degree—and not one of them got the chair.[115]

The villains in the trials were, of course, villainous. Here's Abe Reles, as Burton Turkus described him. "The Kid," Turkus writes,

had eyes there were shiny agates, hard and piercing, and you didn't like them at all. He had a round face, thick lips, and flat nose, and small ears, stuck close to his kinky hair. His arms had not waited for the rest of him. They dangled to his knees, completing a generally gorilla-like figure. Kid Twist's most striking characteristic, though, was in his fingers. They were strong; they strangled men. Where ordinary fingers start to taper at the ends, the Kid's became spatulate. The tips were big and flat. They reminded you of a set of hammers [. . .] You could almost picture this low-browed bandit driving rows of nails into a board merely by snapping the fat heads of his fingers down, one by one. And he was tough. Very, very tough.[116]

The defendants played their gangster roles well. Harry Maione was consistently fierce. Frank Abbandando played the cocky gangster. In May 1940, reporters huddled around Frank Abbandando and Harry Maione after their convictions and shouted questions. Harry Maione scowled and shuffled past them. Abbandando was still the flippant wise guy. Was he surprised at his conviction? Naw, Abbandando said, he'd probably get convicted of some murder or other sooner or later. Did he have any regrets? Well, the Dasher said, "[W]hat burns me up will be to miss the first night Dodgers game, and the fact that Abe Reles won't go the chair with me."[117]

When they acted against role, when Pittsburgh Phil acted crazy or when Buggsy Goldstein burst into tears, their performances were all the more powerful precisely because they ran against their expected role. Gangster Reles proved to be the perfect underworld turncoat; as Turkus put it, Reles was "the star of the show" and "loved that spotlight." [118]

What's so striking about all the figures in the trials is not their "behavior" but rather their "performances."

Shakespeare's famous observation that "all the world's a stage, and all the men and women merely players" (spoken by Jacques, in *As You Like It*, act II, scene 7) was hardly original. The ancients, from Confucius to the Greeks, had a clear sense of "scripted behavior," of roles that people enact. Plato, in the *Laws*, argues that we all must "fall in with our role and spend life in making our play as perfect as possible."[119] Two centuries after Shakespeare, Denis Diderot, the famous encyclopedist, wrote at length about "the play of the world."[120] Certainly since the work of Erving Goffman in the 1950s, social scientists have been acutely sensitive to the ways in which human beings enact roles, to the ways they "perform." Ideas about "performance" extend far beyond theater departments. Andrew Parker and Eve Kosofsky Sedgwick point out that "performance" ranges from "stage to festival," and includes, for instance, "film, photography, television, computer simulation, music, 'performance art,' political demonstrations, health care, cooking, fashion, [and] shamanistic ritual," just to name a few areas where "performance" has become important.[121] Scholars as diverse as Kenneth Burke, Richard Schechner, and Victor Turner have argued that it is just about impossible to talk about any human activity without taking into account the fact that people "perform," that is, they follow certain "scripts," often not of their own making; that their performative behavior sometimes takes on a highly charged, symbolic quality; and that people perform in what Turner calls "social dramas," which enact who people are, what they fear and hope for, who they hate, and who and what they love.[122] Judith Butler argues that categories as fundamental as "masculine" and "feminine" are performative; that is, "gender is an identity tenuously constituted in time, instituted in an exterior space through a *stylized repetition of acts.*" Gender is not so much a matter of "being" as it is of "doing."[123] Patriotic parades, political protests, election debates, all are forms of theater, in which all the players play their parts.

Another name for this sort of "social drama" is what Clifford Geertz calls "deep play." Geertz argues that we should move our thinking about society away from the pneumatic push and pull of "cause and effect" to the interpretation of meanings. What "causes" Balinese cockfighters to engage in cockfights is probably less important to figure out than what they "mean" by their cockfights. Geertz proposed a "semiotic" understanding of human culture. "Believing," Geertz writes,

> with Max Weber, that man is an animal suspended in webs of significance he himself has spun, I take culture to be those webs, and the analysis of it to be therefore not an experimental science in search of law but an interpretive one in search of meaning.[124]

Meaning, Geertz writes, is expressed performatively in "deep play." Jeremy Bentham coined the term; he used it to refer to the sorts of games in which the stakes are so high that no rational person would play them. However, Geertz notes that in, for instance, the traditional Balinese cockfight, what is really going on is not simply a contest between roosters. What is occurring is a bloody ritual that enacts everything from manhood to status to power. Deep play is suffused with moral meaning.[125]

Seeing morality linked to play and theater is not new; Aristotle, after all, insisted that ethics is about action and not just theory. If by "theater" one means something inherently fraudulent, inauthentic, and irreal, then linking morality to theater makes little sense. Morality ought to be true, authentic, and real. If, however, by "theater" one means the symbolic enactment and expression of fundamental values, then morality and theater are integrally related.

Zygmunt Bauman writes that we live in several sorts of "spaces"—physical space, of course, but also cognitive, aesthetic, and moral space. We share physical and cognitive space with the others we merely live *with*. If, however, we agree with Emmanuel Levinas that ethics is all about human relationships,[126] then moral space is where we and others express what we live *for*. These others, Bauman writes, "are resistant to all typification. As residents of moral space, they remain forever specific and irreplaceable."[127] Moral space, then, is the arena, the theater, in which we act, performing morally, with people whose concrete lives matter greatly to us.

Clifford Geertz notes that "there are at least three points where chaos—a tumult of events which lack not just interpretations but *interpretability*—threatens to break in on man: at the limits of his analytic capacities, at the limits of his powers of endurance, and at the limits of his moral insight."[128] The Murder, Inc., killers threated their contemporaries with chaos, not simply with the physical chaos the hoodlums caused—the beatings and shootings and murders and mayhem—but with moral chaos. The killers threatened their contemporaries' moral insight, their ability to make moral sense of their world. If murder goes unpunished, then moral performance becomes incoherent. Therefore, murderers have to be expelled from the moral stage, theatrically expelled in some sort of moral drama, in a kind of deep play, that drives home to audience and participants alike that moral space must be coherent and therefore cannot contain unpunished murderers. The insistent references to the movies, to theater, to acting, throughout the Murder, Inc., trials, all the highly theatrical gestures and mannered language, all the public performances taken before the rapt courtroom audience and the wider media audience, remind us that the trials really were a sort of theater, a kind of deep play, a social drama. Those threatening the wider society not only with physical harm but also with moral chaos had to be ritually purged from the society they threatened. The morally impure had to be denounced, condemned, hidden away somewhere (like Sing Sing), and then literally expunged from the city's moral space. The Murder, Inc., trials might well have been called the Murder, Inc., Theater.

By the summer of 1941, Bill O'Dwyer and Burton Turkus had led four different Murder, Inc., trials (the trial and retrial of Maione and Abbandando; the trials of Goldstein and Strauss, and Nitzberg), and participated in two more (in Los Angeles, the trial of Bugsy Siegel, and in Newark, the trial of Charlie Workman). That summer, they were preparing for their biggest trial yet. In the fall, they'd try Louis Capone, Mendy Weiss, and Lepke Buchalter for the murder of Joe Rosen. Lepke was the biggest target; he was the most powerful underworld leader ever to be charged with homicide. With Reles, Tannenbaum, and all their other witnesses, O'Dwyer and Turkus were sure that in this, their fifth Murder, Inc., trial, they would win convictions and death sentences. And on the horizon were even more dramatic targets—above all, Albert Anastasia. Reles and all the other witnesses had made clear that nothing happened in Brooklyn without Anastasia's approval. Convicting Anastasia, after eliminating Lepke and after Dewey's conviction of Luciano, would fatally cripple, O'Dwyer and Turkus hoped, New York's underworld.

They had no idea, of course, that within months, the Murder, Inc., investigations and trials would come to a shocking, violent, and very sudden end.

8
Ethics of Ambiguity
The Canary Could Sing but Couldn't Fly

Hey Burt, Reles just went out the window.

—*Reporter Harry Feeney to Burton Turkus, November 12, 1941*[1]

In the summer of 1941, District Attorney William O'Dwyer and Assistant District Attorney Burton Turkus prepared their fifth Murder, Inc., trial. This would be the biggest trial ever. Three gangsters—Mendy Weiss, Louis Capone, and, most dramatically, gang lord Louis "Lepke" Buchalter, would be charged with the murder of Joe Rosen. Lepke was the very first top-level gangster in the United States to be charged with murder. Al Capone had been convicted of tax evasion; Lucky Luciano had been convicted of organizing prostitution; if Lepke were convicted he would be the first big name hoodlum to be punished for the worst thing hoodlums did, kill people. Suddenly, though, that fall, the whole Murder, Inc., investigation would come to a screeching end, and for the next decade and more, the whole Murder, Inc., story would be laced with contradiction and confusion. Moral certainty would be rattled by moral ambiguity. What, though, is the place of ambiguity in the moral endeavor? Could ambiguity actually be more moral than certainty? And what happened to Abe Reles?

In that summer of 1941, after four Murder, Inc., trials, after assisting with the trials in Los Angeles and Newark, William O'Dwyer and Burton Turkus prepared their biggest case so far. They charged Louis Capone, Mendy Weiss, and Lepke Buchalter with murder.

Lepke Buchalter, in the 1930s, was one of New York's lords of the underworld. In 1936, after Tom Dewey had convicted Lucky Luciano, Dewey decided to go after Lepke. Other gangland figures, like Frank Costello and Meyer Lansky, covered their tracks skillfully; they would be difficult to catch. Besides, Costello and Lansky were primarily involved with gambling, not murder. Lepke was different.

A teenage "schlammer" (Yiddish slang for someone who beats up people), Lepke, by the mid-1930s, with his lieutenants Jacob "Gurrah" Shapiro[2] and Emmanuel "Mendy" Weiss, had shaken down both the garment and the trucking industries. Lepke and his gang went from business to business and union to union, demanding to be paid off "or else." "Or else" meant a rock through the window, slashed tires, acid in the face, a busted head, or a bullet through the brain. New York City was the center of the nation's garment industry, and most of the garment industry regularly paid off Lepke. New York was totally dependent on the trucking industry for everything from marketing its wares to hauling in its daily bread; Lepke and his hoodlums went methodically from trucking company to trucking company and sometimes from trucker to trucker and demanded to be paid off. Just about everyone paid Lepke. The garment and trucking industries were plagued by threats, extortion, and violence, and the cost to New Yorkers was enormous. Anyone who even threatened to oppose Lepke—by, for instance, going to Prosecutor Dewey—was sure to end up dead.

Lepke was well connected in the New York underworld. His ties to Albert Anastasia were especially strong. When Lepke wanted someone murdered, he often turned to Anastasia to handle the job. Anastasia typically passed the murder contract along to Abe Reles and his Brownsville gang.

After Al Capone's conviction for tax evasion in 1931 and Lucky Luciano's conviction for organizing prostitution in June 1936, Dewey and his gangbusters knew there were many ways to catch gangsters. By the mid-1930s, everyone was hunting Lepke—Tom Dewey, special prosecutor and then Manhattan's (New York County) district attorney; New York State; and the federal government too. Over in Brooklyn, Bill O'Dwyer and Burton Turkus were after Lepke as well. Turkus and O'Dwyer, however, had something the other law officers did not—eyewitnesses who could convict Lepke Buchalter of first-degree murder.

No wonder Lepke disappeared.

In November 1936, federal officials convicted Buchalter and Gurrah Shapiro of violating antitrust laws in the rabbit-fur garment industry in New York. Out on bail, both Buchalter and Shapiro went underground. They were sentenced to two years in prison; their lawyers appealed but, in June 1937, lost. Instead of beginning their prison terms, Buchalter and Shapiro stayed hidden. In November 1937, the federal government offered a $5,000 reward—for most people much more than a year's salary—

for information leading to their capture. Meanwhile, in December 1937, federal officials indicted Buchalter on yet another charge—smuggling narcotics from Asia into the United States.

Shapiro had no stomach for being on the lam; in April 1938, he surrendered. Not Lepke. And in 1938, Lepke became the target of one of the most dramatic manhunts in American history. Beginning from the time he first disappeared, in November 1936, accelerating in 1937, and reaching something like an obsession in 1938, "Where's Lepke?" became a national issue, much like the hunt for John Dillinger four years before. Before he went underground, Lepke made clear that he was coming back. Abe Reles went with him to a meeting on Foster Avenue in New York. They were joined by Longy Zwillman, Tommy "Three Finger Brown" Lucchese, and several others. According to Reles,

> Lepke laid down the law, that the garment district was his for years and years, with no interference by any other mobsters while he was on the outside and so there should be no interference just because he was in hiding. He said that there was no dispute; the territory was his. The others were convinced and agreed.[3]

The media too hunted for Lepke, and at the center of the media hunt for Lepke was one of New York's most remarkable characters, the person who almost single-handedly created mass media celebrity culture—Walter Winchell.[4]

Winchell was the grandchild of Jewish immigrants and grew up in poverty in Harlem. When he was a child, his family moved from tenement to tenement constantly looking for cheaper rent. His father was a failure in the garment business; his mother and father fought constantly. Walter was a poor student and quit school when he was a teenager. He found a way out of this grim situation, however, through show business.

For ten years, from ages thirteen to twenty-three, Walter Winchell was a vaudeville trouper. He was in a kids' act at first; when he got too big for the kids' act, he formed a new act with Rita Greene; they married and later divorced. Their act was pure vaudeville—a little singing, a little dancing, and a few jokes. For years, they followed the tough vaudeville circuit, from little town to little town, from fleabag hotel to fleabag hotel. Some audiences loved them; some threw pickles at them. Most of the little money they made went to agents and managers. Winchell was only a so-so entertainer, but he was a funny storyteller, and he got in the habit of writing a little newsletter, which he called the *Daily Newssense,* and leaving it behind in theaters for the entertainment of the following vaudeville troupes. The *Daily Newssense* was a kind of continuous diary, a proto-blog. Winchell wrote not in paragraphs but in little one and two sentence bursts—"tweets" a later generation might say. He peppered his prose with the era's hottest slang. The *Daily Newssense* was a scandal sheet. Winchell reported who was dating whom; who was cheating on whom; who had said what catty thing about whom. Funny and cynical, hurtful and clever, the *Daily Newssense* was a hit. Winchell sent copies to regular papers like *The Vaudeville News* and *Billboard* and they printed them.

In 1920, when he was twenty-three, *The Vaudeville News* in New York City offered Winchell a job. He was to write a regular column just like his *Daily Newssense* for them. Winchell took the job and roared into action. He spent every night wandering Broadway, slipping in and out of theaters, partying with the singers and dancers and comedians, and soaking up all the latest gossip, which he then hurriedly wrote up in his unique jazzy, slangy, witty, and cruel style. Everyone, of course, denounced Winchell's gossip column— and hurried to read it as soon as it appeared. He moved to bigger papers, to the *New York Graphic* and then the *New York Mirror*. If people were hurt by his columns, they were also thrilled to be in them because Winchell's Broadway gossip column possessed the magical ability to grant celebrity to anyone mentioned. People did not really have to do anything; if they appeared in Winchell's column, they became instant celebrities. Celebrities would turn heads; people would rush to touch them; waiters would insist on giving them the best tables; reporters would ask their opinion on the world situation. How they dressed, what they had for breakfast, whom they dated, and whom they hated all became big news, more fodder for Winchell's column. This celebrity had nothing to do with actual accomplishment or talent or wisdom; it had everything to do with being touched by the magic of the mass media.

Everyone desperately wanted a mention in Winchell's columns and Winchell knew everyone. He himself became a celebrity. Once he started broadcasting his gossipy stories on nationwide radio, his own celebrity soared. As his biographer, Neal Gabler, notes, at Winchell's height, in the 1930s and 1940s, Winchell had an audience of at least fifty million people, or about one-third of the US population. His column was syndicated in two thousand newspapers.[5] Winchell was an enthusiastic networker and made friends with movie stars, agents, promoters, entrepreneurs, and politicians. Federal Bureau of Investigation (FBI) director J. Edgar Hoover, who loved the media's attention, became a Winchell pal.

Walter Winchell also loved gangsters.

In his twenties, patrolling Broadway—the same Broadway Damon Runyon made famous with his comic gangsters—Winchell ran into lots of mob guys. In the Jazz Age, a night on the town in New York meant seeing a show, then having dinner and drinks. During Prohibition, drinks were illegal, so having a drink meant committing a crime. For Winchell, however, and for most Americans, drinking illegal liquor was thrilling, not criminal. Knocking on the speakeasy door, whispering "Joe sent me," and dancing the Lindy Hop to the latest hot jazz, that was what the Roaring Twenties were all about. As for the bootleggers who trucked in the beer and whiskey, people like Dutch Schulz, Legs Diamond, Frank Costello, Waxey Gordon, and all the others, they shared the deliciously dangerous aura of the speakeasies. The New Yorker, in 1940, would remember that

> the intense melodrama of the Twenties accustomed people to an aristocracy of crime, to a superheated vision of America, ruled by an outlaw nobility of vast and incalculable powers. Beer barons and vice lords were a dime a dozen; almost every thug was at least a king. In New York, there were kings of vice, poultry, dope, fur, policy, and artichokes, to mention a few, and each of them commanded a band of desperadoes capable of dealing with the U.S. Marines.[6]

Prowling Broadway after midnight, Winchell did his best to cultivate the gangster look. Inside or out, he wore a snap-brim gray fedora; a Lucky Strike cigarette perpetually dangled from his lips. He spoke like he wrote, in sarcastic, sardonic, flippant clips. He rocked on his toes and jabbed with his fingers like a dancer or a featherweight fighter. His "crisp urban style," biographer Gabler writes, reminded everyone of the actor Jimmy Cagney.[7]

Owney Madden was Winchell's guide to the underworld. Madden was born in Liverpool; after his father's death, he was sent to live with relatives in New York City. A wild teenager in Manhattan's Hell's Kitchen neighborhood, he joined a gang called the Gophers. A thief, burglar, and killer, Madden made millions during Prohibition. All the bootleggers had their own clubs and speakeasies—Legs Diamond ran the Hotsy-Totsy Club; Dutch Schulz, the Hub Social Club; Frank Costello owned part of the Copacabana; and Madden was part owner of Harlem's famous Cotton Club. Later Madden even bought into the exclusive Stork Club. Just a year older than Winchell, Madden loved show business and knew all the stars and Winchell found him fascinating. Madden gave Winchell a Stuz Bearcat automobile as a gift and helped Winchell get an interview with Al Capone. Capone was playing cards when Winchell spoke with him in Miami. Capone waved his friends away. Winchell noted that just under the table, Capone had a gun. Why did he need a gun when he was playing cards with friends, Winchell asked. "I have no friends," Capone replied.[8]

Owney Madden also introduced Winchell to other underworld figures like Lucky Luciano. Once, Winchell said, he had been in Chicago and had been warned by some sinister figures that he had better share with them some of the money he had made in Chicago. Frightened, Winchell called the police for protection; he was a celebrity, after all, so they rushed over a couple of cops to keep an eye on him. Winchell, still nervous, called the FBI, explained that he was a friend of the director's, and asked for help; the bureau sent over a couple of special agents. Still frightened, Winchell contacted friends of Lucky Luciano back in New York. Could Lucky help him in Chicago? Within a few minutes, a couple of hoodlums appeared, vowing to take care of Mr. Winchell. For the rest of the evening, the Chicago cops, the FBI agents, and the underworld gorillas hovered around Winchell and glowered at each other.[9]

There were occasions when Winchell's gangster connection was unsettling. On February 8, 1932, Winchell included this in his gossip column:

Five planes brought dozens of machinegats from Chicago Friday [...] to combat the Town's Capone [...] Local banditti have made one hotel a virtual arsenal and several hot-spots are ditto because Master Coll is giving them the headache [...] One of the better Robin Hoods has a private phone in his cell [...] Haw!

Only hours before the column appeared, "Master Coll" had been shot to pieces in the London Chemist drugstore. Had Winchell known something about Coll's impending murder? Both the law and the underworld wanted to know.[10]

In 1937 and 1938, Walter Winchell turned the hunt for Lepke into a national obsession. Winchell reported all the latest rumors and boasted about having all the inside dope.

Then, on August 5, 1939, Winchell, at the Stork Club, got a scary telephone call. Lepke wanted to come in, the caller said, but Lepke was afraid he would be killed. Lepke would surrender to only Winchell and to J. Edgar Hoover—personally.

The call was an extraordinary scoop for the gossip columnist, but terrifying too. On August 6, he told his radio audience: "Your reporter is reliably informed—that Lepke, the fugitive, is on the verge of surrender, perhaps this week. If Lepke can find someone he can trust (I am told) he will come in [...] I am authorized to state by the G-Men—that Lepke is assured of safe delivery."[11] But for the next three weeks, Winchell got frightening calls, telling him to go here and then go there in the middle of the night. No Lepke. At last, after Hoover angrily vowed to order his agents to shoot Lepke on sight, Winchell got a final call. On August 24, around 10:30 p.m., Winchell parked his car on 24th Street, near Madison Square. A man got in. It was Lepke. Winchell drove to the corner of Fifth Avenue and 28th Street. He and Lepke got out and walked to a waiting car. In it were J. Edgar Hoover and some of his agents. Winchell introduced Lepke to Hoover. Lepke got in the car, and they all sped off to the Federal Building on Foley Square. Winchell drove off to report his extraordinary story.[12] The *Times* headlined the FBI's, and Hoover's, role in Lepke's surrender; Hoover snidely pointed out to the *Times* that "neither the New York Police nor District Attorney Dewey [. . .] had any part in bringing into custody the man whom Mr. Dewey had denounced as the 'worst industrial racketeer in America.'"[13] Although Winchell loved to recount his role in the Lepke adventure, he was content to let Hoover take the credit. It was a huge favor to Hoover, and you never knew when you might need a favor from the FBI in return.[14]

Abe Reles knew all along where Lepke had been hiding. When Lepke went on the lam in 1936, he asked Albert Anastasia for help. Anastasia told Reles to hide Lepke. Reles and his gang arranged for a series of hideouts for Lepke in New York; they brought him food, newspapers, and cigarettes. They kept the curious away. In January 1939, for instance, a neighbor named Eugenio Salvese wondered who the new tenant was in the apartment on Clinton Street, in Brooklyn. Abe Reles noticed Salvese staring at the building, stepped over to him, and said,

> You are a good fellow. Don't talk to anybody about the boarder in the basement of the house. You are a hard-working man. You work hard for a living. If you do as I say and don't talk to anybody and be a good fellow, maybe you won't have to work anymore.[15]

By 1939, though, as the heat got worse, people like Frank Costello, Albert Anastasia, and others decided that Lepke had to come in. Anastasia brought Lepke to Winchell on that August night. Convicted on federal narcotics charges, Lepke thought he was safe. He was sentenced to prison at Fort Leavenworth, Kansas, and he assumed that he would spend the next dozen or so years there. He was not safe. On May 9, 1941, in Brooklyn, Burton Turkus charged Lepke Buchalter with first-degree murder.

Turkus would have to handle the Lepke case mostly without District Attorney O'Dwyer's help because that summer and fall, Bill O'Dwyer was very busy. He was running for mayor against Fiorello La Guardia. The Murder, Inc., trials had done great things for O'Dwyer; they had made him Tom Dewey's gangbuster heir. The New York press was filled with praise for O'Dwyer, and national magazines like *Life* and *Look* published their flattering profiles.[16]

Bill O'Dwyer was determined to ride the gangbuster wave just as Tom Dewey had; O'Dwyer, in 1941, planned to use his gangbuster fame to get himself elected New York's mayor. His Tammany Hall supporters were sure that if anyone could finally defeat Fiorello La Guardia, it would be O'Dwyer. So that summer and fall of 1941, Bill O'Dwyer was running for mayor. Burt Turkus and his staff would handle the Lepke case.[17]

Originally, Turkus had planned to indict Louis Capone for organizing the murder of Joe Rosen in 1936, Mendy Weiss and Harry Strauss for actually killing Rosen, James "Dizzy" Ferraco for acting as lookout, and Philip "Little Farvel" Cohen for helping with the getaway. Strauss had already been convicted of killing Puggy Feinstein. Little Farvel Cohen had already been convicted of narcotics trafficking and was already in prison; anyway, Turkus lacked positive evidence to link Cohen to the Rosen murder. Dizzy Ferraco had disappeared and was presumed dead. So Turkus decided to prosecute the remaining three—Louis Capone, Mendy Weiss, and Lepke Buchalter.[18] Turkus described Lepke, Capone, and Weiss as "big game"; Turkus wrote, "for me, this was the big one."[19]

Jury selection began in August 1941. Jurors were fully aware of what had happened to other witnesses against Lepke; it took some time to find enough people who were willing to serve.

The trial of Louis Capone, Mendy Weiss, and Louis "Lepke" Buchalter for the murder of Joe Rosen began in October 1941. Defending Lepke was Hyman Barshay, a former assistant district attorney. Capone's attorney was Sidney Rosenthal, one of New York's leading defense attorneys. Retired judge Alfred Talley defended Mendy Weiss—a "banner lineup of New York's legal talent," costing, Turkus thought, at least a quarter of a million dollars.[20]

Like all trials, this trial began slowly. Turkus described the victim, Joe Rosen, through the testimony of Rosen's wife and children. Joe Rosen was a simple trucker. Rosen had refused to pay off Lepke and Gurrah. They had gotten him fired. Rosen had opened a little convenience store in Brooklyn; he sold candy, odds and ends, and newspapers. His family lived in the back. Gurrah Shapiro and Mendy Weiss had started hanging around the store. Rosen vowed to go to Dewey; Gurrah and Weiss had tried to buy him off and then threatened him repeatedly. Rosen's son, wife, and daughter swore they had witnessed all this.[21] The police described the murder—early Sunday morning, September 13, 1936, Joe

Rosen had opened his convenience store, stepped outside to retrieve a bundle of newspapers, and walked back into his store. Two men followed and shot Rosen to death. Neighborhood witnesses described the bangs of the guns that they'd heard and the screech of the tires of the getaway car. Then Turkus began to trot out his star witnesses.

Turkus called Sholom Bernstein, the same Bernstein who had tried to help Bugsy Siegel murder Big Greenie out in Los Angeles. Bernstein had worked for Lepke for many years; Turkus wanted Bernstein to explain to the jury just how Lepke intimidated people. Well, for instance, Bernstein patiently explained, he'd get a call from Mendy Weiss, Gurrah Shapiro, or someone else; an accomplice would steal a car to be used on the job and then Bernstein would go on a "shlom" job. At this point, the judge interrupted. A what job? Turkus, Lepke's lawyer, Hyman Barshay, and the judge tried to define "shlom job" while Bernstein sat quietly on the witness chair. A "shlom job"? Was that a beating? A killing? Finally, they asked Bernstein. "It means breaking someone's head with a lead pipe," Bernstein explained. That was the sort of work Bernstein did for Lepke Buchalter.[22]

Turkus called on Max Rubin. Rubin had worked for Lepke for years. Rubin counted the money and helped keep Lepke's labyrinthine books. As the Dewey investigations heated up, Rubin decided to bail out. He knew what had happened to Joe Rosen in 1936, but he had no intention of going to jail to protect Lepke. Word reached Lepke that Rubin was turning canary. In 1937, Rubin turned state's evidence and testified against Lepke. On October 1, 1937, Rubin was walking along a New York street when a car pulled alongside. Someone in the car shouted, "Max!" Rubin looked, and the man who'd called his name shot him in the head. Miraculously, Rubin survived; the would-be assassin was never identified. Sholem Bernstein testified that Mendy Weiss had been in charge of the attempt to kill Rubin. Charlie "the Bug" Workman, Tannenbaum added, had remarked to him that "whoever did the shooting should not have trusted to luck that one shot was sufficient, but should have taken a few shots." Workman, Tannenbaum added, "expressed disappointment for not having been given that assignment."[23] Now, in October 1941, Rubin testified against Lepke. He explained how Lepke's extraordinarily intricate system of inter-locking and fake businesses worked. He told the jury that Lepke boasted of having an "in" with Brooklyn's former district attorney, William F. X. Geoghan,[24] and how he, Rubin, was present when Lepke exploded in anger about Joe Rosen's threats to go to Dewey.[25]

Turkus trotted out Seymour "Blue Jaw" Magoon, who had already testified against Harry Maione, Frank Abbandando, Martin Goldstein, and

Harry Strauss. Magoon testified that he had spoken with Louis Capone about another job along Sutter Avenue; Magoon was nervous about it because Sutter was a busy thoroughfare with lots of potential witnesses. According to Magoon, Capone replied, "Why, I was on the Rosen thing and it was right on Sutter Avenue and I wasn't recognized."[26]

Then Turkus called on Allie "Tick Tock" Tannenbaum. Tannenbaum had carried out special jobs for Lepke, like killing another potential Dewey witness, Irv Ashkenaz.[27] Tannenbaum had agreed to testify for Turkus. He confirmed Bernstein's and Rubin's testimony. That day, back in the summer of 1936, when Lepke was raging on about Joe Rosen, "Lepke's face was flushed; he was angry," Tannenbaum testified. "He was yelling at Max [Rubin]."

> Lepke was yelling that he gave Rosen money to go away and then he sneaks back into a candy store, after he tells him to stay away. Lepke was hollering. He says, 'There is one son of a bitch that will never go down to talk to Dewey about me.' Max was trying to calm him down.

But Lepke would not be calmed. "This is the end of it," Tannenbaum heard him say; "I'm fed up with that son of a bitch and I'll take care of him." Later, Tannenbaum was in Lepke's office when Mendy Weiss reported in after killing Rosen. Tannenbaum reported Weiss's angry comment that "that son of a bitch, Pep" [Harry Strauss] wouldn't stop shooting Rosen. Tannenbaum said that Lepke had replied: "all right, what's the difference [. . .] as long as everybody is clean and you got away all right."[28]

By early November 1941, Turkus's case against Capone, Weiss, and Buchalter was going well, and Turkus had yet to call on his star witness, Abe Reles. Reles had not been part of the Rosen job, but as usual, Reles knew all about it.

Turkus had even greater things in mind for Abe Reles. After convicting Lepke, Turkus was determined to go after Albert Anastasia, Brooklyn's most powerful gangster and one of the most powerful criminals in New York. Reles was the key to destroying Anastasia. Reles had worked with Anastasia for years and had repeatedly killed people on his orders. Insofar as Reles was an accomplice in any of those murders, he was of little use to Turkus. Amazingly, however, Reles was an uninvolved eyewitness to a murder conspiracy in which the chief conspirator was Anastasia.

Morris Diamond was a teamster official who was murdered in 1939. Lepke had feared that Diamond would testify about Lepke's muscling into the trucking industry. Albert Anastasia, according to Reles, had agreed to murder Diamond. Once, in 1939, Reles told Turkus, he had gone over to Anastasia's Brooklyn home. "I came over to talk to Albert about our bookmaking business and these two guys are sitting there." The two guys were the same two Lepke assassins who had killed Dutch Schulz—Mendy Weiss and Charlie "the Bug" Workman. Anastasia, Weiss, and Workman, Reles told Turkus, "are discussing the Diamond matter." Anastasia was complaining that Weiss was too slow in killing Diamond. "Everybody is ready and you still haven't told us where the bum lives," Anastasia complained. "As soon as I get it, I'll give it to you," Weiss replied. "When I get it," Anastasia responded, "we will take care of him."[29] That fragment of conversation, combined with everything else Turkus had, would be enough, Turkus was sure, to send Albert Anastasia to the electric chair.

Bill O'Dwyer waged a bruising campaign for mayor in November 1941, but he was defeated by Fiorello La Guardia. *The New Yorker* was shocked by the name-calling and mudslinging. "By contrast," *The New Yorker* commented,

we thought the testimony of a stool-pigeon killer named Sholom Bernstein at the Brooklyn murder trials furnished a nice exhibition of decorum. For example, O'Dwyer called La Guardia "a paymaster of gangsters," La Guardia called Governor Lehman "a fixer," and the Italian press called Roosevelt "a criminal grafter," but Sholom Bernstein had no stronger term for Abe Reles, confessed murderer of eleven men, than 'that mouse.' A political campaign conducted on the level of "dictator," "clown," "cad," "dope," "cabbage head," "bum," "goniff," "flop," "looney," "faker," and "charlatan," shocks us a bit, and we were relieved when Bernstein carefully addressed all lawyers as "sir" and "counselor," and always referred to the police as "those gentlemen." And who, would you say offhand was accused of being "a welsher," "a criminal lunatic," a "congenital liar," a "hypocrite," and a "cowardly jackal"? Pittsburgh Phil Strauss, Dirty Face Ferraco, Little Farvel Cohen, or the President of the United States? Class dismissed.[30]

O'Dwyer had lost, but he had run a strong race. There was still plenty of publicity to be won from Murder, Inc. He still had a bright political career before him, and there'd be another mayoral race in 1945.

Wednesday morning, November 12, 1941. Burton Turkus would later remember that he was at home, getting ready for court. The telephone rang. On the line was Harry Feeney, the reporter who had dubbed Turkus's defendants "Murder, Inc." Feeney said, "Hey Burt. Reles just went out the window."[31] Turkus was aghast. Reles was in protective custody! He was the key to the entire Murder, Inc., investigation! But now, Abe Reles had gone flying out the window.

What in heaven's name had happened?

Abe Reles had been in protective custody in the Half Moon Hotel on Coney Island, on Brooklyn's southern shore, safe, Turkus hoped, from Brooklyn's gangs. Scores of whispered death threats swirled around Reles, and O'Dwyer and Turkus had taken them seriously.[32] The Half Moon, named after Henry Hudson's ship, had been built in the 1920s for Coney Island tourists. It was a big hotel, shaped like an upside-down *T*. Its base was a long rectangle, with a tall tower in the center. "You may know it," *The New Yorker* wrote in a 1933 description of the Half Moon: "the tall brick building set rather haughtily away from the gaudier sections of Coney Island and inhabited mostly by elderly ladies who look as if they'd be dizzied by a revolving door." The Half Moon's lobby was the meeting place for the "haut monde of Brooklyn politics." Only twenty minutes from Floyd Bennett Air Field, the Half Moon attracted a number of pilots. Busy in the summer, the Half Moon was, *The New Yorker* reported, pretty lonely in the winter.[33] Several businesses had offices in the Half Moon, including the local draft board. That chilly November of 1941, the Half Moon was half empty. New York police had reserved the sixth floor; they called it the "squealer suite."

The Murder, Inc., informers, held in protective custody, lived on the sixth floor with their police guards. That November, four witnesses were being held: Abe Reles, Sholem Bernstein, Allie "Tick Tock" Tannenbaum, and Mickey Sycoff, a loan shark's loan shark, who had played a small but important part in the trials thus far. Sycoff had been involved in the 1935 murders of Joey Amberg and Manny Kessler.[34] All four knew each other. They were all locked onto the sixth floor, but they were not exactly prisoners; Bernstein had his own room, room 622, and so did Reles, room 623. Tannenbaum and Sycoff shared room 626, across the hall. Access to the sixth floor was guarded by the police. The witnesses could not lock their doors, nor were they locked in. They were free to wander around the floor. Half-a-dozen detectives shared the floor with them and mounted a 'round-the-clock guard; the guards had their own room, 620. Other police officers were elsewhere in the hotel standing watch.[35]

For Reles, Bernstein, Tannenbaum, and Sycoff, and their detective warders, life in the Half Moon was tedious at best. They flipped through magazines (carefully screened to keep reporting on the trials away from them); they played endless card games. Reles was not exactly popular. His

The Half Moon Hotel and a sketch of Reles's fall. (*Brooklyn Eagle*, Brooklyn Public Library)

courtroom stardom had gone to his head; he was even more bossy and boastful than ever. He was also gross. He had developed some sort of lung infection. When they ate together, he would hack, cough, spit phlegm into the palm of his hand, and then show it off to his companions. Allie Tannenbaum thought that Reles "had filthy habits."[36]

When one or another witness was needed in court the whole floor would come alive, the witness would dress in his best suit; scowling and heavily armed, detectives would hurry him down the elevator and out the hotel's entrance into a waiting squad car. However, for both police officers and witnesses, most days were spent in mind-numbing boredom.

Witnesses were allowed to have visitors, and on the night of November 11, Rose Reles came to see her husband. The visit was long, from around 7:00 p.m. until nearly 10:00 p.m., and unhappy. Rose was sick to death of gangsters, lawyers, trials, cops, reporters, and death threats. She had two young children now to think of; what kind of life could she possibly have left with Abe? They'd had fights like this before; she'd demand a divorce, Abe would refuse. Whatever they talked about, Tick Tock Tannenbaum thought Rose looked "irate" when she left; she usually asked Tannenbaum about his family, but this time she didn't and it kind of hurt Tannenbaum's feelings.[37]

On Wednesday, November 12, 1941, at 4:30 a.m., four men were sitting around in the lobby of the Half Moon Hotel at Coney Island.[38] George Govans, the night bellhop, was dozing on a sofa. Alfred Wolfarth, the building engineer, was half asleep in a chair; he had been working on the hotel's furnace all night. Officers Charles Burns and Thomas Doyle, from the New York Police Department, were sitting in the lobby, too; they were part of the police unit designated to guard the "squealers' suite." The middle of the night in mid-November is dark and chilly in Coney Island; the dark Atlantic Ocean rumbled nearby, and a cold wind blew across the water. The four men later remembered that they were arguing about the Brooklyn Dodgers. After winning their first pennant in two decades, the Dodgers had just lost the World Series to their archrival, the New York Yankees.

Suddenly, a loud thud startled Alfred Wolfarth. Govans thought it sounded like a car banging into something. But the police officers were not alarmed, and it was too dark to see anything outside anyway.

At 7:00 a.m., William Nicholson, the chief clerk of the Draft Board, which had its office in the Half Moon, arrived at work, settled at his desk, gazed out the window—and saw a human body on the kitchen roof only a few feet away. Nicholson snatched up his phone and called Alexander Lysberg, the hotel's assistant manager. Lysberg ran out of his eleventh-floor office, hurried down the elevator, and joined Nicholson. Nicholson pointed out the window. There, lying facedown, was a corpse.

Lysberg ran to the entrance and grabbed officers Burns and Doyle who were at their posts in front of the hotel. Lysberg, Burns, and Doyle clambered out onto the kitchen roof. The corpse was facedown, its left arm flung out and its face embedded with the roof's gravel. It was dressed casually, in a gray suit, white shirt, blue sweater, and black shoes. Fluttering above them, they noticed two sheets, tied together, flapping out of a sixth-floor window. Fifty-two feet below the sixth-floor window was the corpse. Burns hurried inside; from Nicholson's office, he frantically called his precinct. Within minutes, police cars and an ambulance were howling their way to the Half Moon. The dead guy, Officers Burns and Doyle reported, was Abe Reles.

For the next few hours, everything would be crazy at the Half Moon. Captain Frank Bals, District Attorney O'Dwyer's chief police investigator, and a dozen detectives scrambled out onto the roof and with astonishing carelessness, rolled the body over, and examined it. The officers ran up to the sixth floor and into Reles's room. Reles, or someone else, had tied two sheets together and then tied one end of the sheets to a length of wire; the wire was wound around the room's radiator. Reles, or someone else, had then tossed the knotted-together sheets out the window.

Everyone was shouting questions at everyone else. Detective James Boyle swore he had checked on Reles around 6:45 a.m. and saw Reles asleep in his bed. If that were true, the thud Govans, Wolfarth, Burns, and Doyle had heard around 4:30 a.m. could not have been Reles. Detective Victor Robbins said that he had checked on Reles around 7:10 a.m., and Reles was gone! Robbins saw the sheets out the window and had rushed over to the window and looked out; he had seen Reles's body six floors below. Robbins also insisted that he had immediately notified police headquarters.[39] Reles's corpse was pulled onto a stretcher, hauled back into the hotel, and then hurried downstairs and out to the waiting ambulance.

The media instantly flashed the news. Harry Feeney called Burt Turkus. That day, newspaper headlines shouted the shocking news: "Reles Dies in Hotel Plunge!"[40]

Why did Abe Reles go flying out the window?[41]

The medical examiner determined that Reles probably landed in a kind of sitting position; the tremendous impact of the fifty-two feet fall had broken his back. Had he been drunk? Or drugged? No, the autopsy found no odd chemicals in his body.

Had he committed suicide? His life was a shambles; he had just had a fight with his wife. Maybe he was afraid to testify against Lepke or Anastasia. However, those who knew Reles were sure that he had not killed himself. He had never shown any signs of suicidal behavior and never admitted to any suicidal thoughts. His single strongest trait was a fierce survival instinct, even if his own survival sent others to their deaths. He had never lost his "cocky manner."[42] No one really believed Reles had jumped.

Had he died, then, in an escape attempt? That was what the first newspaper reports said.[43] He had tied those sheets together to make a rope, anchored his homemade rope to his room's radiator with a piece of wire he had found, and then climbed out the window and down the sheets.

But this was as hard to believe as the suicide theory. Reles, despite his famously long arms and powerful hands, was no gymnast. Anyway, the sheets hanging out Reles's sixth-floor window only reached to the fifth-floor window. What had he intended to do, break into the fifth-floor room below him? How did he know the room was not occupied? Even if he gotten into the fifth-floor room, then what? Would he have ridden the elevator down to the lobby and into the arms of Officers Burns, Doyle, and their colleagues? Then too, why in the world would Reles try to escape? He knew that everyone in the underworld wanted to kill him. He knew that the only safe place he had in the whole world was the sixth floor of the Half Moon Hotel.

Police captain Frank Bals had his own peculiar theory. No, Reles had not committed suicide, Captain Bals agreed, and no, this was not an escape attempt. Remember, Bals argued, Abe Reles was quite the jokester. He liked shocking people. Maybe, Captain Bals suggested, this was all a joke gone bad. Maybe Reles planned to climb out his sixth-floor window, climb back in the fifth-floor window, then march upstairs to the sixth floor, and surprise his guards and fellow informers!

No one, aside from Frank Bals, thought Reles was trying to pull off a practical joke.

And so there remained only one, last, grim possibility. Had someone pitched Reles out the window? Had one or more of Reles's fellow informers—Bernstein, Tannenbaum, and Sycoff, each of whom had killed people—simply tired of Reles? Or, had they decided to curry favor with the gangs, and, especially, with Lepke Buchalter and Albert Anastasia, by finally, at long last, silencing Reles? Had one or more of the detectives agreed to look the other way—or even to help?

Had Abe Reles, one of the leaders of Murder, Inc., been murdered?

District Attorney O'Dwyer immediately ordered both an internal police investigation and empaneled a grand jury to investigate Reles's murder. No one discovered anything.[44]

New York's media were enraged. How could the district attorney, how
could the whole New York Police Department, not figure out who killed
Abe Reles? The journalists, however, despite their intensive reporting,
could not solve the mystery either.

Burton Turkus was shocked and deeply frustrated by Reles's death but
cautious in his opinions. Turkus would later write that "the conclusion
[. . .] is that murder by one or two men is the likeliest of all the theories
advanced for Reles' startling and mysterious end."[45] Turkus did not identify the one or two men he thought involved; presumably he meant Tannenbaum, Bernstein, and Sycoff, the other witnesses in the hotel. Albert
Anastasia was obviously the beneficiary of Reles' death, but Turkus provides no proof of Anastasia's direct involvement in the murder. Shortly
after Reles's death, O'Dwyer quietly informed his office and the New
York Police Department that he was ending the investigation of Albert
Anastasia. The media were incredulous, but O'Dwyer insisted that without Reles, there was no case against Anastasia. Anastasia, who had disappeared, suddenly turned up again among his friends on the Brooklyn
docks. Burton Turkus never publicly criticized O'Dwyer's decision, but
in his memoir, Turkus does cite others' vehement criticisms.[46] Out on the
streets, there were no doubts about Reles's fate. As Joe Valachi later commented, "I never met anybody who thought Abe went out that window
because he wanted to."[47]

No one mourned for Abe Reles. Cops laughed that Reles was a canary who could sing but couldn't fly.[48] After the coroner was done with
his body, his relatives quickly retrieved it and quietly buried it in a private
ceremony. Reporter Walter Kiernan wrote a scathing obituary, aimed at
Brooklyn teenage boys who might be tempted by the hoodlum life. Kiernan called his piece, published in the Brooklyn Eagle, "Hey Kids! Reles
Was No Hero, Just a Blubberer with a Grin." Reles, Kiernan wrote, was
"a top-grade No. 1 specimen of gangster and consequently a low-grade
heel without morals, conscience, and not much sense." So, Kiernan continued, "gangsters have glamor—eh? Come around with me some time
and talk to the widow of a man they have rubbed out by mistake. They've
done that, you know [. . .] Watch her sitting there twisting her handkerchief beside the body of her man and try to work up a good case of hero
worship for the rat who killed him." He concluded,

Burton Turkus (*right*) and Lepke Buchalter (*center*) during Buchalter's murder trial.
(*Brooklyn Eagle*, Brooklyn Public Library)

If you want a laugh, step into a police precinct and watch one of these
boys who has been deprived of his gun blubber: "sure, I'll talk—it
wasn't me—it was him [...]." Reles had a couple of youngsters. Say
a little prayer for them. Pray that if he ever did a nice thing for them
they will remember—and forget the rest.[49]

The Lepke trial had yet to conclude, and it still crackled with excitement.
Allie "Tick Tock" Tannenbaum emerged as the key witness; had he actually been a police snitch all along? Tick Tock never admitted anything,
but there were stories that he had been paid by the New York Police
Department's famous detective, Barney Ruditsky, for years.[50] Defense
attorney James Cuff suddenly collapsed; from insulin shock, the doctors
said later.[51] On November 30, 1941, Burton Turkus's birthday, the jury
found Lepke, Capone, and Weiss guilty of the murder of Joe Rosen. All
three were sentenced to death in Sing Sing's electric chair. Lepke was the
first, and only, major crime figure to be sentenced to death.

On February 20, 1942, just after midnight, Harry Maione and Frank
Abbandando were electrocuted in Sing Sing.[52] Both went quietly to their

deaths. Their bodies were shipped back to Brooklyn for burial. There was a ruckus at Frank Abbandando's funeral. A photographer for the *New York Journal-American*, Henry McAllister, showed up at the private funeral and began snapping pictures. Frank Abbandando's brother, Rocco, kicked McAllister out of the funeral home. Rocco was arrested and charged with assault but, at his trial, apologized and received a suspended sentence.[53] In April 1942, Harry Maione's two brothers, Carlo and Louis, were arrested for and later convicted of intimidating witnesses during the Maione and Abbandando trials.[54] A decade after Frank Abbandando's execution, in March 1952, his son, Frank, Jr., now sixteen, was arrested and charged with illegal possession of a loaded gun. The presiding magistrate, Arthur Dunaif, warned Frank, Jr., "This seems to be a second edition of Murder, Inc. You're starting out early on the wrong path." According to the *Times* reporter, Frank Jr., "a dark-haired, undersized lad who wore a gray gabardine zoot suit and a sport shirt with a Windsor-knotted tie seemed unperturbed."[55]

Lepke Buchalter dominated the very last act of the Murder, Inc., story. Lepke was convicted in November 1941; his lawyers immediately filed an appeal. Lepke himself dangled various enticements before intrigued prosecutors. Lepke suggested that he had lots of dirt on lots of politicians. "If I would talk," Lepke warned, "a lot of big people would get hurt."[56] Two of President Roosevelt's leading trade union supporters were Sydney Hillman and Dave Dubinsky from the garment industry; Lepke hinted that he had lots of stories to tell about both. No one doubted Hillman and Dubinsky knew about Lepke; everyone in the garment industry did. However, neither Lepke nor later researchers ever produced any evidence that either Hillman or Dubinsky was a racketeer; in fact, both Hillman and Dubinsky were determined to rid the gangsters from their unions. In March 1944, Lepke offered to cut a deal with Governor Tom Dewey, who then was preparing to run for president against Franklin Roosevelt. However, Dewey was unimpressed with Lepke's stories.

The poet Robert Lowell saw Lepke from a distance when Lowell was imprisoned as a conscientious objector during World War II. In "Memories of West Street Jail and Lepke," the narrator writes that another prisoner, a Jehovah's Witness, taught him how to make his bed with a "hospital tuck," and

[p]ointed out the T-shirted back
of *Murder, Incorporated*'s Czar Lepke,
there piling towels on a rack
or dawdling off to his little segregated cell full

of things forbidden to the common man:
a portable radio, a dresser, two toy American
flags tied together with a ribbon of Easter palm.
Flabby, bald, lobotomized,
he drifted in a sheepish calm,
where no agonizing reappraisal
jarred his concentration on the electric chair
hanging like an oasis in his air
of lost connections.[57]

On Thursday—Sing Sing always conducted its executions on Thursdays—March 4, 1944, at 11:00 p.m.—executions were always at 11:00 p.m.—Louis Capone, Mendy Weiss, and Lepke Buchalter, one after the other, were electrocuted. Each was strapped into the electric chair, and a gurney waited behind the chair to carry the corpse away. Twenty-two hundred volts of electricity were fired into each; they died almost immediately. Sometimes hair or skin burned. Louis Capone went first and had nothing to say. Mendy Weiss said, "I'm innocent. I'm here on a framed-up case. Give my love to my family and everything." Lepke went last. He had no final words.[58]

With Abe Reles's mysterious death, the Murder, Inc., investigations and trials suddenly ended. Reles died in November 1941; weeks later, Japan bombed Pearl Harbor, and the United States went to war. War stories drove gangster stories from the headlines. District attorney and former candidate for mayor Bill O'Dwyer joined the army as a major; by war's end, he would be a brigadier general. His duties were legal and logistical. In December 1942, Major O'Dwyer was briefly back in New York on army business. He was also in New York on political business. O'Dwyer wanted to run for mayor again in 1945 and needed Tammany's backing. He was in New York to begin raising money and aligning friends.

One of the people O'Dwyer quietly met with was Frank Costello. O'Dwyer's rivals got wind of the meeting and never let O'Dwyer live it down. O'Dwyer tried to explain that he was just investigating, for the army, allegations of contract fraud at Wright Air Force Base in Dayton, Ohio. He just went to see Frank Costello because, well, maybe Costello would know something about contract fraud. Yes, Costello was a retired bootlegger and gambler, O'Dwyer admitted, and yes, he had trouble with his taxes, but Costello was someone a person talked to if serious about politics in New York. Of course, Tammany people were there in Costello's apartment that evening too. Costello knew a lot of people. Frank Costello had a lot of friends.[59]

And so, the Murder, Inc., investigations and trials ended on a minor, bleak, uncertain note. What had happened to Abe Reles? Why did O'Dwyer drop the Anastasia investigation? Why did O'Dwyer go to see Frank Costello? After all this time and all this effort, after the Seabury hearings, Dewey's gangbusting, and the Murder, Inc., trials, had anything really been accomplished?

The Murder, Inc., trials had been a kind of moral crusade. Now, however, they had ended in confusion and ambiguity. Morality is about certainty, is it not? Can ambiguity have anything to do with morality? After all, does morality not mean the application of unambiguous moral laws? Is ambiguity, then, not a sign that morality has failed?

Certainly an older sort of ethics would have dismissed ambiguity out of hand. At least since the eighteenth century, moral philosophy has been based on two key principles: (1) religion, with its miracles, its stress on narrative, and its relentless paradoxes, had no place in ethical discourse (religious people could, of course, talk about ethics, but ethical philosophers had no business talking about religion), and (2) moral philosophy should be a kind of moral mechanics, based on universal, inflexible, and predictable laws. All the great Enlightenment-era moralities—Kantian deontology, Lockean contractarianism, and Benthamite utilitarianism—look to Newtonian physics as their model. To be moral, then, meant to identify Newtonian-like moral principles and then, after due deliberation, implement them. As Zygmunt Bauman writes, modern moral thought, like modernity in general, sought "to replace diversity with uniformity and ambivalence with coherent and transparent order."[60] Moral agents ought to be engineers of souls, who apply unquestionable rules with efficient skill. Morality, to switch metaphors, ought to be painted in bold colors, not sketched in chiaroscuro.

Unfortunately, Newtonian ethics, certainly by the twentieth century, had reached a dead end. Even during the Enlightenment, Adam Smith, in addition to describing early capitalism, had developed a "theory of moral sentiments." Calculating reason alone does not lead to moral outcomes, Smith thought. The "sentiments" do. By sentiments, Smith meant emotions but also a whole range of mental states and activities including intuition, sensations of pleasure and disgust, and aesthetic experience. They, and not just arithmetical syllogisms, shape moral judgment. Thus, the cultivation of the sentiments is as vital a part of moral education as logical training. Thus, too, consulting the sentiments is as important a part of moral reflection as parsing arguments, even though sentiments are inherently messy and even contradictory.[61]

Darwin and Marx played a role in undermining Newtonian morality by stressing the ineluctable and dynamic nature of social, cultural, and moral change. Whatever moral philosophy may be, it must be more than the mechanical application of static rules to static situations. Morality must take account of motion, something William James and the Pragmatists attempted to do. The "universe," James argued, is more like a ""multiverse" or "pluriverse" than a "universe." At least since Darwin, the world had become increasingly complicated and monism, the belief that one fixed universe needs only one fixed set of laws, simply will not do. The "absolute" needs to be replaced, James argued, by a much more open notion that might be called the "ultimate"[62] (or, to speak with Emmanuel Levinas, "totality" ought to be replaced with "infinity").[63] If morality is to be compared to science, James insisted it ought to be thought of not as something "deducible all at once from abstract principles" but more as an experimental science, tentative and particular and "ready to revise its conclusions from day to day."[64]

If morality moreover, deals with action, that is, with constructing a future that does not yet exist, then morality, at the point of action, can never be certain of itself. Morality, then, is inherently ambiguous because it deals with choices whose outcomes are unclear. That is why morality requires courage in the face of uncertainty. Indeed, if an action's outcomes were clear, if there were no choices to be made, no real dilemmas to be faced, if responsibility were never an issue because there were no alternatives to be consider anyway, then such an action might be many different things but "moral" would not be one of them.

The twentieth century was seared by ambiguity and uncertainty, by "absurd" moments when "is" and "ought" conflicted, when, as Albert Camus argued, the human yearning for meaning collided with the raw experience of meaninglessness. Morality, at least for Camus, did not mean eliminating the absurd because the absurd was the very condition of the possibility of morality. Morality meant facing the absurd, rebelling against the absurd, and accepting all the contradictions that rebellion might involve.

In any case, as Levinas argued, the distinctly "moral moment" is a specific, concrete, face-to-face encounter when the moral actor recognizes the other as a person, even if the other does not reciprocate. The "Good Samaritan" rescues the one fallen among thieves not because of any kind of reciprocal agreement, not to maximize utility, not to fulfil a social contract, and not even to fulfill a Kantian sense of duty, but because the Good Samaritan, moved by compassion not calculation, recognizes the other as a person, even though the story never indicates that the other ever recognizes the Samaritan as a person too. Simon Critchley, like Levinas, insists that "ethical experience" is "first and foremost, the approval of a demand," that is, the primordial ethical moment arises when I recognize an other as a person for whom I experience concern. It is from that moment, experienced as a kind of "revelation," that moral action begins.[65] Of course, proverbs and principles may then prove useful, but the distinctive thing about moral experience is its concrete, revelatory, coming-to-awareness quality, not its adherence to a physics-like law.

"Revelation" suggests, of course, that the eighteenth-century banning of religion from moral philosophy was a fundamental mistake. In fact, *revelation, apocalypse, redemption, messiah,* and a whole host of other religious terms are absolutely central to ethical thought, at least if one accepts the sorts of arguments made by, among others, a whole generation of German thinkers ranging from Theodor Adorno to Walter Benjamin, from Ernest Bloch to Dietrich Bonhoeffer to Martin Buber and Franz Rosenzweig. As Wayne Cristaudo argues, what links these very diverse writers, and what others, such as Jacques Derrida and Emmanuel Levinas share, is an acceptance of "the defining philosophical gesture of the twentieth century," the attack on "totalism," that is, the rejection of the belief that some "total system," some "philosophical physics," could someday remove mystery, paradox, contingency and ambiguity from human affairs.[66]

This movement away from Newtonian morality is what Zygmunt Bauman means by "postmodern ethics." The term *postmodern* carries with it a heavy baggage; it sometimes is understood to mean some unpleasant thing ranging from relativism to nihilism. For Bauman, *postmodern* means a final departure from eighteenth-century understandings of ethics. "Modern" morality was based on the search for a "non-ambivalent, non-aporetic [that is, non-contradictory] ethical code."[67] However, there is no such thing. "A foolproof—universal and unshakably founded—ethical code will never be found," Bauman insists, because "morality is incurably *aporetic,*"[68] that is, riddled with contradictions. "The moral self moves," Bauman writes, "feels and acts in the context of ambivalence and is shot through with uncertainty. Hence the ambiguity-free moral situation has solely an utopian existence [...] seldom may moral acts bring complete satisfaction [...] uncertainty is bound to accompany the condition of the moral self forever."[69]

All this does not mean that the moral actor should be cynical or despondent; it does mean that the moral actor must be both brave and responsible and that ambivalence, far from meaning that that morality has fled a situation, is often a clear marker that the situation is deeply moral.

The messy Dewey investigations; Dewey's release of Luciano; the chaotic and shocking end to the Murder, Inc., trials, do not detract from the moral intensity of the issues involved. To the contrary—untidy, ambiguous, incomplete, with a murder mystery as its finale, the Murder, Inc., case is, at root, a profoundly moral issue, not despite its ambivalence but precisely because of its ambivalence. The owl of Minerva, as Hegel crisply put it, flies by night; morality's favorite color is noir.

Epilogue
"That Dangerous and Sad City of the Imagination"

> I remember the first day it rained. I unhitched
> the cultivator and went back to the farm. Earl
> Putnam asked me, "Why?" I said: "I thought
> we didn't work when it rained." He replied:
> "We do." So I went back to the field and
> went on cultivating and I never went
> home again when it rained.
>
> —*Tom Dewey, recounting one of his father's favorite anecdotes*[1]

In November 1945, gangbuster and brigadier general Bill O'Dwyer was elected the one hundredth mayor of New York City. Everyone loved Bill O'Dwyer, he was charming, funny, and gregarious; at his inauguration, he lustily joined in a chorus of "It's a Great Day for the Irish."[2] New York City entered a long economic boom in the O'Dwyer years—World War II was over, and the American Century was at its height; Mayor O'Dwyer was in charge of the city's first billion-dollar budget; he was mayor when the United Nations moved its headquarters into town; New York succeeded Paris as the Atlantic World's artistic center. That O'Dwyer easily won reelection in 1949 is no wonder.

But Mayor O'Dwyer never escaped the ghosts of Murder, Inc. Nor had anyone else.

Bill O'Dwyer was a Tammany loyalist. Although O'Dwyer was personally honest, Tammany, despite everything that had happened, was still the center of politics based on winks and nods; patronage and nepotism; secret deals, special privileges, bribes, payoffs, and kickbacks. In Tammany's eyes, everything was for sale, anyone with money was welcome to the political trough, and it made no difference at all where the money came from. People like Frank Costello had lots of money and lots of Tammany friends.

In the 1945 mayoral race, O'Dwyer's Republican–Liberal–Fusion opponent, Jonah Goldstein, denounced O'Dwyer's friendship with Frank Costello, and alleged that Costello really ran the city of New York.[3] In the 1949 race, O'Dwyer's Republican–Liberal–Fusion opponent, Fiorello La Guardia's old ally Newbold Morris, again alleged that O'Dwyer, in particular, and Tammany, in general, were still linked to mobsters.[4] In both races, O'Dwyer's failure to solve the mystery of Abe Reles's death and his refusal, after Reles's death, to go after Albert Anastasia were displayed as evidence of O'Dwyer's unsavory gangster connections. Then, in 1950, in one of New York's great political ironies, a new Brooklyn district attorney, Miles McDonald, announced that he had solid evidence that the newly reelected mayor had accepted dirty campaign money. Denying the charge, O'Dwyer, nevertheless, on September 2, 1950, resigned. Lots of people still loved him, however; President Harry Truman named him ambassador to Mexico.[5]

But then the ghosts of the gangsters returned. In 1950, the US Senate created a special committee to investigate the impact of organized crime on interstate commerce. The special committee was chaired by Senator Estes Kefauver of Tennessee. The Kefauver Committee traveled around the country looking for gangsters; they unearthed scores, each with hair-raising stories to tell. The Kefauver Committee hit the jackpot in New York. There, on live television (the Kefauver Committee hearings were the very first Senate hearings televised live), the senators interrogated some of New York's most notorious mobsters, including Frank Costello. Costello's raspy voice, silk suit, and twitching figures seemed to incarnate the very archetype of the underworld boss. The Kefauver Commission also commented on Abe Reles's death. They questioned Captain Frank Bals, District Attorney O'Dwyer's lead investigator, and guffawed at Bals's argument that Reles had been trying to pull off a practical joke. Senator Charles Tobey, a Republican from Wisconsin, was incredulous that Captain Bals really thought Reles planned to sneak out his sixth-floor window, climb back in a fifth-floor window, sneak back up to the sixth floor, and shout, "Boo," to his guards. Senator Tobey mocked this as a "peekaboo" theory. "Six policemen going to sleep at the same time, and you in charge of them!" Tobey shouted at Bals. "Why, this is ridiculous! O. Henry in all his wonderful moments never conceived of such a wonderful silly story as this!" Tobey insisted that obviously someone gave Abe Reles the old heave-ho.[6]

The Kefauver Committee demanded that newly named Ambassador O'Dwyer return to New York for questioning; they grilled O'Dwyer furiously, and he seemed both truculent and clueless. The senators were astonished that O'Dwyer had failed to solve the Reles murder, that he had dropped the case against Albert Anastasia, and that he, personally, and his political aides had associated with Frank Costello. Burton Turkus dryly recounts O'Dwyer's response to the committee's question about the 1942 meeting among O'Dwyer, his Tammany associates, and Costello, in Costello's apartment. One of the committee members asked: "'A funny thing what magnetism that man (Costello) had. How can you analyze it; what is the attraction he has?' O'Dwyer responded, 'It doesn't matter whether it is a banker, a businessman, or a gangster; his pocketbook is always attractive.'"[7]

In his account of O'Dwyer's testimony to the committee, Kefauver wrote, "To me, the position of Mr. O'Dwyer was particularly lamentable—a melancholy essay on political morality [. . .] the committee's final judgment on Mr. O'Dwyer's official conduct as Kings County district attorney and mayor of New York, was summed up in our report [. . .] as follows:

> "Neither he [O'Dwyer] nor his appointees took any effective action against the top echelons of the gambling, narcotics, waterfront, murder, or bookmaking rackets. In fact, his actions impeded promising investigations of such rackets [. . .] his failure to follow up concrete evidence of organized crime, particularly in the case of Murder, Inc., and the waterfront, have contributed to the growth of organized crime, racketeering, and gangsterism in New York City."[8]

Meantime, yet another grand jury, inspired by the Kefauver Hearings, investigated, yet again, Reles's death. After hearing from some two hundred witnesses, the only conclusion this grand jury arrived at was that then district attorney O'Dwyer had bungled the Reles investigation and had unjustifiably dropped the Anastasia case.[9]

Burton Turkus's career demonstrated just how powerfully the Murder, Inc., ghosts had infested not just New York City politics but the wider culture as well.

The Murder, Inc., case made Burton Turkus a star. During the trials, he was swamped by requests for speaking engagements. Everyone in Brooklyn, from the Kiwanis to the Rotary to the American Legion to the Masons, from churches, synagogues and men's clubs to good government civic groups, wanted to meet him, shake his hand, and hear him speak.[10] In April 1942, for example, Turkus spoke in Paterson, New Jersey. A bold headline in the *Paterson Evening News* announced "Burton Turkus, Famed N.Y. Crime Buster, to Speak Here." The paper went on to explain that Turkus was a "dynamic prosecutor," who called the hoodlums he had prosecuted "wild dog packs that prey on labor, the dog packs that tear tribute from labor and everybody else." The article continued: "always immaculate, Turkus wears a diamond ring on the little finger of his left hand, smokes a pipe and cigars, and continually dreams of his favorite sport—golf."[11]

In November 1942, Turkus ran for a Brooklyn judgeship but lost; his campaign material, including a faux tabloid newspaper called the *Murder, Inc. News*, focused on his role as gangbuster.[12] Turkus left criminal law and became a highly respected labor arbitrator. The revival of interest in gangsters in the early 1950s, triggered by the Kefauver hearings, renewed Turkus's celebrity.

The Reles affair, particularly the notion of a protected witness being pitched out a window, had, in addition, inspired both a play, Leonard Kanto's *Dead Pigeon* (1953), and a film based on the play, *Tight Spot* (1955), starring Edward G. Robinson, Ginger Rogers, Lorne Greene, and Brian Keith.[13] Meanwhile, the phrase "Murder, Inc." began its long career as a free-floating meme. "Murder, Inc." surfaces in surprising places. In 2013, for example, Adam LeBor, reviewed Stephen Kinzer's *The Brothers. John Foster Dulles, Allen Dulles, and Their Secret World War.* According to Kinzer, LeBor notes, President Lyndon Johnson was deeply suspicious of Allen Dulles's Central Intelligence Agency (CIA) operations in the Caribbean; Johnson complained that the CIA was running "a goddamn Murder, Inc. in the Caribbean."[14]

For a time, in the 1930s and 1940s, everyone, it seemed, had gangsters on his or her minds; gangsters seemed as uniquely American as pilgrims or cowboys. In 1942, Louis Sohol, a columnist for the *New York Journal-American,* wrote that he, too, thought a lot about gangsters. In fact, he wrote, he had purchased a pistol so he could protect himself from the mob. The first night he carried the pistol, he was in a restaurant when two rough-looking men came in; one was carrying a violin case. Sohol had seen enough movies to know what gangsters carried in violin cases. Sohol whipped out his new pistol, shouted at the men to drop the violin case and put their hands in the air, and nervously told the restaurateur to call the cops. The cops arrived and snapped open the violin case. Out fell a violin and a set of men's underwear.[15]

"Gangster" by the end of the Murder, Inc., trials, had become a key metaphor for moral evil. In 1940, running for the Republican nomination for president, Tom Dewey, speaking about Hitler, Mussolini, and the Japanese militarists, remarked that "as a nation, we face a bitter truth [...] this has become a gangster world. I know something about gangsters."[16] On December 9, 1941, in a national radio address two days after Pearl Harbor, Franklin Roosevelt tried to explain to Americans just why they had to go to war. Referring to Imperial Japan, Nazi Germany, and Fascist Italy, Roosevelt argued that "powerful and resourceful gangsters have banded together to make war upon the whole human race."[17] We had all come to live in what critic Robert Warshow, writing about the gangster world, called "that dangerous and sad city of the imagination."[18]

The gangster had become one central focus for modern American moral accusation and reflection and both as archetype and social phenomenon, the gangster refused to disappear. Against the gangster there would be no final victories. As Tom Dewy liked to say, retelling a story his father liked to tell, sometimes you have to keep working in the field even in the rain.

The gangsters never went away. In New York, in 1943, two years after the Murder, Inc., story had ended, a new gangster scandal erupted. An FBI wiretap caught this conversation between a candidate for New York State Supreme Court judge, Thomas Aurelio, and Frank Costello. Costello had helped Aurelio be nominated for the seat:

AURELIO: Good morning, Francesco! How are you? And thanks for everything!
COSTELLO: Congratulations! It went over perfect! When I tell you something is in the bag, you can rest assured.
AURELIO: It was perfect. Right now I want to assure you of my loyalty for all you have done. It's undying.
COSTELLO: I know.

When the press got hold of the story, Aurelio found himself in very hot water. He survived politically and actually went on to a respectable judicial career. However, his call to Costello seemed to show that gangsters still shaped the city's politics.[19] In 1951, *Look* magazine, responding to the Kefauver hearings, published a story titled "The Shame of New York." According to its authors, "the biggest and richest city in the country relaxes while thugs and hoodlums pull strings and fill their pockets."[20] It sounded like not much had changed.

Still, some things had changed. There had been a moral victory, no matter how tenuous, ambiguous, and temporary. On July 1, 1942, Burton Turkus and a Brownsville crowd rallied on the corner of Livonia and Saratoga Avenues. After some speech making, they displayed a huge American flag, crowded around it, and mugged for the camera. Their

The Corner. Midnight Rose's Candy Store on the corner of Livonia and Saratoga avenues, Brownsville, Brooklyn. (New York City Municipal Archives)

photograph appeared in the New York papers.[21] The crowd around the flag on The Corner seemed to say that if the ghosts of Kid Twist, Pittsburgh Phil, the Dasher, Happy, and the others had not been exorcized, at least they had been driven away from that particular corner at that particular time. Burton Turkus insisted that he'd "gone to war" against Murder, Inc., "to make Brooklyn safe."[22] That bright July day, Brooklyn, if not completely safe, was a little safer than it had been in years, and that at least was something, in what Dutch Schulz had called "this tough world."

Acknowledgments

Many people helped me put this story together, and I'd like to take a final moment to thank them all.

At Queens University of Charlotte, thanks to Carolyn G. McMahon and Sam H. McMahon Jr., benefactors of the McMahon Professorship in History, and to Dr. Jerry Greenhoot and Dr. Kathryn Greenhoot, benefactors of the Noble Fellowship, both of which provided funding for this project. Thanks as well to the Queens Everett Library interlibrary loan staff, especially Sharon Barham, who helped me track down often-obscure gangster lore.

As the notes and bibliography demonstrate, I owe a debt of thanks to a great many archivists and librarians, especially Sam Shapiro of the Charlotte Mecklenburg Public Library; Ellen Belcher at the Lloyd Sealy Library of the John Jay College of Criminal Justice, City University of New York; Douglas Di Carlo at the La Guardia and Wagner Archives, La Guardia Community College, City University of New York; Ken Cobb and Michael Lorenzini at the New York City Municipal Archives; and Alla Roylance at the Brooklyn Public Library. Thanks also to Coreen Hallenbeck for her research at the New York State Archives in Albany, New York.

At Fordham University Press, thanks to Fredric Nachbaur, Eric Newman, Will Cerbone, Ann-Christine Racette, and their colleagues for their professional skill and great patience. Thanks to Ford Editing for a splendid job copy editing the manuscript. I would like to thank as well Fordham's two anonymous readers for their wise counsel.

This book is for Meg, my wife and best friend, and for our children, James, Julia, and Cecilia, with my love. Thank you for putting up with the ghosts of gangsters and gangbusters for all these years. Now those old ghosts can finally move out from around our kitchen table and into the pages of their very own book.

Notes

Prologue: Naked City

1. Anthony W. Lee and Richard Meyer, *Weegee and Naked City* (Berkeley: University of California, 2008), 10.

2. Jenna Weissman Joselit, *Our Gang. Jewish Crime and the New York Jewish Community, 1900—1940* (Bloomington: Indiana University, 1983), 155; Harry Feeney was the police reporter for the *New York World Telegram;* he first coined the term; other papers quickly picked it up.

3. On the "syndicate" film, see Carlos Clarens, *Crime Movies* (New York: Da Capo, 1997), chap. 8, "The Syndicate," 234–58.

4. E. E. Rice, *Murder, Inc.* (Cincinnati, Ohio: Zebra Picture Books, 1949), 24, 57.

5. Robert Lacey, *Little Man. Meyer Lansky and the Gangster Life* (New York: Little, Brown, 1991), 314.

6. Rich Cohen, *Tough Jews. Fathers, Sons, and Gangster Dreams* (New York: Simon and Schuster, 1998), 35.

7. Ibid., 35, 28, 33.

8. Letters, scripts, and related materials can be found in BPL, Burton Turkus Papers, Folder 1.

9. Burton Turkus and Sid Feder, *Murder, Inc.* (New York: Da Capo Press, 1979, originally published in 1951). "36 Hours from Murder," *Look,* November 20, 1951, and "The Mob Invades California," *Look,* December 4, 1951, both in Folder 1, Burton Turkus Papers, BPL. The Kefauver Hearings, officially, the US Senate Special Committee to Investigate Crime in Interstate Commerce, were held in 1950 and 1951 and were chaired by Tennessee senator Estes Kefauver. The first such investigation to be televised live, the Kefauver Hearings fueled an immense public interest in gangsters and organized crime.

10. For related correspondence and other materials, see BPL, Burton Turkus Papers, Folder 1.

11. David E. Ruth, *Inventing the Public Enemy* (Chicago: University of Chicago, 1994), 1.

12. Neil Kleid and Jake Allen, *Brownsville. A Graphic Novel* (New York: Nantier Beall Minoustchine, 2006).

13. Kenneth Williams, *The Saga of Murder, Inc.*, accessed March 18, 2014, http://www.merkki.com/murderinc.htm.

14. Bruce Springsteen, *Murder, Inc.* (1982), on Bruce Springsteen, *Greatest Hits* (New York: Columbia Records, 1995).

15. William James, "The Moral Philosopher and the Moral Life," in *Pragmatism and Other Essays* (New York: Washington Square Press, 1963), 226.

16. In English, although not in most other languages, the terms *morality* and *ethics* cause considerable confusion. Some writers use *morality* to refer to specific actions and choices and *ethics* to refer to critical thought about those actions and choices. However, other writers reverse this usage and use *ethics* to refer to practices and the rules governing practices and *moral philosophy* to refer to critical reflection on those rules and practices. To simplify matters, this text uses *morals* and *ethics* as synonyms.

17. Susan Neiman, *Evil in Modern Thought. An Alternative History of Philosophy* (Princeton, N.J.: Princeton University, 2002), 2–3.

18. Ibid.

19. Ibid., xii.

20. Ibid., xviii.

21. Eyal Press, *Beautiful Souls. The Courage and Conscience of Ordinary People in Extraordinary Times* (New York: Picador, 2012), 179–80.

22. James Bryce, *The American Commonwealth* (New York: John D. Morris, 1906), 236, 241.

23. Ibid., 241.

24. See William Kennedy, introduction to Damon Runyon, *Guys and Dolls* (New York: Penguin, 1992), ix–xv.

25. These notes about Fellig's biography are from Anthony W. Lee and Richard Meyer, *Weegee and* Naked City (Berkeley: University of California, 2008), 8. Another possible origin of the nickname "Weegee"—Fellig remarked that one of his many part-time jobs was as a "squeegee boy" washing car windows; maybe that's where "Weegee" came from; Lee, *Weegee*, 8.

26. Lee, *Weegee*, 10.

27. Ibid., 25.

28. Ibid., 51–55.

29. Ibid., 57–59.

30. Ellen Handy Barth, "Picturing New York, the Naked City: Weegee and Urban Photography," in *Weegee's World, ed. Miles Barth* (Boston: Bulfinch, 1997), 149.

31. Lee, *Weegee*, 56–57.

32. Ibid., 1.

33. Ibid., 41.

34. Martha Nussbaum, *Political Emotions* (Cambridge, Mass.: Harvard, 2013), 162.

35. Mary Midgley, *Wickedness. A Philosophical Essay* (New York: Routledge, 1992), 3.

36. Ibid., 131.

37. Humorist James Thurber's quote is "All men should strive to learn, before they die, what they are running from and to and why." The quotation is from his *Further Fables for Our Time* (London: Hamish Hamilton, 1956), available online at Project Gutenberg.

38. Paul Sann, *Kill the Dutchman! (New York: Popular Library, 1971)*, 231.

1. Reel Gangsters—Mobsters and the Movies

1. George Raft, in George Walsh, *Public Enemies. The Mayor, The Mob, and the Crime that Was* (New York: Norton, 1980), 28.

2. Colonel Henry Barrett Chamberlain, of the Chicago Crime Commission, coined the term *public enemy*. Later, J. Edgar Hoover and the FBI recognized the media power of the term and used to especially to refer to the midwestern bandits of the mid-1930s, like Dillinger, Pretty Boy Floyd, Bonnie and Clyde, and others. See Thomas Repppetto, *American Mafia* (New York: Holt, 2004), 113.

3. Not the famous "red dress" of legend. See Bryan Burrough, *Public Enemies* (New York: Penguin, 2004), 403.

4. Dillinger might better be described as a "bandit" or an "outlaw" rather than a "gangster," if *gangster* refers to urban criminals who are members of more or less permanent gangs. Dillinger was more of a small-town than an urban criminal; although he had "partners," he was not exactly a member of a "gang."

5. The account follows Burrough, *Public Enemies, 401–15.*

6. Laurence Bergreen, *Capone. The Man and the Era* (New York: Simon and Schuster, 1994), 523.

7. Richard Greene and Peter Vernezze, eds., *The Sopranos and Philosophy* (Chicago: Open Court, 2004), 1.

8. Jack Shadoian, *Dreams and Dead Ends. The American Gangster Film* (New York: Oxford, 2003), 32.

9. Carlo Clarens, *Crime Movies* (New York: Da Capo Press, 1997), 54, 56.

10. Bergreen, *Capone*, 525.

11. Shadoian, *Dreams*, 55.

12. Clarens, *Crime Movies,* 91.

13. Fran Mason, *American Gangster Cinema* (New York: Palgrave, 2002), 25.

14. Robin Wood, "*Scarface*," in *Gangster Film Reader, ed. Alain Silver and James Ursini* (Pompton Plains, N.J.: Limelight Editions, 2007), 19.

15. Bergreen, *Capone*, 524.

16. Clarens, *Crime Movies*, 82–83.

17. Mason, *Gangster Cinema,* 28.

18. Ibid., 29.

19. Steve Neal, *Happy Days Are Here Again* (New York: Harper, 2005), 11.

20. Mason, *Gangster Cinema*, 32.

21. Saverio Giovacchini, *Hollywood Modernism. Film and Politics in the Age of the New Deal* (Philadelphia: Temple University, 2001), 48, 53.

22. Clarens, *Crime Movies*, 82.

23. Tim Newark, *Lucky Luciano. The Real and the Fake Gangster* (New York: St. Martin's Press, 2010), 136.

24. Clarens, *Crime Movies*, 234–58; reference to the "Last Just Man," 246.

25. Slavoj Žižek, *Violence* (New York: Pacador, 2008), 3–4.

26. There are innumerable accounts of Dillinger's last moments. See, for example, Burrough, *Public Enemies,* 401–15, as well as John Toland, *The Dillinger Days* (New York: Da Capo Press, 1995), 319–331.

27. Steeves, "Dying," in Greene and Vernezze, *The Sopranos,* 116.

28. Shadoian, *Dreams*, 54.

29. Rich Cohen, *Tough Jews* (New York: Vintage, 1999), 29.

30. Newark, *Lucky Luciano*, 217.

31. Ibid., 249.

32. Clarens, *Crime Movies,* 82.

33. Patrick Downey, *Legs Diamond, Gangster* (Lexington, Ky.: CreateSpace, 2011), i.

34. Ibid., iii.

35. William Kennedy, *Legs* (New York: Penguin, 1975).

36. Richard Norton Smith, *Thomas E. Dewey and his Times* (New York: Simon and Schuster, 1982), 122.

37. Joel Sayre, "Profile: Big Shot-At," *TNY,* June 13, 1931, 24–27.

38. "Talk of the Town—Gangster at Home," *TNY,* July 25, 1931, 11.

39. "Talk of the Town," *TNY,* August 22, 1931, 9.

40. David Ruth, *Inventing the Public Enemy. The Gangster in American Culture, 1918–1934* (Chicago: University of Chicago, 1996).

41. Vincent Patrick, "This You Call a Stick-Up?" A Review of Rich Cohen's *Tough Jews," NYT Archive*, April 12, 1998.

42. "Reles Described as Vicious Thug," *NYT Archive*, March 24, 1940.

43. "Arrested 71 Times, Racketeers Freed," *NYT Archive,* August 26, 1937.

44. "Reles Described as Vicious Thug," *NYT Archive*, March 24, 1940; "'Lenient' Jury Chided on Assault Verdict," *NYT Archive*, May 9, 1934.

45. Raft, in Walsh, *Public Enemies*, 28.

46. E. L. Doctorow, *Billy Bathgate* (New York: Random House, 2010), 25. Doctorow's novel first appeared in 1989; the film version, starring Dustin Hoffman as Dutch Schulz and Loren Dean as Billy Bathgate, of the novel premiered in 1991.

47. Ibid., 26.

48. Ibid., 27.

49. Clarens, *Crime Movie,* 110.

50. H. Peter Steeves, "Dying in our Own Arms: Liberalism, Communitarianism, and the Construction of Identity in *The Sopranos,*" in Greene and Vernezze, *The Sopranos,* 116; James Harold, "A Moral Never-Never Land, Identifying with Tony Soprano," in Greene and Vernezze, *The Sopranos,* 140.

51. "Memo for the Director—RE: Location of Louis Buchalter," July 5, 1939, FBI files, Buchalter file #60-1501-3222, BACM Research/Paperless Archives.

52. Jonathan Munby, *Public Enemies, Public Heroes: Screening the Gangster from "Little Caesar" to "Touch of Evil"* (Chicago: University of Chicago, 1999).

53. Shadoian, *Dreams and Deadends,* 3–4.

54. Ibid.

55. Mason, *Gangster Cinema,* 5.

56. Gwyn Symonds, "Show Business or Dirty Business?" in *Reading the Sopranos,* ed. David Lavery (New York: Palgrave Macmillan, 2006), 127.

57. Noël Carroll and Jinhee Choi, eds., *Philosophy of Film and Motion Pictures* (New York: Blackwell, 2006), 323.

58. Amartya Sen, *The Idea of Justice* (Cambridge, Mass.: The Belknap Press of Harvard University, 2009), 155.

59. Ibid.

60. Sen writes at length of the Smithian "impartial spectator." See, for example, Sen's comparison of Smith's "spectator" to John Rawls's ideas about social contract, in ibid., 130–38.

61. Sam Girgus, *Levinas and the Cinema of Redemption* (New York: Columbia University, 2010), 60–62.

62. Mason, *Gangster Cinema,* 32–33.

63. Robert Warshow, "The Gangster as Tragic Hero (1949)," in Silver and Ursini, *Gangster Film Reader,* 11–16.

64. Reynold Humphries, "A Gangster unlike the Others: Gordon Wiles, *The Gangster,*" in Silver and Ursini, *Gangster Film Reader,* 121.

2. Real Gangsters: Abe Reles and the Origins of Murder, Inc.

1. Edmund Elmaleh, *The Canary Sang but Couldn't Fly* (New York: Union Square Press, 2009), 9.

2. David Ruth, *Inventing the Public Enemy* (Chicago: University of Chicago Press, 1996), 1.

3. Herbert Asbury, *The Gangs of New York* (New York: Vintage, 2008), xx.

4. Irving Howe, *World of Our Fathers* (New York: Harcourt Brace Jovanovich, 1976), 264.

5. H. Paul Jeffers, *Commissioner Roosevelt. The Story of Theodore Roosevelt and the New York Police, 1895–1897* (New York: Wiley, 1994), 57.

6. Ibid., 181.

7. William Foote Whyte, *Street Corner Society* (Chicago: University of Chicago Press, 1973).

8. Burton Turkus and Sid Feder, *Murder, Inc.* (New York: Da Capo, 1992), 56.

9. "An Old Maxim of Pittsburgh Phil Profitable to Jamaica Patrons," *BE*, April 29, 1931; Damon Runyon, *Guys and Dolls (New York: Penguin, 1992)*, 5; "Pittsburgh Phil Is Dead of Consumption," *NYT Archive*, February 2, 1905; "Pittsburg [*sic*] Phil Buried," *NYT Archive*, February 6, 1905; "E.W. Cole Is Dead; Was Turf Writer," *NYT Archive*, February 25, 1928.

10. Turkus and Feder. *Murder, Inc.*, 129.

11. Elmaleh reports that Max Zweibach worked for the labor racketeer Monk Eastman. Just how Zweibach got the name "Kid Twist" is not clear. "Kid" was a common nickname for young criminals (as in "Billy the Kid"). The German word *zweibach* literally means "twice backed"; Germans used a kind of *zweibach* bread as a kind of teether for babies. That bread sometimes was "twisted," so maybe, through some sort of linguistic gymnastics, *zweibach* turned into" twisted" and Max Zweibach became "Kid Twist." In any case, Zweibach and his bodyguard, Cyclone Lewis, a circus strongman, were gunned down in 1908 by Louis "Louie the Lump" Pioggi. Pioggi and Zweibach were rivals for the attentions of the same young woman. Pioggi also was a member of a rival gang, which may have influenced his shooting. See Elmaleh, *Canary*, 4; see also Neil Hanson, *Monk Eastman* (New York: Knopf, 2010), 125–26.

12. Edmund Elmaleh refers to Abe Reles's father as "Sam"; Elmaleh, *Canary*, 5. Rich Cohen refers to him as "Sol"; Rich Cohen, *Tough Jews* (New York: Vintage, 1999), 26. Elmaleh's source is Abe Reles's birth certificate, #27650/1906; Elmaleh, *Canary*, 191.

13. Elmaleh, *Canary*, 5.

14. Howe, *World*, 131–32.

15. Wendell Pritchett, *Brownsville, Brooklyn. Blacks, Jews, and the Changing Face of the Ghetto* (Chicago: University of Chicago Press, 2002), 11.

16. Turkus and Feder, *Murder, Inc.*, 30.

17. Pritchett, *Brownsville, Brooklyn*, 16.

18. Ibid., 18.

19. The "Zionist" movement, inspired by the Austrian journalist Theodor Herzl, was born in 1897; it included dozens of factions with competing agendas. The "Bund" was also born in 1897. Created by Jewish labor union activists and socialists, it tried to merge a concern with the rights of the Jewish ethnic minority with a wider demand for social justice. Zionists and Bundists were often rivals; both competed against conservatives, liberals, democrats, anarchists, and scores of other groups within the Jewish community.

20. Alter Landesman, *Brownsville. The Birth, Development, and Passing of a Jewish Community in New York* (New York: Bloch, 1969), 7.

21. Ibid., 2.

22. Pritchett, *Brownsville,* 14.

23. Ibid., 15.

24. Landesman, *Brownsville,* 324. In general, Landesman argues, Jews had an overall crime rate about one-third that of other ethnic groups.

25. Pritchett, *Brownsville,* 46.

26. Ibid.

27. Ibid.

28. Landesman, *Brownsville,* 333.

29. Ibid., 8.

30. Ibid., 333.

31. Louis "Lepke" Buchalter, FBI file #60-1501-980, undated.

32. "Notes and Comment," *TNY,* April 20, 1940, 13. Also, Turkus and Feder, *Murder, Inc.,* 206–12.

33. "'Death Kiss Girl' Held in $50,000," *NYT Archive,* April 2, 1940.

34. Turkus and Feder, *Murder, Inc.,* 192–93.

35. Ibid., 205–6.

36. Carlos Clarens, *Crime Movies* (New York: Da Capo Press, 1997), 154–55.

37. Jack Katz, *Seductions of Crime* (New York: Basic Books, 1988).

38. Robert Lacey, *Little Man. Meyer Lansky and the Gangster Life* (New York: Little, Brown, 1991), 37.

39. Landesman, *Brownsville,* 8.

40. Albert Fried, *The Rise and Fall of the Jewish Gangster in America* (New York: Holt, Rinehart and Winston, 1980), 37.

41. Elmaleh, *Canary,* 6–7.

42. Ibid., 9.

43. Pritchett, *Brownsville,* 46.

44. Turkus and Feder, *Murder, Inc.,* 56.

45. Ibid., 57.

46. All the relevant criminal records can be found among the Sing Sing prison files, NYSA, "Sing Sing Prison Records," BO 143-80, Box 61 (Maione); BO 143-80, Box 61 (Abbandando); BO 143-80, Box 62 (Goldstein); BO 143-80, Box 63 (Weiss); BO 143-80, Box 66 (Buchalter).

47. NYSA, "Sing Sing Records," BO 147-80, Box 2, "Harry Strauss." The report, untitled, is a carbon copy of the original, which was presumably submitted to the court; it has signature blocks for Joseph C. Hayden, investigating probation officer; Edmond Fitzgerald, chief probation officer; and Joseph Astarita, first deputy probations officer. The report is dated September 25, 1940.

48. For instance, the articles by H. Peter Stevens, "Dying in Our Own Arms: Liberalism, Communitarianism, and the Construction of Identity on *The Sopranos,*" and Scott Wilson's "Staying within the Family: Tony Soprano's Ethical Obligations," in *The Sopranos and Philosophy,* ed. Richard Greene and Peter Vernezze (Chicago: Open Court, 2004), assume this *Godfather* image of the gangsters' gang.

49. Turkus and Feder, *Murder, Inc.,* 69.
50. Ibid., 68.
51. Ibid., 3.
52. Marc Mappen, *Prohibition Gangsters. The Rise and Fall of a Bad Generation* (New Brunswick, N.J.: Rutgers University, 2013), 6.
53. Joseph Freeman, "Murder Monopoly. The Inside Story of a Crime Trust," *The Nation,* May 25, 1940, 645.
54. Paul Kavieff, *The Life and Times of Lepke Buchalter* (Fort Lee, N.J.: Barricade Books, 2006), 78.
55. Jack Shadoian, *Dreams and Dead Ends. The American Gangster Film* (New York: Oxford University Press, 2003), 176–77, 196–218.
56. Ibid., 175.
57. Lacey, *Little Man,* 57.
58. Ibid., 55.
59. Ibid., 50, 66.
60. Robert B. Pippin, *Modernism as a Philosophical Problem* (New York: Blackwell, 1999), 168–70.
61. Steven Connor, *Postmodernist Culture* (New York: Blackwell, 1989), 237.
62. Pauline Marie Rosenau, *Post-modernism and the Social Sciences* (Princeton, NJ: Princeton University Press, 1992), 10. Rosenau distinguishes between "skeptical" and "affirmative" postmodernists and notes that while the skeptics avoid ethical debate, the affirmatives "do not shy away from affirming an ethic, making normative choices, and striving to build issue-specific political coalitions" (16).
63. See, for instance, Jean Baudrillard, "The Map Precedes the Territory," in *The Truth about the Truth,* ed. Walter Truett Anderson (New York: Jeremy P. Tarcher, 1995), 79–81.
64. Chris Hedges, *Empire of Illusion. The End of Literacy and the Triumph of Spectacle* (New York: Nation Books, 2010).
65. Neil Postman, *Amusing Ourselves to Death* (New York: Penguin, 2005).
66. Fredric Jameson, *Postmodernism, or, the Cultural Logic of Late Capitalism* (Durham, N.C.: Duke University Press, 1992), 235–36.
67. Pippin, *Modernism,* 2. Also, Rosenau, *Postmodernism,* 90.
68. For a useful outline of Levinas's thought about "the same" and "the other," see Colin Davis, *Levinas. An Introduction* (Notre Dame, Ind.: University of Notre Dame, 1996), 34–62.
69. John McGowan, *Postmodernism and its Critics* (Ithaca, N.Y.: Cornell University Press, 1991), 91.

3. Gangster City

1. Leonard Katz, *Uncle Frank: The Biography of Frank Costello* (New York: Pocket Books, 1975), 193.

2. Patrick Downey, *Gangster City* (New York: Barricade Books, 2004).

3. Francis Fukuyama, *Political Order and Political Decay* (New York: Farrar Straus Giroux, 2014), especially chap. 36, "Political Order and Political Decay."

4. Burton Turkus and Sid Feder, *Murder, Inc.* (New York: Da Capo, 1992), 56.

5. Fran Mason, *American Gangster Cinema* (New York: Palgrave Macmillan, 2002), 75–76.

6. "Terranova Charges He Is 'Political Goat,'" *NYT Archive*, December 28, 1929; "Terranova Freed in Vitale Holdup," *NYT Archive*, January 24, 1930; "Terranova Dead; Once Racket King," *NYT Archive*, February 20, 1938; *Thomas* Reppetto, *American Mafia (New York: Holt, 2004)*, 135–36.

7. Paul Sann, *Kill the Dutchman!* (New York: Popular Library, 1971), 150.

8. Robert Lacey, *Little Man. Meyer Lansky and the Gangster Life* (New York: Little, Brown, 1991), 33.

9. David Pietrusza, *Rothstein* (New York: Basic Books, 2011), 131–34.

10. Tim Newark, *Lucky Luciano. The Real and the Fake Gangster* (New York: St. Martin's Press, 2010), 26–34.

11. Martin Gosch and Richard Hammer, *The Last Testament of Lucky Luciano* (New York: Dell, 1974), 48.

12. George Wolf and Joseph DiMona, *Frank Costello. Prime Minister of the Underworld* (New York: William Morrow, 1974), 101. On November 4, 1928, Rothstein was shot in the stomach. Rushed to a hospital, he died of his wounds. His murder was never solved.

13. Gosch and Hammer, *Luciano*, 87.

14. Katz, *Uncle Frank*, 55.

15. Neil Hanson, *Monk Eastman* (New York: Knopf, 2010), 44.

16. "Racket Fund Story to be Sifted Today," *NYT Archive*, September 29, 1933.

17. "People v. Maione and Abbandando," March 1941, NYCMA, Murder, Inc., Case Files, Folder 13, Roll 1.

18. Thomas Kessner, *Fiorello La Guardia* (New York: Penguin, 1989), 226.

19. Sann, *Dutch Schulz*, 13–14, 10.

20. See "1934–36," in *100 Years of U.S. Consumer Spending: Data for the Nation, New York, City, and Boston*, report 991 (Washington, DC: US Department of Labor, 2006), 15–20, accessed August 26, 2013, www.bls.gov/opub/uscs/1934-36.pdf.

21. "$20,000,000 Racket Aim of Dewey Raid," *NYT Archive*, October 16, 1935; "Luciana Indicted as Vice Ring Head," *NYT Archive*, April 3, 1936.

22. "Reles Loan Racket Is Exposed by Amen; Profits of Murder Gangsters' $1,000,000 Usury Held to Have Gone to Police," *NYT Archive*, January 25, 1941.

23. Richard Norton Smith, *Thomas E. Dewey and his Times* (New York: Simon and Schuster, 1982), 129.

24. John Baxter, "The Gangster Film," in *Gangster Film Reader*, ed. Alain Silver and James Ursini (Pompton Plains, N.J.: Limelight Editions, 2007), 29.

25. "Gang Kills Gunman, 2 Bystanders Hit," *NYT Archive*, August 12, 1922; Newark, *Luciano*, 24.

26. Sann, *Dutchman*, 132.

27. "Gang Murder of Boy Stirs Public Anger," *NYT Archive*, July 30, 1931; "Wide Aid Offered in Gangster Hunt," *NYT Archive*, July 31, 1931; "Eyewitness Gives Clue to Gangsters Who Killed Child," *NYT Archive*, August 3, 1931; "Coll Trial Begins Today," *NYT Archive*, December 16, 1931; Sann, *Dutchman*, 139.

28. "2 Policemen, 3 Thugs, and Child Slain in Battle during 12-Mile Hold-up Chase; 12 Wounded as Gunfire Rakes Street," *NYT Archive*, August 22, 1931; "Bandit Victim, 4, Is Buried in Bronx," *NYT Archive*, August 27, 1931.

29. "Same Gang Killed Coll and his Aides," *NYT Archive*, February 10, 1932.

30. "Coll Is Shot Dead in a Phone Booth by Rival Gunmen," *NYT Archive*, February 8, 1932; Sann, *Dutchman*, 144–48.

31. There are innumerable accounts of this famous gangland war. Joe Valachi provides a vivid account; see, for instance, Peter Maas, *The Valachi Papers* (New York: Perennial, 2003), 75–85. Salvatore Maranzano's famous meeting at which he claimed to be the new "boss of all the bosses" has inspired an enormous commentary. See, for instance, Marc Mappen follows Valachi's account; see Marc Mappen, *Prohibition Gangsters. The Rise and Fall of a Bad Generation* (New Brunswick, N.J.: Rutgers University, 2013), 56. The notoriously unreliable "Last Testament of Lucky Luciano," also follows Valachi; see Gosch and Hammer, *Last Testament*, 137–38; Thomas Reppetto refers to "several meetings" among Maranzano and gang leaders; see Thomas Reppetto, *American Mafia* (New York: Holt, 2004), 139; Selwyn Raab, in *Five Families* (New York: Thomas Dunne, 2006), reports that the meeting took place in "a resort hotel in tiny Wappingers Falls, seventy-five miles north of Times Square." Raab says that Al Capone also attended; see Raab, *Five Families*, 29. Luciano's biographer, Tim Newark, however, writes that the meeting actually took place in the same restaurant where Masseria was killed; it was, Newark reports, a "three day banquet to which all the top mafiosi from around the country were invited"; see Newark, *Luciano*, 61.

32. "Racket Chief Slain by Gangster Gunfire," *NY Archive*, April 16, 1931.

33. Ibid.

34. Newark, *Lucky Luciano*, 59.

35. "Gang Kills Suspect in Alien Smuggling," *NYT Archive*, September 11, 1931; "Seek Official in Alien Smuggling," *NYT Archive*, September 12, 1931.

36. Peter Maas, based on his conversations with Joe Valachi, says that about forty Maranzano supporters were killed; Maas, *Valachi Papers*, 91; Reppetto thinks that number is too high; Reppetto, *Mafia*, 139.

37. "Gunman Imperils Children at Play," *NYT Archive*, May 17, 1932.

38. H. Paul Jeffers, *Commissioner Roosevelt. The Story of Theodore Roosevelt and the New York Police, 1895–1897* (New York: Wiley, 1994), 5.

39. Kessner, *La Guardia*, 24.

40. Ibid., 26; Fiorello La Guardia, *The Making of an Insurgent* (New York: Lippincott, 1948), 70–74.

41. "Reles Is Telling Story of Murders Done by His Gang," *NYT Archive*, March 24, 1940.

42. "Reles Described as a Vicious Thug," *NYT Archive*, March 24, 1940.

43. "Five More Seized in Drive on Usury," *NYT Archive*, November 24, 1935.

44. "Two in Murder Ring Quickly Convicted," *NYT Archive*, May 24, 1940.

45. "Strauss to Bare Murders of Ring," *NYT Archive*, May 9, 1940.

46. "Witness Uphold Reles Testimony," *NYT Archive*, May 17, 1940.

47. Sann, *Dutchman*, 130.

48. Reppetto, *American Mafia*, 146.

49. Lacey, *Little Man*, 55.

50. Turkus and Feder, *Murder, Inc.*, 20–21.

51. Lincoln Steffens, *The Shame of the Cities* (Mineola, N.Y.: Dover, 2004), 69.

52. Steffens, *Shame*, 4–5.

53. David Kirp, *Shakespeare, Einstein, and the Bottom Line* (Cambridge, Mass.: Harvard, 2003), 3.

54. Ibid., 6.

55. Ibid., 6–7.

56. Michael Sandel, *Justice* (New York: Farrar Straus Giroux, 2009), 102.

57. Ibid., 265. Sandel develops his argument in his book *What Money Can't Buy. The Moral Limits of Markets* (New York: Farrar Straus Giroux, 2013). See also Robert Kutner, *Everything for Sale. The Virtues and Limits of Markets* (Chicago: University of Chicago Press, 1999); Debra Satz, *Why Some Things Should Not Be For Sale. The Moral Limits of Markets* (New York: Oxford, 2010).

58. Mason, *Gangster Cinema*, 75–76.

59. Fred Gardaphé, *From Wise Guys to Wise Men. The Gangster and Italian American Masculinities* (New York: Routledge, 2006), xvi.

60. Ibid., 213–14.

4. Fiorello La Guardia and the Cinema of Redemption

1. Thomas Kessner, *Fiorello La Guardia and the Making of Modern New York* (New York: Penguin, 1989), 362.

2. Jonathan Munby, *Public Enemies, Public Heroes: Screening the Gangster from "Little Caesar" to "Touch of Evil"* (Chicago: University of Chicago, 1999), 105.

3. Sam Girgus, *Levinas and the Cinema of Redemption. Time, Ethics, and the Feminine* (New York: Columbia University, 2010).

4. "The Way We Are: Of Artichokes and Liberty," *NYT Archive*, November 6, 2013.

5. "Mayor Puts a Ban on Artichoke Sale to Curb Rackets," *NYT Archive*, December 22, 1935.

6. Kessner, *La Guardia*, 362.

7. "The Mayor Trains His Guns on Rackets," *NYT Archive*, December 6, 1936.

8. Girgus, *Levinas*.

9. Leonard Katz, *Uncle Frank. The Biography of Frank Costello* (New York: Pocket Books, 1975), 62; David Pietrusza, *Rothstein* (New York: Basic Books, 2011), 284–93; Kessner, *La Guardia*, 162–63.

10. Low would go on to a noble career in public service. From 1907 to 1916, Low was chair of Alabama's Tuskegee Institute. He would be president, too, of the National Civic Federation, which acted as mediator in labor-management disputes. Low would also serve on the boards of New York's Academy of Sciences and numerous charitable and good government groups. He was an enthusiastic champion of agricultural and consumer cooperatives. Low died in 1916.

11. Becker's arrest, trial, and conviction dominated New York news from 1912 until his execution in 1915. For more on the case, see Rose Keefe, *The Starker. New York City's First Great Gangster Boss* (Nashville, Tenn.: Cumberland House, 2008); Thomas Reppetto, *American Mafia* (New York: Holt, 2004), 75; Michael Bookman's *God's Rat: Jewish Mafia on the Lower East Side* (New York: PublishAmerica, 2000), *and* Mike Dash, *Satan's Circus* (New York: Three Rivers Press, 2008). For fictional treatment of the case, see Kevin Baker, *Dreamland* (New York: Harpers, 2006). The fictional gangster Meyer Wolfsheim, in F. Scott Fitzgerald's *The Great Gatsby*, also discusses the Becker case.

12. For an overview of the investigation, see Herbert Mitgang, *The Man Who Rode the Tiger. The Live of Samuel Seabury* (New York: Viking, 1963).

13. Ibid., 216–17.

14. "Seabury Is Ready to Draft Charges against Walker," *NYT Archive*, May 30, 1932; "Walker's Statement Explaining his Decision to Resign as Mayor," *NYT Archive*, September 2, 1932; Mitgang, *Tiger*, 295–99; Walsh, *Gentleman Jimmy Walker*, 326–27.

15. Ernest Cuneo. *Life with Fiorello* (New York: Macmillan, 1951), 170. Cuneo does not say in which campaign this occurred; it appears that it was during the 1933 campaign.

16. Ibid., 175.

17. Reppetto, *Mafia*, 146.

18. Kessner, *La Guardia*, 364.

19. Charles Garrett, *The La Guardia Years. Machine and Reform Politics in New York* (New Brunswick, N.J.: Rutgers, 1961), 159.

20. Kessner, *La Guardia*, 356.

21. M. Lowell Limpus and Burr Leyson, *The Man La Guardia* (New York: Dutton, 1938), 394.

22. Lewis J. Valentine, *Night Stick* (New York: The Dial Press, 1947), 20–21.

23. Ibid., 21.

24. Jack Alexander, "Profile: Independent Cop—I," *TNY*, October 3, 1936, 21.

25. Jack Alexander, "Profile: Independent Cop—III," *TNY*, October 17, 1936, 30.

26. "Lewis J. Valentine Dies in Hospital," *NYT Archive*, December 17, 1946; A. G. Sulzberger, "La Guardia's Tough and Incorruptible Police Commissioner," *NYT Archive*, November 11, 2009.

27. Alexander, "Independent Cop—III," 30; Kessner, *La Guardia*, 356.

28. Alexander, "Independent Cop—II," *TNY*, October 10, 1936, 26.

29. "Police Get Orders to Terrorize Thugs; 'Muss 'Em Up Is Valentine's Edict," *NYT Archive*, November 27, 1934.

30. Alexander, "Independent Cop—II," 28.

31. Ibid., 28.

32. "Police Get Orders."

33. August Heckscher, *When La Guardia Was Mayor* (New York: Norton, 1978), 109; Kessner, *La Guardia,* 356; Arthur Nash, *New York City Gangland* (Charleston, S.C.: Arcadia Publishing, 2010), 48.

34. Kessner, *La Guardia*, 351.

35. Ibid.

36. "Slot Machines Sunk in Sound," *NYT Archive,* October 14, 1934.

37. Ibid.

38. Kessner, *La Guardia*, 358; "Mayor Denounces Vice Protectors," *NYT Archive,* June 20, 1936.

39. Alyn Brodsky, *The Great Mayor. Fiorello La Guardia and the Making of the City of New York* (New York: St. Martin's, 2003), 10.

40. Kessner, *La Guardia,* 73–74.

41. Ibid., 71.

42. William Manners, *Patience and Fortitude: Fiorello La Guardia* (New York: Harcourt Brace Jovanovich, 1976), 176.

43. Brodsky, *The Great Mayor*, 46.

44. Hannah Arendt, *The Human Condition* (Chicago: University of Chicago, 1958), 2.

45. Ibid., 31.

46. Ibid., 32.

47. Ibid., 220.

48. Manners, *Patience*, 16. The letter, it appears, was not sent.

49. Ibid., 191.

50. Ibid., 174.

51. Brodsky, *The Great Mayor*, 258.

52. Ibid., 289.

53. Robert Lacey, *Little Man. Meyer Lansky and the Gangster Life* (New York: Little, Brown, 1991), 48.

54. Girgus, *Levinas*, 50.

55. Levinas is a notoriously difficult philosopher; his prose is invariably dense, arcane, and often obscure. He has, though, been enormously influential. For an

introduction to his thought, see, for example, Colin Davis, *Levinas. An Introduction* (Notre Dame, Ind.: University of Notre Dame Press, 1996); Simon Critchley and Robert Bernasconi, eds., *The Cambridge Companion to Levinas* (New York: Cambridge University Press, 2002); B. C. Hutchins, *Levinas. A Guide for the Perplexed* (New York: Continuum, 2004); and Samuel Moyn, *Origins of the Other. Emmanuel Levinas between Revelation and Ethics* (Ithaca, N.Y.: Cornell University Press, 2005).

56. Girgus, *Levinas*, 61–65.

57. Ibid., 53.

58. Kessner, *Fiorello La Guardia,* 82–83.

59. Simon Critchley, *Infinitely Demanding. Ethics of Commitment, Politics of Resistance* (New York: Verso, 2007), 13.

60. Kessner, *La Guardia*, 82.

61. Ibid., 37; La Guardia, *Insurgent*, 113.

62. Arendt, *Human Condition*, 52.

63. Ibid., 242.

64. Ibid., 53.

65. Ibid., 77.

66. Martha Nussbaum, *Political Emotions* (Cambridge, Mass.: Harvard, 2013), 3.

67. Ibid., 380.

68. Paul Kavieff, *The Life and Times of Lepke Buchalter* (Fort Lee, N.J.: Barricade Books, 2006), 8.

5. Gangbuster: Thomas Dewey and Imperfect Justice

1. Thomas Dewey, *Twenty against the Underworld* (Garden City, N.Y.: Doubleday, 1974), 137–38.

2. "Bail Bond Inquiry Will Open Monday," *NYT Archive,* February 22, 1935; "Smash Policy Ring, Mayor Warned," *NYT Archive,* February 28, 1935; Dewey, *Twenty*, 149.

3. "Schulz in Hiding; Ran Policy Racket," *NYT Archive*, February 27, 1935; Dewey, *Twenty*, 149.

4. Dewey, *Twenty*, 149.

5. "Dodge's Statements to 'Runaway' Jury in 1935," *NYT Archive*, February 21, 1939; "Lee T. Smith, 77, Realtor, Is Dead," *NYT Archive*, December 9, 1963.

6. Richard Norton Smith, *Thomas E. Dewey and His Times* (New York: Simon and Schuster, 1982), 148; Dewey, *Twenty*, 150.

7. Dewey, *Twenty*, 57.

8. Ibid., 65.

9. Ibid., 68.

10. Ibid., 68.

11. Ibid., 69.

12. Ibid., 79. Also, "George Z. Medalie, Big-Game Prosecutor, Goes Back to Private Practice Tuesday," *JTA Archive*, November 19, 1933, accessed July 30,

2013, http://www.jta.org/1933/11/19/archive/george-z-medalie-big-game
-prosecutor-goes-back-to-private-practice-tuesday.
  13. Richard Norton Smith, *Thomas E. Dewey and his Times* (New York:
Simon and Schuster, 1982), 115, 130.
  14. Dewey, *Twenty*, 80.
  15. Ibid., 82.
  16. "Grand Jury Ponders Diamond 'Tampering,'" *NYT Archive*, August 11,
1931; "Diamond Is Facing Maximum Sentence," *NYT Archive*, August 12, 1931.
  17. Dewey, *Twenty*, 118.
  18. Ibid., 121.
  19. Ibid., 123.
  20. "Gordon Locked Up as His Trial Opens," *NYT Archive*, November 21,
1933; Dewey, *Twenty*, 125.
  21. "Gordon Refused $600,000 for Plant," *NYT Archive*, November 29,
1933; Dewey, *Twenty*, 128–36.
  22. "Dewey Is Sworn for Medalie Post," *NYT Archive*, November 23, 1933.
  23. Dewey, *Twenty*, 137–38.
  24. Ibid., 143.
  25. Ibid., 146.
  26. "Dewey Won Fame as 'Racket Buster,'" *NYT Archive*, November 3, 1937.
  27. Smith, *Dewey*, 54.
  28. Ibid., 53.
  29. Ibid., 57.
  30. Ibid., 60.
  31. Ibid., 67.
  32. Ibid., 496.
  33. Dewey, *Twenty*, 155. For a general account of Dewey's investigation of
Luciano and Dutch Schulz's plot against Dewey's life, see Burton Turkus and
Sid Feder, *Murder, Inc.* (New York: Da Capo, 1992), chap. 6, 128–51.
  34. Dewey describes all this at length in Dewey, *Twenty*, 155–60.
  35. Ibid., 160.
  36. Ibid., 169.
  37. Ibid., 174.
  38. "$20,000,000 Racket Aim of Dewey Raid," *NYT Archive*, October 16,
1935; "Painters Are Raided in Rackets Inquiry," *NYT Archive*, January 16, 1936;
Dewey, *Twenty*, 180.
  39. Dewey, *Twenty*, 184.
  40. Paul Sann, *Kill the Dutchman!* (New York: Popular Library, 1971), 257.
Just who said what at this meeting, or these meetings, is a matter of guesswork.
The first reports of such a session came from Abe Reles, who told the story to
Burton Turkus. Reles, however, as a minor hoodlum, was not a participant, and
his story was secondhand. For a general discussion of this 1935 crisis, see ibid.,
251–70.

41. Ibid., 258; Tim Newark, *Lucky Luciano. The Real and the Fake Gangster* (New York: St. Martin's Press, 2010), 80–81; Martin Gosch and Richard Hammer, *The Last Testament of Lucky Luciano* (New York: Dell, 1974), 188–89.

42. This account follows Sann, *Dutchman*, 9–27.

43. Stanley Walker, "An Inquiry into the Literary Significance, if Any, and the Basic Ideology of the Late Mr. Flegenheimer," *TNY*, April 5, 1941, 28.

44. Dewey, *Twenty*, 186.

45. Ibid., 187.

46. "110 Arrested in 41 Secret Raids by Dewey in Drive on Chain of 200 Disorderly Houses," *NYT Archive*, February 2, 1936; "Valentine Seeks Way to Curb Vice," *NYT Archive,* February 5, 1936.

47. Dewey, *Twenty*, 192; "Vice Raids Smash $12,000,000 Ring; Leaders in Jail," *NYT Archive*, February 3, 1936.

48. "Grand Jury Hears Dewey Cases," *NYT Archive*, February 6, 1936; "Ten are Indicted as Vice Ring Heads," *NYT Archive*, February 7, 1936.

49. "Luciana Indicted as Vice Ring Head; Named with 11 Henchmen," *NYT Archive*, April 3, 1936.

50. "Dewey Says Lucania Seized Vice Industry," *BE*, May 13, 1936.

51. James Benet, "New York's Vice Ring," *TNR,* June 10, 1936, 124–26; Tim Newark, *Lucky Luciano. The Real and the Fake Gangster* (New York: St. Martin's Press, 2010), 117–27; Martin Gosch and Richard Hammer, *The Last Testament of Lucky Luciano* (New York: Dell, 1974), 203–26; also Marc Mappen, *Prohibition Gangsters. The Rise and Fall of a Bad Generation* (New Brunswick, N.J.: Rutgers University, 2013), 152–70.

52. Wolcott Gibbs and John Bainbridge, "St. George and the Dragnet," *TNY*, May 25, 1940, 28.

53. Ibid., 28.

54. Ibid., 30.

55. Ibid., 27.

56. "2 Girls Unmask Vice Racket," *NYDN*, May 14, 1936.

57. "Woman Bares Threat of Death in Vice Probe," *BE*, May 29, 1936.

58. "Business Women Whose Trade Was Vice Take Stand," *NYDN*, May 15, 1936.

59. "Woman Swears Vice Overlords Ruled by Gun," *BE*, May 15, 1936.

60. "Mistress of Bordello Vents Spite on Aides of Luciano at Trial," *NYDN*, May 16, 1936; "Luciana Trial Ends Second Week Today," *NYT Archive,* May 18, 1936.

61. "Prey of Vice Ring Tells of Beatings," *NYT Archive*, May 16, 1936.

62. "Lucania's Girl Is Threatened," *BE*, May 26, 1936.

63. "Aid Names Lucky City Vice Czar," *NYDN*, May 22, 1936.

64. "Vice Dictatorship's Iron Rule Bared," *NYDN*, May 19, 1936.

65. "Woman Swears Vice Overlords Ruled by Gun," *BE*, May 15, 1936.

66. "Boro Woman Names Lucania as Vice Chief," *BE*, May 18, 1936.

67. "Vice Lords Split Girls' Tongues for 'Squealing,' Jury Is Told," *BE*, May 25, 1936.

68. "Ex-Aide Draws Net on Lucania at Vice Trial," *BE*, May 20, 1936.

69. "Claims Lucania Vice Fees Were for Prosecutor," *BE*, May 19, 1936.

70. "Held Prisoner in Vice House, Girl Testifies," *BE*, May 21, 1936.

71. "Dewey Exhibits Record of 154 Vice Cases," *BE*, May 28, 1936.

72. "Big Hotel Suite Luciana's 'Office,'" *NYT Archive*, May 23, 1936; "Convict Calls Luciano Czar of City's Vice," *NYDN*, May 22, 1936.

73. "Vie Ring Trial Nears End," *NYT Archive*, May 25, 1936; "Vice Ring Threats of Death, Torture, Told by Girl at Trial," *NYDN*, May 26, 1936; "'Friend' of Luciana's Acts as Accuser," *NYT Archive*, May 26, 1936.

74. Dewey, *Twenty*, 221.

75. "Giant Vice Chain Aim of Luciano," *NYDN*, May 23, 1936.

76. Dewey, *Twenty*, 215.

77. See, for instance, "Luciano Named by Cokey Flo," *The Miami News*, May 22, 1936, accessed July 31, 2013, http://news.google.com/newspapers?nid=2206&dat=19360522&id=PAktAAAAIBAJ&sjid=pdcFAAAAIBAJ&pg=5665,1818895.

78. "Lucania Is Named Again as Vice Chief," *NYT Archive*, May 23, 1936.

79. "Hide Girls Baring Vice Ring's Rule," *NYDN*, May 27, 1936.

80. "Lawyer, 2 Women Jailed as Vice Perjury Plotters," *NYDN*, May 28, 1936.

81. Carlos Clarens, *Crime Movies (New York: Da Capo Press, 1997)*, 157; "Lucky to Plead Girls Lied as Dope Addicts," *NYDN*, June 1, 1936; "Vice Ring Stickup Man Denies Knowing Lucky," *NYDN*, June 2, 1936.

82. Photograph, caption: "Change of Habits for Lucky," *NYDN*, May 26, 1936.

83. "Assistant D.A. Helps Luciano Fight Vice Rap," *NYDN*, June 3, 1936.

84. "Lucania Takes Witness Stand in Vice Trial," *BE*, June 3, 1936.

85. "Luciano is Forced to Admit Crimes," *NYT Archive*, June 4, 1936.

86. "Luciano Cringes on Stand, Admits 'Record' Under Fire," *NYDN*, June 4, 1936.

87. Dewey, *Twenty*, 235; "Dewey Riddles Lucky on Stand," *NYDN*, June 4, 1936.

88. "Dewey Accused of Trial 'Deals,' by Vice Chief," *BE*, June 2, 1936; "Vice Defense Paints Dewey as 'Glorifier,'" *NYDN*, June 5, 1936; "Claims Dewey Aides Cannot Back Charges," *BE*, June 5, 1936.

89. Dewey's summation can be found in TDP, *Early Career*, "Dewey's Summation at Luciano Trial," file 1-90-4; "Dewey Blasts Vice Lords in His Summation," *BE*, June 6, 1936; Dewey, *Twenty*, 256, 258.

90. Dewey had originally indicted thirteen people; three pled guilty, and only ten were put on trial; then Jack Ellenstein, a booker, pled guilty, reducing the number of defendants to nine. See "Lucania Aide Pleads Guilty," *BE*, June 1, 1936; "State Rests; Vice Aide to Admit Guilt," *NYDN*, May 30, 1936. Those

convicted were Charlie Luciano, Meyer Berkman, Jesse Jacobs, James Frederico, Abbie Wahrman, Davie Betillo, Ralph Ligouri, Tommy Bull, and Bennie Spiller—see "Lucky Guilty; 8 Aides, also for Life," *NYDN*, June 8, 1936.

91. "Jury Debates Lucania's Fate," *BE*, June 7, 1936; "Luciano and Eight Guilty, Face Life as Vice Lords," *NYDN*, June 8, 1936; "Luciana Convicted with 8 in Vice Ring on 62 Counts Each," *NYT Archive*, June 8, 1936; "Dewey Reveals Bribery Offers in Vice Inquiry," *BE*, June 8, 1936.

92. "Luciana Sentenced to 30 to 50 Years," *NYT Archive*, June 19, 1936; *Twenty*, 262–66; "Lucania Faces Life Term on Vice Conviction," *BE*, June 8, 1936.

93. "Luciana Convicted with 8 in Vice Ring on 62 Counts Each," *NYT Archive*, June 8, 1936.

94. "Valentine Hails Dewey Victory as Racket Blow," *BE*, June 8 1936.

95. Newark, *Luciano*, 127.

96. For Sen's discussion of Rawls, see Amaryta Sen, *The Idea of Justice* (Cambridge, Mass.: Belknap Press of Harvard University Press, 2009), 52–74.

97. Ibid., 129.

98. Ibid., vii.

99. Ibid., vii.

100. Ibid., 20–21.

101. Ibid., 7.

102. Richard Rorty, "Postmodernist Bourgeois Liberalism," cited in John Patrick Diggins, *The Promise of Pragmatism* (Chicago: University of Chicago, 1994), 453.

103. Richard Rorty also argues along these lines. See, for instance, David L. Hall, *Richard Rorty. Prophet and Poet of the New Pragmatism* (Albany: State University of New York), 174.

104. Sen, *Justice*, 44–46.

105. Ibid., 187ff.

106. For an intriguing exploration of Smith's notion of "moral sentiments," see Eyal Press, *Beautiful Souls. The Courage and Conscience of Ordinary People in Extraordinary Times* (New York: Picador, 2012), 66–67.

107. Sen, *Justice*, 110.

108. Ibid., 155.

109. Dewey, *Twenty*, 137–38.

110. Smith, *Dewey*, 216.

111. Ibid., 234.

112. The texts of Dewey's radio addresses can be found in TDP, Early Career, "Radio Addresses," Series 9–Speeches; Smith, *Dewey*, 236.

113. Smith, *Dewey*, 234.

114. Memo from Mr. De Loach, to: [deleted], Subj: "Record by Walter Winchell," November 16, 1960, FBI files, Abe Reles file, #62-57444. Director Hoover, it seems, listened to the recording on November 17, 1960.

115. "Talk of the Town," *TNY*, November 13, 1937, 15.

116. Smith, *Dewey*, 26–28.
117. Newark, *Luciano*, 130.
118. Gibbs and Bainbridge, "St. George," 28; Smith, *Dewey*, 224.
119. Newark, *Luciano*, 151–78.
120. "Dewey Commutes Luciano Sentence," *NYT Archive*, January 4, 1946.
121. "Luciano Plea Cites His Aid to U.S. Army," *NYT Archive*, May 23, 1945; "Luciano War Aid Called Ordinary," *NYT Archive*, February 27, 1947; "Dewey Silent on Luciano," *NYT Archive*, May 15, 1951; "Dewey Assailed on Luciano Parole," *NYT Archive*, July 18, 1951; Norton, *Dewey*, 570–73; Newark, *Luciano*, 172–78; Gosch and Hammer, 275–77.
122. Memo from A. Rosen to A.A. Tam, Subj: "Charles Lucky Luciano Parole," April 18, 1946, FBI files, Charles Luciano file, #39-2141.
123. Smith, *Dewey*, 572–73.
124. "Secret Report Cites Luciano on War Aid," *NYT Archive*, October 9, 1977; The Herlands Report (1954) can be found in TDP, Governor Dewey Papers, "The Herlands Report, 1954," 13-17-2.
125. Newark, *Luciano*, 217–20.

6. Murder, Inc.: "I Got Used to It"

1. Burton Turkus and Sid Feder, *Murder, Inc.* (New York: Da Capo, 1992), 65.
2. Lars Svendsen, *A Philosophy of Evil*, translated by Kerri A. Pierce (Champaign, Ill.: Dalkey Archive Press, 2010), 30.
3. Turkus and Feder, *Murder, Inc.*, 56.
4. This description comes from Reles's autopsy: "Autopsy Report, Reles," November 12, 1941, NYCMA, Murder, Inc., Case Files, Folder 52, Roll 8.
5. "RE: Louis Capone," JJC, Burton Turkus Papers, "DA Files," Box 1; Turkus and Feder, *Murder, Inc.*, 119.
6. Turkus and Feder, *Murder, Inc.*, 108.
7. Ibid., 107.
8. Ibid., 107.
9. Ibid., 109.
10. Edmund Elmaleh, *The Canary Sang but Couldn't Fly* (New York: Union Square Press, 2009), 9.
11. Turkus and Feder, *Murder, Inc.*, 8. There were rumors that Pittsburgh Phil went off on assignment to other cities to kill people, although solid evidence of his alleged murders outside New York was never found.
12. Ibid., 112.
13. "RE: The Killing of Irving Feinstein," undated, NYCMA, Murder, Inc., Case Files, Folder 223, Roll 15.
14. Turkus and Feder, *Murder, Inc.,* 9.
15. Ibid., 107.
16. Ibid., 113–14.

17. Albert Fried, *The Rise and Fall of the Jewish Gangster in America* (New York: Holt Rinehart and Winston, 1980), 203.

18. The following narrative is based on Turkus and Feder's account of the Reles–Shapiro war in *Murder, Inc.*, chap. 5, 107–27. See also Elmaleh, *Canary*, 17–20; and Paul R. Kavieff, *The Life and Times of Lepke Buchalter* (New York: Barricade Books, 2006), chap. 6. Rich Cohen recounts this struggle in Cohen, *Tough Jews* (New York: Vintage, 1999), 70–88.

19. Elmaleh, *Canary*, 18.

20. Turkus and Feder, *Murder, Inc.*, 109–10, 117; Jenna Weissman Joselit, *Our Gang. Jewish Crime and the New York Jewish Community, 1900–1940* (Bloomington: Indiana University Press, 1983), 152.

21. Turkus and Feder, *Murder, Inc.*, 114.

22. Ibid., 111–12.

23. "Criminals on Run, Police Heads Say," *NYT Archive*, September 1, 1931.

24. "Gang Shoots Imperil Crowd, One Hits Car," *NYT Archive*, September 7, 1931.

25. Turkus and Feder, *Murder, Inc.*, 117.

26. Ibid., 118–19.

27. Ibid., 123.

28. "Mrs. Rose Gold Reaches Out to Son," *NYJA,* May 8, 1939; and "Woman, 68, Held as Key Figure in Racket Empire," *NYDN,* May 5, 1939, both in JJC, Burton Turkus Papers, Scrapbooks, Box 5.

29. "Rose Gold Held as Racket Key," *NYS*, May 5, 1939, JJC, Burton Turkus Papers, Scrapbooks, Box 5.

30. Turkus and Feder, *Murder, Inc.,* 114.

31. Ibid., 121.

32. "Reles Described as Vicious Thug," *NYT Archive*, March 24, 1940.

33. "People v. Maione and Abbandando," March 1941, NYCMA, Murder, Inc., Case Files, Folder 13, Roll 1.

34. "Reles Described as Vicious Thug," *NYT Archive*, March 24, 1940.

35. "Arrested 71 Times, Racketeers Freed," *NY T Archive,* August 26, 1937.

36. See Chapter 1. No one was ever convicted for Snyder's murder.

37. "RE: Abraham Meer and Irving Amron," April 2, 1940, NYCMA, Murder, Inc., Case Files, Folder 218, Roll 15; "RE: Killing of Abraham Meer and Irving Amron," undated, NYCMA, Murder, Inc., Case Files, Folder 223, Roll 15.

38. "Information furnished by Seymour Magoon, RE: Killing of Joey Amberg," undated, NYCMA, Murder, Inc., Case Files, Folder 1, Roll 7.

39. "The Shooting and Killing of Joseph Amberg and Morris Kessler," September 30, 1935, NYCMA, Murder, Inc., Case Files, Folder 1, Roll 7.

40. "RE: Shooting and Killing of Joey Amberg and Morris Kessler," March 25, 1942, NYCMA, Murder, Inc., Case Files, Folder 9, Roll 7.

41. "RE: Shooting and Killing of Joey Amberg and Morris Kessler," March 25, 1942, NYCMA, Murder, Inc., Case Files, Folder 1, Roll 7.

42. Patrick Downey, *Gangster City* (Fort Lee, N.J.: Barricade, 2004), 250–57; Albert Fried, *The Rise and Fall of the Jewish Gangster in America* (Ithaca, N.Y.: Cornell University, 2009), 203, 218; "RE Joey Amberg and Manny Kessler," undated, NYCMA, Murder, Inc., Case Files, Folder 1, Roll 7.

43. Turkus and Feder, *Murder, Inc.,* 125–26.

44. Ibid., 127.

45. "Memorandum in Behalf of Defendant Att'ny David Price, Leon Fishbein," March 1940, NYCMA, Murder, Inc., Case Files, Folder 4, Roll 1.

46. Max Rubin Oral Statement, undated, Burton Turkus Papers, BPL, Box 1, Folder 4. Police reports pertaining to the Rosen murder can be found in NYCMA, Murder, Inc., Case File, Box 4, Roll 5.

47. Max Rubin Oral Statement, undated, BPL, Burton Turkus Papers, Box 1, Folder 4.

48. "Ester Rosen's Testimony," undated, NYCMA, Murder, Inc., Case Files, Folder 1, Roll 6.

49. "Ester Rosen's Testimony," September 23, 1936, NYCMA, Murder, Inc., Case Files, Folder 1, Roll 7.

50. Undated memorandum titled "Motive," BPL, Burton Turkus Papers, Box 1, Folder 4.

51. Paul Kavieff, *The Life and Times of Lepke Buchalter* (Fort Lee, N.J.: Barricade Books, 2006), 155.

52. "Rosen Grand Jury," NYCMA, Murder, Inc., Case Files, Folder 1, Roll 6; Turkus and Feder, *Murder, Inc.,* 378.

53. "Rosen Grand Jury," undated, NYCMA, Murder, Inc., Case Files, Folder 1, Roll 6.

54. "Rosen Information," undated, NYCMA, Murder, Inc., Case Files, Folder 1, Roll 6.

55. Turkus and Feder, *Murder, Inc.,* 381. This account of Rosen's murder follows Turkus and Feder, *Murder, Inc.*, 363–95.

56. Ibid., 393.

57. "Witness Interviews, Rosen Shooting," undated, NYCMA, Murder, Inc., Case Files, Folder 43, Roll 7.

58. Turkus and Feder, *Murder, Inc.,* 216–19.

59. Ibid., 219.

60. Ibid., 229.

61. Ibid.

62. Ibid., 230.

63. Ibid.

64. Ibid., 232.

65. Ibid.

66. Ibid., 304.

67. Reles's account of the Feinstein murder can be found at "RE: Irving Feinstein," April 2, 1940, NYCMA, Murder, Inc., Case Files, Folder 218, Roll 15.

68. "Memorandum given by Abe Reles, RE: Killing of Irving ('Puggy') Feinstein," undated, NYCMA, Murder, Inc., Case Files, Folder 223, Roll 15.

69. Ibid.

70. Ibid.

71. "He's Burnin' Me' Goldstein Cries," *Brooklyn Eagle*, September 17, 1940; "Memorandum given by Abe Reles, RE: Killing of Irving ('Puggy') Feinstein," undated, NYCMA, Murder, Inc., Case Files, Folder 223, Roll 15.

72. Turkus and Feder, *Murder, Inc.*, 298.

73. "Goldstein Yells in Court: 'Guy Is Burnin' Us!'" *NYT Archive*, September 18, 1940.

74. Turkus and Feder, *Murder, Inc.*, 297.

75. Ibid., 71.

76. Ibid.

77. "People v. Maione and Abbandando," March 1941, NYCMA, Murder, Inc., Case Files, Folder 13, Roll 1.

78. Turkus and Feder, *Murder, Inc.,* 45–47.

79. "Drucker Guilty of Ice-Pick Murder; Brooklyn Ring's Finger Man Is Convicted of Second Degree Murder," *NYT Archive*, May 6, 1944.

80. "Crimes of Harry (Happy) Maione," undated, JJC, Burton Turkus Papers, "DA Files," Box 1; Turkus and Feder, *Murder, Inc.,* 213.

81. "Re: Rape of D.W.", undated, NYCMA, Murder, Inc., Case Files, Folder 11, Roll 1.

82. "RE: Vito Gurino," undated, NYCMA, Murder, Inc., Case Files, Folder 226, Roll 15.

83. David Ruth, *Inventing the Public Enemy* (Chicago: University of Chicago Press, 1996), 92.

84. Fred Gardaphé, *From Wiseguys to Wise Men. The Gangster and Italian American Masculinities* (New York: Routledge, 2006), 18.

85. Turkus and Feder, *Murder, Inc.,* 43–44; Downey, *Gangster City*, 267–68.

86. "People v. Buchalter," September 1941, NYCMA, Murder, Inc., Case Files, Folder 41, Roll 5.

87. Mary Midgley, *Wickedness. A Philosophical Essay* (New York: Routledge, 1992), 49.

88. Judith Butler, *Precarious Life. The Powers of Mourning and Violence* (New York: Verso, 2004), 16.

89. See Eyal Press, *Beautiful Souls. The Courage and Conscience of Ordinary People in Extraordinary Times* (New York: Picador, 2012), 101.

90. Slavoj Žižek, *Violence. Six Sideways Reflections* (New York: Picador, 2008), 4.

91. See Svendsen, *Evil*, 143–47.

92. Carlos Clarens, *Crime Movies* (New York: Da Capo Press, 1997), 93–101.

93. Ibid., 116.

94. Ibid., 149.

95. Thomas Dewey, *Twenty against the Underworld* (Garden City, N.Y.: Doubleday, 1974), 186.

96. Turkus and Feder, *Murder, Inc.,* 53–54, 57.

97. Ibid., 61.

98. Ibid., 3.

99. Ibid., 106.

100. Lewis J. Valentine, *Night Stick: The Autobiography of Lewis J. Valentine, Former Police Commissioner of New York* (New York: Dial Press, 1947), 148.

101. Dewey, *Twenty,* 174.

102. "Crimes of Harry (Happy) Maione," undated, JJC, Burton Turkus Papers, "DA Files," Box 1.

103. "Kings County Homicide Report," March 3, 1935, NYCMA, Folder 5, Roll 1.

104. "People v. Abbandando," NYCMA, Folder 2, Roll 1.

105. "RE: Joseph Ciancemino," undated, NYCMA, Murder, Inc., Case Files, Folder 1, Roll 1.

106. "Statement by D.A. O'Dwyer, January 30, 1942," NYCMA, Murder, Inc., Case Files, Folder 4, Roll 1. Here, O'Dwyer notes that Nestfield had finally, in 1940, identified Max "the Jerk" Golub as one of the assailants. Although the police were sure that Frank Abbandando and Harry Maione were also involved, that had little evidence to go on.

107. "Statement of Minnie Jones," undated, NYCMA, Murder, Inc., Case Files, Folder 7, Roll 1.

108. See, for example, Bettina Stangneth, *Eichmann before Jerusalem,* translated by Ruth Martin (New York: Knopf, 2014). Stangneth demonstrates that Eichmann, far from being simply stupidly evil, was a vehement anti-Semite.

109. Svendson, *Evil,* 137–87.

110. Elmaleh, *Canary,* 6–7.

111. Turkus and Feder, *Murder, Inc.,* 65.

112. "Testimony of Julie Catalano," 1940, NYCMA, Murder, Inc., Case Files, Folder 228, Roll 15.

113. Ibid.

114. "People v. Maione and Abbandando," March 1941, NYCMA, Murder, Inc., Case Files, Folder 16, Roll 2.

115. "Testimony of Julie Catalano," 1940, NYCMA, Murder, Inc., Case Files, Folder 228, Roll 15.

116. "RE: Siciliano/ Lattaro Killing of February 6, 1939," undated, NYCMA, Murder, Inc., Case Files, Folder 226, Roll 15; Turkus and Feder, *Murder, Inc.,* 167–71.

117. Charles Norton Coe, *Demi-Devils. The Character of Shakespeare's Villains* (New York: Bookman, 1963), 19.

118. Charlotte Spivack, *The Comedy of Evil on Shakespeare's Stage* (Cranbury, N.J.: Associated University Presses, 1978), 9.

119. Arthur O. Lovejoy, *The Great Chain of Being*, cited in Spivack, *Comedy*, 24.
120. Spivack, *Comedy*, 26.
121. Ibid., 18.
122. Clarens, *Crime Movies*, 155.
123. Ibid., 139.
124. "Cars Killers Used Are Found Junked," *NYT Archive*, April 4, 1940.
125. "Crimes Committed by Harry (Happy) Maione," undated, JJC, Burton Turkus Papers, "DA Files," Box 1.
126. Turkus and Feder, *Murder, Inc.*, 30.

7. A Theater of Ethics: Mr. Arsenic and the Murder, Inc., Trials

1. Burton Turkus and Sid Feder, *Murder, Inc.* (New York: Da Capo, 1992), 30.
2. George Walsh, *Public Enemies. The Mayor, the Mob, and the Crime That Was* (New York: Norton, 1980), 116–17.
3. "O'Dwyer to Out Geoghan's Staff," *NYT* Archive, December 2, 1939.
4. "Complaint," October 30, 1935, NYCMA, Murder, Inc., Case Files, Folder 1, Roll 7.
5. "Anonymous Letter," February 9, 1940, NYCMA, Murder, Inc., Case Files, Folder 8, Roll 1.
6. "Anonymous letter," April 22, 1940, NYCMA, Murder, Inc., Case Files, Folder 8, Roll 1.
7. Letter from Meier Steinbrink to Bascom Slemp, February 3, 1925, in BPL, Burton Turkus Papers, Box 4, Folder 6. There is, unfortunately, no indication of whether young Turkus did meet the president.
8. "Burton B. Turkus, 80, Prosecutor of Murder, Inc. in the 1940s, Dies," *NYT Archive*, November 24, 1982.
9. "Boxer," *The Brooklyner,* July 8, 1933, BPL, Burton Turkus Papers, Box 3, Folder 3/4.
10. BPL, Burton Turkus Papers, Box 1, Folder 1.
11. Turkus's picture was regularly in the newspapers during the trials. One striking photograph of him shows him, earnest and intense, standing before the judge, Lepke Buchalter beside him. A 1942 photo shows a smiling and perfectly groomed Turkus escorting his mother from a voting booth during Turkus's unsuccessful run for a judgeship in Brooklyn. See BPL, Burton Turkus Papers, "Photos," Box 2, Folder 8.
12. In the 1940s, Turkus would be an enthusiastic supporter of progressive Republican Tom Dewey. For a collection of materials showing Turkus's support of Dewey, see, BPL, Burton Turkus Papers, Box 2, Folder 8.
13. Turkus and Feder, *Murder, Inc.*, 27.
14. Ibid., 31.
15. Ibid.
16. Ibid., 49.

17. Meyer Berger, "What Makes a Successful Detective?," *NYT Archive*, September 10, 1944.

18. Turkus and Feder, *Murder, Inc.*, 33.

19. Ibid., 35.

20. "Reles—Buggsy Hoodlums Sent to Workhouse," *BE*, March 5, 1940; "2 Reles Hoodlums Guilty of Vagrancy," *BE*, March 8, 1940.

21. Turkus and Feder, *Murder, Inc.,* 44.

22. "O'Dwyer Grills Wives of Reles and Goldstein," *BE*, March 15, 1940; Turkus and Feder, *Murder, Inc.,* 50.

23. "Detective 59 Years Quits with Regret; Murder Ring's Abe Reles Would Talk Only to 'Honest Cop,'" *NYT Archive*, November 27, 1952.

24. "Reles to Blow Lid off Murder Ring," *BE*, March 23, 1940.

25. Turkus and Feder, *Murder, Inc.,* 58.

26. Ibid., 54.

27. Ibid., 61.

28. Ibid., 60.

29. "Interrogation of Harry Maione," February 23, 1940, NYCMA, Murder, Inc., Case Files, Folder 11, Roll 1.

30. Turkus and Feder, *Murder, Inc.,* 60.

31. Ibid., 55.

32. "Abe Reles Criminal Record," NYCMA, Murder, Inc., Case Files, Folder 77, Roll 10, lists forty-three arrests between 1920 and 1940. He was first arrested in 1920, when he was fourteen, and charged with juvenile delinquency, for which he received five months in reform school; he was thereafter arrested at least once each year; Turkus and Feder, *Murder, Inc.,* 55.

33. Turkus and Feder, *Murder, Inc.,* 66.

34. Ibid., 67.

35. Ibid., 64.

36. Ibid., 70.

37. Ibid., 65.

38. "Reles to Blow Lid off Murder Ring," *BE*, March 23, 1940; "Reles Bares Ring Secrets; 2 More Grilled in Killings," *BE*, March 24, 1940; "A Gangster 'Sings,'" *BE*, March 25, 1940.

39. "Terror Reign Seen in Scared Gangs," *BE*, March 27, 1940; "F.B.I. Seeks Adonis in Far-Flung Hunt," *BE*, May 1, 1940; "Fugitive Named Racket Boss—Anastasia, 3-Time Suspect in Murders, Sought in Panto Case," *BE*, May 1, 1940; "Adonis Gives Up to Amen, Ends Wide Kidnapping Hunt," *BE*, May 9, 1940; "Lepke, 5 Others, Indicted in Boro Gang Slayings," *BE*, May 24, 1940.

40. "'Little Guy' Ready to Squeal on Bosses in Murder Ring," *BE*, March 25, 1940.

41. "Murder Inquiry Holds Man who Scarred Capone," *NYHT,* March 28, 1940.

42. "Grill Louis Capone on Murder Ring—Seek Head of Fantastic Syndicate," *BE*, March 18, 1940.

43. "Grill Mystery Women in 3 Slayings," *BE*, March 22, 1940.

44. "Gang Tries to Bribe O'Dwyer Witness," *BE*, March 19, 1940; "Froschs Called 'Fixers' for Murder Syndicate," *BE*, March 20, 1940; "Ring Raises Fund to Free Squealers," *BE*, March 21, 1940. The Frosch family ran a bail bonds business; they were accused of falsifying bail applications and bribing witnesses. "O'Dwyer is Guarded against Murder Mob," *Brooklyn Eagle*, March 29, 1940.

45. "A 'Murder for Money' Racket," *BE*, March 15, 1940.

46. Turkus and Feder, *Murder, Inc.*, 190.

47. "Woman Tells Grand Jury of Gang Slaying," *NYHT*, March 26, 1940; "2 Indicted in Murder Ring; First in O'Dwyer's Crusade," *BE*, March 28, 1940.

48. "State Splits Boro Gang Trial," *BE*, May 8, 1940.

49. "Two Indicted as Gangster's Hired Killers," *NYHT*, March 29, 1940; "Murder Squealers May Take Stand," *BE*, May 9, 1940.

50. Turkus and Feder, *Murder, Inc.*, 223.

51. "Stole Death Car, Maffetore Admits," *BE*, May 14, 1940.

52. "Ring Members Tell of Stealing Car for Murder," *NYHT*, May 15, 1940.

53. "Reles Tells Murder Ring Trial He Killed or Helped Kill 16 Men," *NYHT*, May 16, 1040.

54. "People v. Maione and Abbandando," March 1941, NYCMA, Murder, Inc., Case Files, Folder 13, Roll 1. This is actually from the retrial; testimony at the retrial was exactly the same as at the original trial.

55. "People v. Maione and Abbandando," March 1941, NYCMA, Murder, Inc., Case Files, Folder 13, Roll 1.

56. Ibid.

57. "Reles Depicts Brutal Slaying for Gang Jury," *BE*, May 15, 1940.

58. "People v. Maione and Abbandando." This is the testimony from the second Maione and Abbandando trial, which repeated, word for word, testimony from the first trial. NYCMA, Murder, Inc., Case Files, Folder 14, Roll 2.

59. Turkus and Feder, *Murder, Inc.*, 228.

60. "Maione Shouts Defiance as Gang Cases Nears Jury," *BE*, May 23, 1940; Turkus and Feder, *Murder, Inc.*, 235.

61. "Witness Backs Reles' Story of Mob Murder," *BE*, May 16, 1940.

62. "Witness Rivals Reles' Expose of Murder Ring," *NYHT*, May 17, 1940.

63. "Maione Pins His Lie on Grandma's Death," *BE*, May 20, 1940.

64. "Witness Blasts Murder Alibi, Admits Perjury," *BE*, May 22, 1940.

65. "Maione and Pal Chorus They Were Framed," *BE*, May 21, 1940.

66. "RE: Greenie," NYCMA, undated, Folder 80, Roll 11.

67. "Barney Ruditsky, Detective, Dead," *NYT Archive*, October 19, 1962.

68. Turkus and Feder, *Murder, Inc.*, 270.

69. Ibid., 278. This account of Siegel in Los Angeles follows Turkus and Feder, *Murder, Inc.*, 264–83.

70. Ibid., 280.

71. "RE: Puggy Feinstein," April 2, 1940, unsigned memorandum, NY-CMA, Murder, Inc., Case Files, Folder 218, Roll 15.

72. "Strauss Loses Plea for a Sanity Test as Trial is Begun," *BE*, September 9, 1940.

73. Turkus and Feder, *Murder, Inc.,* 313.

74. Ibid., 300.

75. Ibid.

76. Ibid.

77. "Judge May Hold Court All Night in Strauss Case," *BE*, September 11, 1940.

78. "Gurino Admits Murder Role," *BE*, September 12, 1940; "Jury Indicts Gurino in three Boro Slayings," *BE*, September 13, 1940.

79. "Gangster in Court Pleads for Life," *NYT Archive,* September 18, 1940.

80. "Buggsy Is Mentioned 1st Time in Testimony," *BE*, September 13, 1940; "Abe Reles' 'Song' Scheduled Next at Gang Trial," *BE*, September 14, 1940.

81. Turkus and Feder, *Murder, Inc.,* 302.

82. "Reles Testifies in Talking Part in 11 Murders," *NYHT*, September 17, 1940.

83. "Reles Admits 10 Murders, Squeals on Strauss, Buggsy," *BE*, September 16, 1940.

84. "Reles Loan Racket Exposed by Amen," *NYT* clipping, January 2, 1941, in NYCMA, Murder, Inc., Case Files, Folder 72, Roll 11.

85. "He's Burnin' Me' Goldstein Cries," *BE*, September 17, 1940.

86. "Goldstein Yells in Court: 'Guy is Burnin' Us,'" *NYHT*, September 18, 1940; Turkus and Feder, *Murder, Inc.,* 314.

87. Turkus and Feder, *Murder, Inc.,* 318.

88. "Jury May Decide Strauss' Fate by Nightfall," *BE*, September 18, 1940; "Strauss Case Goes to Jury Today," *BE*, September 19, 1940.

89. "Strauss, Goldstein, Guilty; to Get Chair," *BE*, September 20, 1940, JJC, Burton Turkus Papers, Scrapbook, Box 5.

90. "'Killer' Begs Turn to Plead at Death Trial," *NYJA*, September 19, 1940, JJC, Burton Turkus Papers, Scrapbook, Box 5; "Strauss, Buggsy, Will Hear their Doom Wednesday," *BE*, September 20, 1940; "Strauss and Goldstein Guilty; Must Die for Brooklyn Murders," *NYHT,* September 20, 1940, *NYHT*, JJC, Burton Turkus Papers, Scrapbook, Box 5; "Two Ring Killers Guilty; Must Die," *NYDM*, December 20, 1940, JJC, Burton Turkus Papers, Scrapbook, Box 5.

91. "Strauss, Buggsy Doomed to Die," *BE*, September 26, 1940.

92. "Murder Ring Conviction Is Good News for Brooklyn," *BE*, September 20, 1940.

93. "3 in Death House Win New Trials," *NYDN,* January 1, 1941, JJC, Burton Turkus Papers, Scrapbooks, Box 5.

94. "2 In Murder, Inc. Can't Pay Lawyers," *NYWT*, February 24, 1941, JJC, Burton Turkus Papers, Scrapbook, Box 5; "2 In Murder, Inc. Slated to Face

New Trial Monday," *NYWT,* February 28, 1941, JJC, Burton Turkus Papers, Scrapbook, Box 5; "The People v. Harry Maione and Frank Abbandando," Stenographic minutes, February 1941, NYCMA, Murder, Inc., Case Files, Folder 13, Roll 1.

95. "Excuse Women from Jury at Murder Trial," *NYDN,* March 7, 1941, JJC, Burton Turkus Papers, Scrapbook, Box 5.

96. "Charges Actual Rudnick Slayer Won Immunity," *BE,* March 10, 1941; "Rudnick's Mother Tells of Identifying His Mutilated Body," *BE,* March 11, 1941; "Thugs Torture Ex-Convict, Threaten Material Witness," *BE,* March 13, 1941; "O'Dwyer Checks Tales of Gangster Threats," *BE,* March 14, 1941.

97. "Drove Gang's Death Cars, Witness Says," *BE,* March 12, 1941.

98. "People v. Maione and Abbandando," March 1941, NYCMA, Murder, Inc., Case Files, Folder 13, Roll 1.

99. "Reles Big Mogul in the Rackets, He Tells Court," *BE,* March 17, 1941.

100. "Maione Attacks Reles, Throws Court in Uproar," *BE,* March 19, 1941; "Maione Goes on Rampage at Murder Trial," *NYDM,* March 19, 1941, JJC, Burton Turkus Papers, Scrapbook, Box 5.

101. "Julius Helfand Is Dead at 84," *NYT Archive,* August 18, 1987. Helfand would later become a judge and a commissioner in the New York State Athletic Commission, where he would play a key role in reforming boxing in New York.

102. "Gangster's Trial to Uncover New Murder Ring Tie," *BE,* April 16, 1941.

103. "Gang Killer Tells of Ring's System," *NYT Archive,* May 20, 1941.

104. "Testimony of Abe Reles," 1941, NYCMA, Murder, Inc., Case Files, Folder 229, Roll 15.

105. "Gang Killer Tells Why He 'Reformed,'" *NYT Archive,* May 17, 1941.

106. "Nitzberg Held Guilty after 18 Minutes," *NYT Archive,* May 24, 1941; "Nitzberg Sentenced to Chair," *NYT Archive,* June 3, 1941.

107. "Twice Condemned, Reles Aide Freed," *NYT Archive,* June 2, 1943.

108. "Workman Goes to Prison," *NYT Archive,* June 13, 1941, 15. Also Paul Sann, *Kill the Dutchman (New York: Popular Library, 1971),* 19–27; Turkus and Feder, *Murder, Inc.,* 141–51.

109. "Doomed Pair Eagerly Await Appeal Plea," *NYDN,* March 9, 1941, JJC, Burton Turkus Papers, Scrapbook, Box 5.

110. Turkus and Feder, *Murder, Inc.,* 320–21.

111. Ibid., 330.

112. "Widow Claims Double Indemnity for Buggsy's Death," *BE,* October 28, 1941.

113. Edmund Elmaleh, *The Canary Sang but Couldn't Fly* (New York: Union Square Press, 2009), 62.

114. *Look,* June 4, 1940. A copy can be found in the Turkus Papers, BPL.

115. Turkus and Feder, *Murder, Inc.,* xii.

116. Ibid., 51.

117. "2 Guilty, Get Chair, in 'Trust' Murder," *NYM*, JJC, Burton Turkus Papers, Scrapbooks, Box 5; "2 Gang Slayers Sentenced to Die," *BE*, May 27, 1940.

118. Turkus and Feder, *Murder, Inc.,* 228.

119. Plato, excerpt from *The Laws,* in *The Psychology of Society,* ed. Richard Sennett (New York: Vintage, 1977), 94.

120. Denis Diderot, "The Paradox of Acting," in Sennett, *Psychology,* 101.

121. Erving Goffman, *The Presentation of Self in Everyday Life* (Garden City, N.Y.: Anchor Doubleday, 1959). Andrew Parker and Eve Kosofsky, eds., *Performativity and Performance* (New York: Routledge, 1995), 2. Also Richard Sennett, *The Fall of Public Man* (New York: Vintage, 1974), especially 33–38.

122. See "The Performance of Culture," in Marvin Carlson, *Performance. A Critical Introduction* (New York: Routledge, 1996), 12–30.

123. Judith Butler, *Gender Trouble* (New York: Routledge, 1990), 191. For a comparison of Butler's ideas with those of Foucault and Derrida, see Jeffrey T. Nealon, *Alterity Politics. Ethics and Performative Subjectivity* (Durham, N.C.: Duke University, 1998), 17–30.

124. Clifford Geertz, *The Interpretation of Cultures* (New York: Basic Books, 1973), 5.

125. Geertz, "Deep Play: Notes on the Balinese Cockfight," in *Cultures,* 412–53.

126. Simon Critchley, *Ethics, Politics, Subjectivity* (New York: Verso, 1999), 97.

127. Zygmunt Bauman, *Postmodern Ethics* (New York: Blackwell, 1993), 165.

128. Geertz, *Culture,* 100.

8. Ethics of Ambiguity: The Canary Could Sing but Couldn't Fly

1. Burton Turkus and Sid Feder, *Murder, Inc.* (New York: Da Capo, 1992), 435.

2. No one knows how Shapiro got his odd nickname. One theory is that Shapiro had a kind of verbal tick; after a conversation with someone, he would grunt, "Get outta here," which sounded something like "gurrah."

3. "Material for use in connection with the cross-examination of Louis (Lepke) Buchalter," undated, JJC, Burton Turkus Papers, "DA Files," Box 1.

4. The discussion of Winchell that follows is based primarily on Neal Gabler, *Walter Winchell* (New York: Vintage, 1994).

5. Ibid., xi.

6. Wolcott Gibbs and John Bainbridge, "St. George and the Dragnet," *The New Yorker,* May 25, 1940, 28.

7. Gabler, *Winchell,* caption to a photograph of Winchell with Cagney, between 172–73.

8. Ibid., 155, 120.

9. Ibid., 197–98.

10. No, a very nervous Wincell told everyone; he knew nothing about Coll's murder. He was just doing what he always did, repeat rumors that he'd heard. Ibid., 155.

11. Ibid., 276.

12. Ibid., 278–79; Paul Kavieff, *The Life and Times of Lepke Buchalter* (Fort Lee, N.J.: Barricade Books, 2006), 131–32.

13. "Lepke Surrenders to F.B.I.; Racketeer Never Left City," *NYT Archive,* August 25, 1939.

14. Marc Mappen, *Prohibition Gangsters. The Rise and Fall of a Bad Generation* (New Brunswick, N.J.: Rutgers University, 2013), 197–212; Kavieff, *Lepke,* 131–32.

15. "Statement by Eugenio Salvese," April 12, 1940, NYCMA, Folder 42, Roll 7.

16. Edmund Elmaleh, *The Canary Sang but Couldn't Fly* (New York: Union Square Press, 2009), 62; *Look,* June 4, 1940. A copy can be found in the BPL, Turkus Papers.

17. Elmaleh, *Canary,* 63–64.

18. Turkus and Feder, *Murder, Inc.,* 366, 369.

19. Ibid., 369–70.

20. Ibid., 370–71.

21. "Murdered Man's Son Puts Finger on Lepke," *BE,* October 22, 1941; "Slain Man's Kin Names Shapiro in Lepke Trial," *BE,* October 23, 1941.

22. "Experts Stumped by 'Shlom Job,'" *BE,* October 30, 1941.

23. "Memorandum of Information RD: Charles (the Bug) Workman," April 29, 1941, NYCMA, Folder 42, Roll 7; Turkus and Feder, *Murder, Inc.,* 394; Kavieff, *Lepke,* 118.

24. "Lepke's Boast of Geoghan 'In' Disrupts Trial," *BE,* November 14, 1941.

25. "Lepke, Lucania, Linked in Murder of Rosen, *BE,* October 31, 1941; "Lepke Helped Rosen, Rubin Admits," *BE,* November 6, 1941.

26. Turkus and Feder, *Murder, Inc.,* 398.

27. Ibid., 391.

28. "Memorandum of Information RE: Charles (the Bug) Workman," April 29, 1941, NYCMA, Folder 42, Roll 7; "Memorandum of Information given by Albert Tannenbaum," June 5, 1941, NYCMA, Folder 42, Roll 7; Turkus and Feder, *Murder, Inc.,* 393.

29. Elmaleh, *Canary,* 62.

30. "Talk of the Town," *TNY,* November 15, 1941, 17.

31. Turkus and Feder, *Murder, Inc.,* 435.

32. Elmaleh, *Canary,* 67–69.

33. "Coney Island Eyrie," *TNY,* September 9, 1933, 12.

34. "Memorandum of Information, supplied by Meyer Sycoff, RE: Amberg-Kessler Killings, September 30, 1935," undated, NYCMA, Murder, Inc., Case Files, Folder 44, Roll 7.

35. For a map of the room layout, see Elmaleh, *Canary,* 74.

36. Ibid., 80.

37. Ibid., 79.

38. This account follows Elmaleh, *Canary,* xv–xvii.

39. Ibid., 87–88.

40. "Reles Dies in Hotel Plunge," *BE,* November 12, 1941.

41. The most thorough discussion of Reles's death is Elmaleh, *Canary.*

42. "Reles Dies in Hotel Plunge," *BE,* November 12, 1941.

43. Ibid.

44. "Five Reles Guards 'Broken' as Mayor Opens Wide Probe," *BE,* November 13, 1941.

45. Turkus and Feder, *Murder, Inc.,* 458.

46. Ibid., 485–87.

47. Peter Maas, *The Valachi Papers* (New York: Perennial, 2003), 155.

48. Elmaleh explains that this comment is the origin of the title of his book about Reles's murder; Elmaleh, *Canary,* 98.

49. Walter Kiernan, "Hey Kids! Reles Was No Hero, Just a Blubberer with a Grin," *BE,* November 13, 1941.

50. "Lepke Witness Boasts Killings, Denies He's a Rat," *BE,* November 13, 1941.

51. "Gurrah May Testify to Save Lepke's Life," *BE,* November 20, 1941.

52. "2 in Murder Ring Are Put to Death," *NYT Archive,* February 20, 1942. There was some confusion about the time of the execution; Sing Sing was still on Standard Time, an hour later than, as the *Times* reported, "usual" time. The official time of execution, then, was just after midnight on February 20, 1942; however, down in New York City, the time was just after 11:00 p.m. on February 19.

53. "Gangster's Brother Apologizes," *NYT Archive,* April 19, 1942.

54. "Brother of Slayer Held in Conspiracy," *NYT Archive,* March 17, 1942.

55. "Son of Executed Man Held in Pistol Case," *NYT Archive,* March 9, 1952.

56. Turkus and Feder, *Murder, Inc.,* 416.

57. Robert Lowell, "Memoires of West Street and Lepke," accessed December 6, 2013, http://www.americanpoems.com/poets/robert-lowell/13671.

58. Turkus and Feder, *Murder, Inc.,* 414–15.

59. George Walsh, *Public Enemies. The Mayor, the Mob, and the Crime That Was* (New York: Norton, 1980), 3–5; Leonard Katz, *Uncle Frank. The Biography of Frank Costello* (New York: Pocket Books, 1975), 126.

60. Zygmunt Bauman, *Postmodern Ethics* (Cambridge, Mass.: Blackwell, 1993), 5.

61. For a compelling illustration of the role moral sentiment plays in actual moral dilemmas, see Eyal Press, *Beautiful Souls. The Courage and Conscience of Ordinary People in Extraordinary Times* (New York: Picador, 2012), 66–69.

62. William James, "The One and the Many," in *Pragmatism and Other Essays* (New York: Washington Square Press, 1963), 71.

63. Emmanuel Levinas, *Totality and Infinity,* trans. Alphonso Lingis (Pittsburgh, Pa.: Duquesne University, 1969).

64. James, "The Moral Philosopher and the Moral Life," in James, *Pragmatism*, 231.

65. Simon Critchley, *Infinitely Demanding. Ethics of Commitment, Politics of Resistance* (New York: Verso, 2007), 16–17.

66. Wayne Cristaudo and Wendy Baker, eds., *Messianism, Apocalypse, and Redemption in 20th Century German Thought* (Adelaide, Australia: ATF Press, 2006), xiii.

67. Bauman, *Postmodern Ethics*, 9.

68. Ibid., 10–11.

69. Ibid., 11–12.

Epilogue: "That Dangerous and Sad City of the Imagination"

1. Thomas Dewey, *Twenty against the Underworld* (Garden City, N.Y.: Doubleday, 1974), ix.

2. "O'Dwyer as Mayor Pledges his Regime to Do Good Work," *NYT Archive*, January 2, 1946.

3. "Goldstein Presses Costello Charges," *NYT Archive*, October 19, 1945.

4. "Morris Sees City Run by Costello," *NYT Archive,* October 4, 1949.

5. "Impellitteri Takes Full City Powers," *NYT Archive*, September 3, 1950; "O'Dwyer Is Dead; Ex-Mayor Was 74," *NYT Archive*, November 25, 1964.

6. Estes Kefauver, *Crime in America* (New York: Doubleday, 1951), 290–91.

7. Burton Turkus and Sid Feder, *Murder, Inc.* (New York: Da Capo, 1992), 102–3.

8. Kefauver, *Crime*, 284.

9. "Jury Reopens 10-Year-Old Reles Inquiry; Investigation Follows O'Dwyer Testimony," *NYT Archive,* November 27, 1951; "Inquiry Discredits O'Dwyer for Calling Reles Important," *NYT Archive*, December 22, 1951. Edmund Elmaleh discusses all this in great detail in his *Canary*, especially chapter 15. O'Dwyer returned to Mexico, and then New York. He died in 1964. Bill O'Dwyer's brother, Paul, was also a leading New York politician. Paul O'Dwyer published a memoir of his and his brother's lives; Paul argues that not only was Bill innocent of corruption charges but that the charges were also fabrications hatched by the FBI and CIA. See Paul O'Dwyer, *Beyond the Golden Door* (New York: St. John's University, 1987); and Michael O'Neill, "Surrounded by Rascals," a review of Paul O'Dwyer's memoir, *NYT Archive*, August 16, 1987.

10. Scores of such invitations can be found in the BPL, Burton Turkus Papers, Box 4, Folder 1.

11. "Burton Turkus, Famed N.Y. Crime Buster to Speak Here," *Patterson Evening News,* April 27, 1942, JJC, Burton Turkus Papers, Scrapbook, Box 5.

12. "Turkus Named by Republicans for Kings County Court Judge," *NYHT,* July 14, 1942, JJC, Burton Turkus Papers, Scrapbook, Box 5; "Murder, Inc. News Boosts Turkus," *NYWT,* October 21, 1942, JJC, Burton Turkus Papers, Scrapbook, Box 5; BPL, Burton Turkus Papers, Box 2, Folder 1.

13. *Tight Spot* was directed by Phil Karlson and written by William Bowers. It is a classic "noir" film of the 1950s. The film merges the media's interest in Bugsy Siegel's onetime companion, Virginia Hill, with the Abe Reles experience of a defenestration of a protected witness.

14. Adam LeBor, "Overt and Covert," a review of Stephen Kinzer, *The Brothers. John Foster Dulles, Allen Dulles and Their Secret World War, New York Times Book Review,* November 10, 2013, 50.

15. Louis Sohol, "New York Cavalcade," *NYJA,* May 29, 1942, JJC, Burton Turkus Papers, Scrapbook, Box 5.

16. "Dewey Demands Strong War Steps," *NYT Archive,* June 18, 1940; Susan Dunn, *1940. FDR, Willkie, Lindbergh, Hitler. The Election amid the Storm* (New Haven, Conn.: Yale, 2013), 73.

17. "Radio Address Delivered by President Roosevelt from Washington, December 9, 1941," accessed August 3, 2013, https://www.mtholyoke.edu/acad/intrel/WorldWar2/radio.htm.

18. Robert Warshow, "The Gangster as Tragic Hero," in *Gangster Film Reader,* ed. Alain Silver and James Ursini (Pompton Plains, N.J.: Limelight Editions, 2007), 13.

19. "Frank Costello," October 26, 1944, FBI Report #62-76543, section 1; "Aurelio Describes Costello Backing," *NYT Archive,* October 27, 1943.

20. Rudolph Halley and Ed Reid, "The Shame of New York," *Look,* November 16, 1951, in NYCMA, Murder, Inc. Case Files, Clippings, Roll 11.

21. Caption: "Service Flag Rules 'Murder, Inc.' Haunt," *NYJA,* July 1, 1942, JJC, Burton Turkus Papers, Scrapbook, Box 5.

22. Robert Williams, "Brooklyn on Trial in Turkus Bid for Bench," political flyer, undated (1942?), JJC, Burton Turkus Papers, Box 5, Scrapbook.

Bibliography

Unpublished Sources

Brooklyn Public Library, Brooklyn Collection, Burton Turkus Papers
City of New York, Municipal Archives, Murder, Inc. Case Files
Federal Bureau of Information, Case Files, BACM Research/Paperless Archives
John Jay College of Criminal Law, Lloyd Sealy Library, Special Collections,
    Burton Turkus Papers
New York State Archives, Sing Sing Records
University of Rochester, Department of Rare Books and Special Collections,
    Thomas E. Dewey Papers

Newspapers and Magazines

Brooklyn Eagle
Life
Look
The Nation
New York Daily News
New York Herald Tribune
New York Journal-American
New York Mirror
New York Sun
New York Times
New York World-Telegram
The New Republic
Time

Published Primary and Secondary Sources

Appiah, Kwame Anthony. *The Honor Code. How Moral Revolutions Happen.* New York: Norton, 2010.

Arendt, Hannah. *The Human Condition.* Chicago: University of Chicago, 1958.

Arons, Ron. *The Jews of Sing Sing.* New York: Barricade Books, 2008.

Asbury, Herbert. *The Gangs of New York.* New York: Knopf, 1927.

Baker, Kevin. *Dreamland.* New York: Harpers, 2006.

Barth, Miles, ed. *Weegee's World,* Boston: Bulfinch, 1997.

Bauman, Zygmunt. *Postmodern Ethics.* Cambridge, Mass.: Blackwell, 1993.

Bell, Graham. *Murder, Inc.* New York: The History Press, 2010.

Bergreen, Laurence. *Capone. The Man and the Era.* New York: Simon and Schuster, 1994.

Bookman, Michael. *God's Rat: Jewish Mafia on the Lower East Side.* New York: PublishAmerica, 2000.

Brodsky, Alyn. *The Great Mayor. Fiorello La Guardia and the Making of the City of New York.* New York: St. Martin's, 2003.

Buenker, John. *Urban Liberalism and Progressive Reform.* New York: Norton, 1973.

Burrough, Bryan. *Public Enemies.* New York: Penguin, 2004.

Butler, Judith. *Gender Trouble.* New York: Routledge, 1990.

Camus, Albert. *The Rebel.* Translated by Anthony Bower. New York: Vintage Books, 1956.

Carlson, Marvin. *Performance. A Critical Introduction.* New York: Routledge, 1996.

Clarens, Carlos. *Crime Movies.* New York: Da Capo Press, 1997.

Cipolini, Christian. *Murder, Inc.* New York: Strategic Media, 2015.

Coe, Charles Norton. *Demi-Devils. The Character of Shakespeare's Villains.* New York: Bookman, 1963.

Cohen, Rich. *Tough Jews.* New York: Vintage, 1999.

Critchley, Simon. *Ethics, Politics, Subjectivity.* New York: Verso, 1999.

———. *Infinitely Demanding. Ethics of Commitment, Politics of Resistance.* New York: Verso, 2007.

Cuneo, Ernest. *Life with Fiorello.* New York: Macmillan, 1951

Dash, Mike. *Satan's Circus.* New York: Three Rivers Press, 2008.

Davis, Colin. *Levinas. An Introduction.* Notre Dame, Ind.: University of Notre Dame, 1996.

Dewey, Thomas. *Twenty against the Underworld.* Garden City, N.Y.: Doubleday, 1974.

Diggins, John Patrick. *The Promise of Pragmatism.* Chicago: University of Chicago, 1994.

Doctorow, E. L. *Billy Bathgate.* New York: Random House, 2010.

Downey, Patrick. *Gangster City.* Fort Lee, N.J.: Barricade, 2004.

———. *Legs Diamond, Gangster.* Lexington, Ky.: CreateSpace, 2011.

Duggins, John Patrick. *The Promise of Pragmatism.* Chicago: University of Chicago, 1994.

Dunn, Susan. *1940. FDR, Willkie, Lindbergh, Hitler. The Election amid the Storm.* New Haven, Conn.:Yale University, 2013.

Elmaleh, Edmund. *The Canary Sang but Couldn't Fly.* New York: Union Square Press, 2009.

Fisher, James T. *On the Irish Waterfront. The Crusade, the Movie, and the Soul of the Port of New York.* Ithaca, N.Y.: Cornell University, 2009.

Fried, Albert. *The Rise and Fall of the Jewish Gangster in America.* New York: Holt Rinehart and Winston, 1980.

Fromm, Erich. *The Anatomy of Human Destructiveness.* New York: Fawcett Crest, 1973.

Gabler, Neil. *Walter Winchell.* New York: Vintage, 1994.

Gardaphé, Fred. *From Wise Guys to Wise Men. The Gangster and Italian American Masculinities.* New York: Routledge, 2006.

Garrett, Charles. *The La Guardia Years. Machine and Reform Politics in New York.* New Brunswick, NJ: Rutgers University Press, 1961.

Giovacchini, Saverio. *Hollywood Modernism. Film and Politics in the Age of the New Deal.* Philadelphia: Temple University, 2001.

Girgus, Sam. *Levinas and the Cinema of Redemption. Time, Ethics, and the Feminine.* New York: Columbia University, 2010.

Glaeser, Edward. *Triumph of the City. How our Greatest Invention Makes Us Richer, Smarter, Greener, Healthier, and Happier.* New York: Penguin, 2011.

Gosch, Martin, and Richard Hammer. *The Last Testament of Lucky Luciano.* New York: Dell, 1974.

Greene, Richard, and Peter Vernezze, eds. *The Sopranos and Philosophy.* Chicago: Open Court, 2004.

Hall, David. *Richard Rorty. Prophet and Poet of the New Pragmatism.* Albany: State University of New York, 1994.

Hanson, Neil. *Monk Eastman.* New York: Knopf, 2010.

Heckscher, August. *When La Guardia Was Mayor.* New York: Norton, 1978.

Howe, Irving. *World of our Fathers.* New York: Harcourt Brace Jovanovich, 1976.

James, William. *Pragmatism and Other Essays.* New York: Washington Square Press, 1963.

Jeffers, H. Paul. *Commissioner Roosevelt. The Story of Theodore Roosevelt and the New York Police, 1895–1897.* New York: Wiley, 1994.

———. *The Napoleon of New York. Mayor Fiorello La Guardia.* New York: Wiley, 2002.

Joselit, Jenna Weissman. *Our Gang. Jewish Crime and the New York Jewish Community, 1900–1940.* Bloomington: Indiana University, 1983.

Kabaservice, Geoffrey. *Rule and Ruin. The Downfall of Moderation and the Destruction of the Republican Party from Eisenhower to the Tea Party.* New York: Oxford, 2012.

Katz, Jack. *Seductions of Crime. Moral and Sensual Attractions in Doing Evil.* New York: Basic Books, 1988.

Katz, Leonard. *Uncle Frank. The Biography of Frank Costello.* New York: Pocket Books, 1975.

Kavieff, Paul. *The Life and Times of Lepke Buchalter.* Fort Lee, N.J.: Barricade Books, 2006.

Keefe, Rose. *The Starker. New York City's First Great Gangster Boss.* Nashville, Tenn.: Cumberland House, 2008.

Kefauver, Estes. *Crime in America.* New York: Doubleday, 1951.

Kekes, John. *The Roots of Evil.* Ithaca, N.Y.: Cornell University Press, 2005.

Kennedy, William. *Legs.* New York: Penguin, 1975.

Kessner, Thomas. *Fiorello La Guardia.* New York: Penguin, 1989.

Kleid, Neil, and Jake Allen. *Brownsville. A Graphic Novel.* New York: Nantier Beall Minoustchine, 2006.

Lacey, Robert. *Little Man. Meyer Lansky and the Gangster Life.* New York: Little, Brown, 1991.

Landesman, Alter. *Brownsville. The Birth, Development, and Passing of a Jewish Community in New York.* New York: Bloch, 1969.

Lavery, David, ed. *Reading the Sopranos.* New York: I. B. Tauris, 2006.

Lee, Anthony W., and Richard Meyer. *Weegee and Naked City.* Berkeley: University of California, 2008.

Levinas, Emmanuel. *Totality and Infinity.* Translated by Alphonso Lingis. Pittsburgh, Penn.: Duquesne University, 1969.

Limpus, Lowell M., and Burr Leyson. *The Man La Guardia.* New York: Dutton, 1938.

Maas, Peter. *The Valachi Papers.* New York: Perennial, 2003.

Manners, William. *Patience and Fortitude: Fiorello La Guardia.* New York: Harcourt Brace Jovanovich, 1976.

Mappen, Marc. *Prohibition Gangsters. The Rise and Fall of a Bad Generation.* New Brunswick, N.J.: Rutgers University Press, 2013.

Mason, Fran. *American Gangster Cinema.* New York: Palgrave Macmillan, 2002.

Midgley, Mary. *Wickedness. A Philosophical Essay.* New York: Routledge, 1992.

Mitgang, Herbert. *The Man Who Rode the Tiger. The Life of Judge Samuel Seabury.* New York: Viking, 1963.

Morrow, Lance. *Evil. An Investigation.* New York: Basic Books, 2003.

Munby, Jonathan. *Public Enemies, Public Heroes: Screening the Gangster from "Little Caesar" to "Touch of Evil."* Chicago: University of Chicago Press, 1999.

Nash, Arthur. *New York City Gangland.* Charleston, S.C.: Arcadia Publishing, 2010.

Neal, Steve. *Happy Days Are Here Again.* New York: Harper, 2005.

Nealon, Jeffrey T. *Alterity Politics. Ethics and Performative Subjectivity.* Durham, N.C.: Duke University, 1998.

Newark, Tim. *Lucky Luciano. The Real and the Fake Gangster.* New York: St. Martin's Press, 2010.

Nussbaum, Martha, and Joshua Cohen, eds. *For Love of Country.* Boston: Beacon Press, 2002.

Okrent, Daniel. *Last Call. The Rise and Fall of Prohibition.* New York: Scribner, 2010.
Parker, Andrew, and Eve Kosofsky, eds. *Performativity and Performance.* New York: Routledge, 1995.
Pietrusza, David. *Rothstein.* New York: Basic Books, 2011.
Pritchett, Wendell Pritchett. *Brownsville, Brooklyn. Blacks, Jews, and the Changing Face of the Ghetto.* Chicago: University of Chicago Press, 2002.
Press, Eyal. *Beautiful Souls. The Courage and Conscience of Ordinary People in Extraordinary Times.* New York: Picador, 2012.
Puzo, Mario. *The Godfather.* New York: Signet, 1983.
Raab, Selwyn. *Five Families.* New York: Thomas Dunne, 2006.
Repppetto, Thomas. *American Mafia.* New York: Holt, 2004.
Rice, E. E. *Murder, Inc.* Cincinnati, Ohio: Zebra Picture Books, 1949.
Riis, Jacob. *The Battle with the Slum.* New York: Dover, 1998.
———. *How the Other Half Lives.* New York: Dover, 1971.
Runyon, Damon. *Guys and Dolls.* New York: Penguin, 1992.
Ruth, David. *Inventing the Public Enemy.* Chicago: University of Chicago Press, 1996.
Sandel, Michael. *Justice.* New York: Farrar Straus Giroux, 2009.
———. *What Money Can't Buy: The Moral Limits of Markets.* New York: Farrar Straus Giroux, 2012.
Sann, Paul. *Kill the Dutchman!* New York: Popular Library, 1971.
Satz, Debra. *Why Some Things Should not Be for Sale: The Moral Limits of Markets.* New York: Oxford University Press, 2010.
Sennett, Richard. *The Fall of Public Man.* New York: Vintage, 1974.
Sennett, Richard, ed. *The Psychology of Society.* New York: Vintage, 1977.
Shadoian, Jack. *Dreams and Dead Ends. The American Gangster Film.* New York: Oxford University Press, 2003.
Silver, Alain, and James Ursini, eds. *Gangster Film Reader.* Pompton Plains, N.J.: Limelight Editions, 2007.
Smith, Richard Norton. *Thomas E. Dewey and his Times.* New York: Simon and Schuster, 1982.
Spivack, Charlotte. *The Comedy of Evil on Shakespeare's Stage.* Rutherford, N.J.: Fairleigh Dickinson University, 1978.
Svendsen, Lars. *A Philosophy of Evil.* Translated by Kerri A. Pierce. Champaign, Ill.: Dalkey Archive Press, 2010.
Toland, John. *The Dillinger Days.* New York: Da Capo Press, 1995.
Turkus, Burton, and Sid Feder. *Murder, Inc.* New York: Da Capo, 1992.
Valentine, Lewis J. *Night Stick.* New York: The Dial Press, 1947.
Walsh, George. *Gentleman Jimmy Walker. Mayor of the Jazz Age.* New York: Praeger, 1974.
———. *Public Enemies. The Mayor, the Mob, and the Crime That Was.* New York: Norton, 1980.

Whyte, William Foote. *Street Corner Society*. Chicago: University of Chicago Press, 1973.

Wolf, George, and Joseph DiMona. *Frank Costello. Prime Minister of the Underworld*. New York: William Morrow, 1974.

Žižek, Slavoj. *Violence. Six Sideways Reflections*. New York: Picador, 2008.

Index

Craig, Charles, 90
Crime Doesn't Pay (radio show), 3
Crime Movies (Clarens), 6
criminals: Brownsville as breeding ground, 41–43; families of origin, 39, 40; start of criminal life, 40–43; as types, 150–51. *See also* gangsters
culture of death, 74
Cummings, Homer, 150
Cuneo, Ernest, 82–83

d'Amello, Florence, 64
Dead Pigeon (Kanto), 212
death. *See* violent death
deep play, 183
democracy, corruption and, 71
Depression-era organized crime, 47–48
Dewey, George, 103–4
Dewey, George Martin, Jr., 105
Dewey, Thomas E., xii, 2, *99*, 150; background, 98, 100–1; celebrity, 120–21; college career, 105; courtroom behavior, 111–12; death threats, 122–23; Diamond, Jack "Legs," 101–2; district attorney election, 121; Gordon, Waxey, 102–3; Hines conviction, 121; justice and, 117; Lepke and, 125; letters to "The Rackbuster," 120; literature, 6; Luciano commuted sentence, 122–23, 124; the Mafia, 107; Manhattan corruption investigation, 106–7; Medalie and, 100–1; plans to murder, 107; Progressive Reform, 103–6; Quinlivan, Jimmie, 101; radio talks, 121; Republican activism, 106
Dewey investigations, income numbers, 63
Diamond, Jack "Legs," xii, 21; bodyguard for Arnold Rothstein, 22; Dewey and Medalie, 101–2; Hotsty-Totsy Club shootings, 22; *Legs* (novel), 21; *New Yorker* profile, 21–22; *The Rise and Fall of Legs Diamond* (film), 21
Dillinger, John: death outside movie house, 19–20; gangster movies and, 13–15
The Dillinger Days (Toland), 6
Divino, Samuel, 64
Doctorow, E. L., *Billy Bathgate*, 6, 26
Dodge, William Copeland, grand jury, 98

Downey, Patrick: *Gangster City,* 6; *Legs Diamond, Gangster,* 5
Dwyer, "Big Bill," 61

Egglineger, Agnes, 64
Eichmann, Adolf, 152
The Enforcer (film), 3, 19
ethics: human relationships and, 183; Levinas on, 92–93; *versus* morality, 220n16; Newtonian, 205–6; postmodern, 207; religious terms and, 207
ethnic gangs, 45. *See also* Italian American gangs; Jewish gangs
ethnic mix in gangs, 46; postnational identities, 50
evil, 7; agency and responsibility, 149; banality of, 152–53; comic, 155–56; grotesque, 154–55; radical evil, 149–50; stupid, 152–53

families: Cain and Abel motif, 40–41; criminals' original, 39, 40; gang makeup and, 46; immigrant relationship with children, 41–43
Farley, Tom, 81
Feder, Sid, *Murder, Inc.,* 2
Feeney, Harry, Murder, Inc., 1, 69
Feinstein, Puggy, 126; murder, 135, 141–44; murder trial, 169–70
Fellig, Arthur "Weegee," 9–12
Feraco, Jimmy, 137
films. *See* movies
Fiorello La Guardia (Kessner), 6
Five Families (Raab), 5
Five Points Gang, 60
Flegenheimer, Arthur "Dutch Schulz." *See* Schulz, Dutch
flower shop, Maione, 68
freedom, polis and, 90
Fried, Albert, *The Rise and Fall of the Jewish Gangster in America,* 5
Friedman, Oscar "the Poet," 154
friendships between gangsters and police force, 69
Friscia, John "Mummy," 154–55
From Wise Guys to Wise Men: The Gangster and Italian American Masculinities (Gardaphé), 6, 73–74

morality: ambiguity and, 205–7; Camus, 206; *versus* ethics, 220n16; Good Samaritan, 206–7; rationality and, 149–50; revelation and, 207; theater and, 182–83
morality plays, gangster movies as, 29–30
morals, 7–8
Morello, Giuseppe, 55
movies, 27–28; alienation effect, 29; *Angels with Dirty Faces,* 40–41; *Behind Red Light,* 120; boom in gangster movies, 18; *The Brothers Rico,* 47; commodification of life, 73–74; *Counsel for Crime,* 19; Dillinger and, 13–15; Dillinger's death, 19–20; *The Enforcer,* 3, 19; gangster-as-policeman, 18; *The Godfather,* 4; *The Godfather* Trilogy, 15; *Guns Don't Argue,* 120; *Guys and Dolls,* 4; Hays Office and, 17–18; *I Am a Fugitive from a Chain Gang,* 26–27; influence on gangsters, 20–21; *Lepke,* 19; *Little Caesar,* 3, 15; *Manhattan Melodrama,* 13–15; *Marked Woman,* 19, 120; *Missing Witnesses,* 19; as morality plays, 29–30; MPPDA, 17; *Murder, Inc.,* 19; *Murder at Dawn,* 17; *Musketeers of Pig Alley* (Griffith), 14; *On the Waterfront,* 19; persona of the gangster, 25–26; *The Phenix City Story,* 19, 47; positionality and, 29–30; *The Public Enemy,* 3, 15, 16; *The Racket* (Milestone), 14–15; *Racket Busters,* 19; Raft, George, 25–26; *Scarface,* 3, 16–17; *Smashing Rackets,* 19; syndicate, 47; *Tight Spot,* 212; *Underworld* (von Sternberg), 14; villain as protagonist, 29
MPPDA (Motion Pictures Producers and Distributors Association), 17
Mr. Arsenic (television show), 3
Mr. Smith Goes to Washington (Capra), 92–93
mugging, 146
Munby, Jonathan, *Public Enemies, Public Heroes: Screening the Gangster Film from "Little Caesar" to "Touch of Evil,"* 6
murder: evil and, 149–50; as favor, 145–47; psychopaths and, 148–49; reasons for, 148–49

Murder, Inc. (Rice), 2
"Murder, Inc." (Springsteen), 4
Murder, Inc. (Turkus & Feder), 2
Murder, Inc., gang, 1, 31; Ladies Night, 40
Murder, Inc., meme, 212
Murder, Inc. (film), 19
Murder, Inc., record label, 4
"Murder, Inc." rock band, 4
Murder, Inc., trials: Abbandando, 166–67, 177; appeals for Maione and Abbandando, 175; arrests, 160–65; Capone, Louis, 192–95; defense tactics, 176; Goldstein, 169–70, 172–75; Gurino, 173; housing witnesses, 166; investigations' end, 204–5; jury selection for Lepke, 192; Lepke, 185–87, 191–95, 202; Magoon testimony, 174; Maione, 166–67; Maione conviction, 177; Nitzberg, 177–78; O'Dwyer, Bill, 157–58; Reles's claims of reform, 176–77; Reles's escape from protective custody, 195–201; Reles's mother-in-law, 173; Reles's testimony, 168–69, 173–74; Rudnick, 166–67; Schulz murder, 178–80; state's evidence, 164–66; Strauss, 169–70, 172–75; theatrics, 180–81; Turkus, Burton, 159–60; Weiss, 192–95; women jurors, 175
Murder at Dawn (film), *17*
Murtha, John "Spider," 151–52
Musketeers of Pig Alley (Griffith), 14

New Lots, Brooklyn, 36
New York City as "Gangster City," 54
New York Evening Mail, La Guardia interview, 94
The New Yorker: Legs Diamond profile, 21–22; Schulz's last words, 108–9; Valentine profile, 84, 86
Newark, Tim, *Lucky Luciano: The Real and the Fake Gangster,* 5
Newtonian ethics, 205–6
Nicholson, William, 198
nicknames, 33
Nieman, Susan, 7
nihilism, postmodern nihilists, 52
niti, justice and, 119–20
Nitzberg, Irving "Knadles," trial, 177–78

ESE SELECT TITLES FROM EMPIRE STATE EDITIONS

Salvatore Basile, *Fifth Avenue Famous: The Extraordinary Story of Music at St. Patrick's Cathedral.* Foreword by Most Reverend Timothy M. Dolan, Archbishop of New York

Andrew J. Sparberg, *From a Nickel to a Token: The Journey from Board of Transportation to MTA*

Daniel Campo, *The Accidental Playground: Brooklyn Waterfront Narratives of the Undesigned and Unplanned*

John Waldman, *Heartbeats in the Muck: The History, Sea Life, and Environment of New York Harbor, Revised Edition*

John Waldman (ed.), *Still the Same Hawk: Reflections on Nature and New York*

Gerard R. Wolfe, *The Synagogues of New York's Lower East Side: A Retrospective and Contemporary View, Second Edition.* Photographs by Jo Renée Fine and Norman Borden, Foreword by Joseph Berger

Howard Eugene Johnson with Wendy Johnson, *A Dancer in the Revolution: Stretch Johnson, Harlem Communist at the Cotton Club.* Foreword by Mark D. Naison

Joseph B. Raskin, *The Routes Not Taken: A Trip Through New York City's Unbuilt Subway System*

Phillip Deery, *Red Apple: Communism and McCarthyism in Cold War New York*

North Brother Island: The Last Unknown Place in New York City. Photographs by Christopher Payne, A History by Randall Mason, Essay by Robert Sullivan

Stephen Miller, *Walking New York: Reflections of American Writers from Walt Whitman to Teju Cole*

Tom Glynn, *Reading Publics: New York City's Public Libraries, 1754–1911*

Greg Donaldson, *The Ville: Cops and Kids in Urban America, Updated Edition.* With a new epilogue by the author, Foreword by Mark D. Naison

David Borkowski, *A Shot Story: From Juvie to Ph.D.*

Craig Saper, *The Amazing Adventures of Bob Brown: A Real-Life Zelig Who Wrote His Way Through the 20th Century*

R. Scott Hanson, *City of Gods: Religious Freedom, Immigration, and Pluralism in Flushing, Queens.* Foreword by Martin E. Marty

Pamela Lewis, *Teaching While Black: A New Voice on Race and Education in New York City*

Mark Naison and Bob Gumbs, *Before the Fires: An Oral History of African American Life in the Bronx from the 1930s to the 1960s*

Joanne Witty and Henrik Krogius, *Brooklyn Bridge Park: A Dying Waterfront Transformed*

Visit www.empirestateeditions.com for a complete list.